Continuo Realization
in Handel's Vocal Music

Studies in Music, No. 104

George J. Buelow, Series Editor
Professor of Music
Indiana University

Other Titles in This Series

No. 92	*The Calov Bible of J. S. Bach*	Howard H. Cox, ed.
No. 95	*The Church Music of Heinrich Biber*	Eric T. Chafe
No. 99	*Handel Tercentenary Collection*	Stanley Sadie and Anthony Hicks, eds.
No. 100	*Handel, Haydn, and the Viennese Classical Style*	Jens Peter Larsen
No. 103	*Musical Ensembles in Festival Books, 1500–1800: An Iconographical and Documentary Survey*	Edmund A. Bowles
No. 105	*French Musical Thought, 1600–1800*	Georgia Cowart, ed.
No. 106	*The Letters and Documents of Heinrich Schütz, 1656–1672: An Annotated Translation*	Gina Spagnoli
No. 107	*Church, Stage, and Studio: Music and Its Contexts in Seventeenth-Century Germany*	Paul Walker, ed.

Continuo Realization
in Handel's Vocal Music

Patrick J. Rogers

UNIVERSITY OF ROCHESTER PRESS

Excerpts from the *Hallische Händel-Ausgabe* reprinted by permission of Bärenreiter-Verlag, Kassel and Basel, and VEB Deutscher Verlag für Musik. © Bärenreiter-Verlag.

Excerpts from *The Practical Harmonist at the Harpischord*, by Francesco Gasparini, Frank S. Stillings, trans., David L. Burrows, ed., © 1963 *The Journal of Music Theory*, Yale School of Music, New Haven, Connecticut.

Excerpts from *Essay on the True Art of Playing Keyboard Instruments* by Carl Philipp Emanuel Bach, translated and edited by William J. Mitchell, reprinted by permission of W. W. Norton and Company, Inc., © 1949 by W. W. Norton and Company, Inc.; copyright renewed 1976 by Alice L. Mitchell.

Excerpts from *Handel's Dramatic Oratorios and Masques*, by Winton Dean, and *Thorough-Bass Made Easy*, by Nicolo Pasquali, reprinted by permission of Oxford University Press.

Copyright © 1989 Patrick John Francis Rogers

All Rights Reserved. Except as permitted under current legislation, no part of this work may be photocopied, stored in a retrieval system, published, performed in public, adapted, broadcast, transmitted, recorded, or reproduced in any form or by any means, without the prior permission of the copyright owner.

Originally produced and distributed 1990 by
UMI Research Press
an imprint of
University Microfilms Inc.
Ann Arbor, Michigan 48106

Transferred to digital printing and reprinted in paperback 2010
University of Rochester Press
668 Mt. Hope Avenue, Rochester, NY 14620, USA
www.urpress.com
and Boydell & Brewer Limited
PO Box 9, Woodbridge, Suffolk IP12 3DF, UK
www.boydellandbrewer.com

Paperback ISBN: 978-1-58046-361-4
Cloth ISBN-13: 978-0-83571-875-2
Cloth ISBN-10: 0-8357-1875-1

Library of Congress Cataloging-in-Publication Data

Rogers, Patrick John.
  Continuo realization in Handel's vocal music / by Patrick J. Rogers
    p. cm. — (Studies in music ; no. 104)
  Includes bibliographical references and index.
  ISBN 0-8357-1875-1 (hardcover: alk. paper)
    1. Handel, George Frideric, 1685-1759—Criticism and interpretation. 2. Thorough bass. I. Title. II. Series: Studies in music (Ann Arbor, Mich.) ; no. 104.
  ML410.H13R65 1989
    781.3'2'0924—dc19   88-37937

A catalogue record for this title is available from the British Library.
This publication is printed on acid-free paper.

To my father

Contents

List of Documents   *ix*

Preface   *xi*

Acknowledgments   *xiii*

List of Abbreviations   *xv*

Corrigenda   *xvi*

Introduction: The Importance of Continuo Figuring   *1*
    The Source Materials: Preliminary Clarifications
    Problems Confronting the Performer of Figured Bass
    Previous Studies on Thoroughbass Accompaniment
    Previous Scholarship on Handel's Figured Bass
    Design of the Present Study

Part One   Bass Figuring in Handel Source Materials

1 Bass Figuring in Handel's Autographs   *13*
    Functions of Bass Figuring in Handel's Autographs
    Some Details concerning Handel's Figuring
    Handel's Method of Composition
    Figuring That Became Obsolete during the Compositional Process
    Discarded Figurings
    Problematic Figurings: Definitions and Examples

2 Bass Figuring in Handel's Conducting Scores   *43*
    Handel's Figuring of *Rodelinda*

3 Bass Figuring in Opera and Oratorio Continuo Parts   *53*
    The Hamburg *Cembalopartituren*
    RCM 900
    RM. 19. a. 10.
    Aylesford Keyboard Parts

viii   Contents

4   Bass Figuring in Scribal Copies of the Operas and Oratorios   65
    Charles Jennens's Bass Figuring

5   Bass Figuring in the Royal Academy Opera Editions, 1720-1728   83
    The Figuring of Specific Printed Editions

Part Two   Realization Problems

6   *Unisono* Textures   95
    Evidence from C. P. E. Bach
    Evidence from Handel's Autograph Figuring

7   Plain Recitative   109
    Detached or Sustained Chords?
    Melodic and Harmonic Support
    Foreshortened Cadences

8   Short Rests in the Bass   141
    Handel's Practice
    Theoretical References

9   Pedal Points   155

10 Continuo Harmonization   165
    Standard Formula Progressions
    Harmonization of Sample Excerpts

Part Three   Appendixes

Appendix A   Aylesford Cembalo/Organo Parts for Handel's Operas and Oratorios   197

Appendix B   Manuscript Scores of Handel's Operas, Oratorios, and Odes with Supplementary Figuring   211

Appendix C   Unpublished Autograph Figuring   219
    Rinaldo, Ouverture
    Ottone, "Falsa imagine"
    Duetto X, "Tacete, ohimè, tacete"

Appendix D   Unpublished Compositions   235
    Radamisto, "Cara sposa"
    [Amen, alleluja], HWV 275

Notes   243

Bibliography   259

Index   263

Documents

1. Continuo Figures in Handel's Music   *14*
2. Handel Autographs with Substantial Figuring   *15*
3. Figurings Incompatible with the Composed Parts   *30*
4. Corrections of Figuring in Handel's Autograph Manuscripts   *35*
5. Autograph Figuring in Handel's Conducting Scores   *44*
6. Figuring Mistakes in the H-G Edition of *Rodelinda*   *46*
7. Figuring Discrepancies between the Cluer Printed Edition and the Hamburg Conducting Score of *Rodelinda*   *50*
8. Hamburg *Cembalopartituren*   *54*
9. Hamburg Manuscripts with Excerpts in Continuo Format   *55*
10. Contents of the Harpsichord Part for *Alexander's Feast*   *57*
11. Contents of the Organ Part for *Alexander's Feast*   *59*
12. Newman Flower Keyboard Continuo Parts for the Oratorios   *63*
13. Nine Royal Academy Prints   *86*
14. Short *Unisono* Passages with Sparse Figuring   *105*
15. Repetition of Figuring during Long Bass Notes in Handel's Plain Recitative   *134*
16. Delayed or Semidelayed Cadences in Handel's Plain Recitative   *136*

Preface

A few words are needed concerning the musical examples. Continuo figuring has been placed below the bass staff, regardless of the position in the original sources, but alternate harmonizations are normally placed above the bass. The autograph manuscripts have been consulted as much as possible to eliminate the inaccuracies of Chrysander's figuring, so frequently the reader may notice discrepancies with the Händel-Gesellschaft edition. Vocal texts have only been included when they seem relevant to the points under discussion. All musical examples are by Handel unless otherwise indicated.

Bernd Baselt's system of numbering works and movements, detailed in his *Händel-Handbuch*, is used extensively.

Unfortunately we have no convenient set of terms to describe many of the special types of thoroughbass figuring found in the works of Handel and his contemporaries. I have coined the term "supplementary figuring" to describe figuring which is contained in eighteenth-century manuscripts and printed editions and which is much fuller than the sparse figuring present in most of Handel's autographs and conducting scores. Special types of continuo figuring that are prominent in the autographs are defined at the end of chapter 1.

Acknowledgments

It would be impossible to express adequately my appreciation to many generous teachers, colleagues, and friends.

Dr. Roland Jackson of Claremont Graduate School has been of enormous assistance; his perceptive suggestions have helped immeasurably to clarify and organize the material. Other members of the CGS faculty, especially Dr. Frank Traficante, Dr. Helen Smith, Dr. Alfred Louch, and Prof. Preethi de Silva, have also made valuable comments. J. Merrill Knapp, Professor Emeritus, Princeton, supervised my research on the printed editions during a summer seminar, and has been always ready to share information and offer advice on many other aspects of this book. Dr. Graydon Beeks, of Pomona College, assisted in many ways throughout the project, and was especially helpful in providing details on the Aylesford cembalo parts in the Library of Congress. Prof. Roswitha Burwick of Scripps College offered valuable assistance with the German translations. Betty Roleder, music librarian of the Claremont Colleges, has always been interested and helpful.

The American Philosophical Society, the British Fulbright Commission, the National Endowment for the Humanities, the William Andrews Clark Memorial Library, and Claremont Graduate School have provided substantial grants which made this and related research possible. This study would have been impossible without research trips to Britain and West Germany, so I am especially grateful for the Fulbright and APS fellowships.

Winton Dean and Hans Dieter Clausen were unfailingly hospitable and generous with their time. Terence Best graciously consented to guide me during a year of research in Britain; his approach to the Handel sources was a considerable influence. I am also grateful to Anthony Hicks for allowing me to bounce off ideas on several occasions, and giving me the benefit of his vast expertise in Handelian matters.

Many other reputable Handel scholars deserve to be thanked for stimulating discourse and enlightening letters: Paul Henry Lang, Alfred Mann, Donald Burrows, William Gudger, Elwood Derr, Howard Serwer, William

Weber, Carole Taylor, Graham Pont, Ellen Harris, and Martha Ronish. Donald Burrows has always been ready to answer questions relating to dating and paper characteristics of source materials. William Gudger provided his own extensive notes on the Fitzwilliam Museum Lennard Collection. I am especially grateful to Howard Serwer, the Maryland Handel Festival, and the University of Maryland Center for Renaissance and Baroque Studies for the opportunity to discuss thorny thoroughbass problems with many renowned Baroque specialists.

The staffs of the following institutions were inordinately helpful: The British Library, The Royal College of Music, Westminster Central Music Library, University of London, The Fitzwilliam Museum, Henry Watson Music Library, Manchester, The Clark Library (UCLA), and the Staats- und Universitäts-Bibliothek Carl von Ossietzky, Hamburg.

I am very grateful to Prof. George Buelow for support, encouragement, and advice. Prof. Knapp and Dr. Beeks read portions of the manuscript and offered constructive criticism. The errors that remain should be attributed to me.

Dr. Traficante, Mary Bennett, Mary Wood, and the administrative staff of Claremont University Center have shared word processing expertise and computer facilities; this has greatly expedited the completion of the book. Andrew Glick mastered the staggering complexities of computer music-writing software in the process of inputting most of the musical examples; his tenacity and cooperation were an enormous advantage. My deepest gratitude goes to my wife and son for understanding and patience during extended periods of writing and revision.

Finally, I beg the indulgence of anyone I have inadvertently neglected.

Abbreviations

H-G   *G. F. Händels Werke.* Leipzig, 1858-94. Reprint, Ridgewood, N.J.: Gregg Press, 1965. Volume numbers for H-G are given in references only when a given work does not constitute a complete volume unto itself.

HHA   *Hallische Händel-Ausgabe.* Kassell: Bärenreiter, 1955-.

NBA   *Neue Bach-Ausgabe.* Kassell: Bärenreiter, 1954-.

NMA   *W. A. Mozart: Neue Ausgabe Sämtlicher Werke.* Kassell: Bärenreiter, 1955-.

RM   Royal Music Library Collection, British Library, London.

RCM   Royal College of Music, London.

Corrigenda

P. 77: the S2 figuring on beat 4 of measure 4 should read $^6_5$.

P. 80: the key signature for example 4.6 should contain three sharps.

P. 88, document 13: under "Admeto, Arias or duets missing," the text should read "1 (?)" rather than 0.

P. 102, line 19: "enabling the listener to interpret the downbeats of the third and fourth measures as suspensions" should read "revealing dramatically dissonant chords on the downbeats of the third and fourth measures."

P. 197: under the title of the appendix add: "The RM and RCM keyboard parts, probably used in actual performances of *Alexander's Feast* under Handel's direction, are discussed on pp. 55–61."

P. [225] (appendix C): the MS number for the Ottone excerpt is RM.20.b.9.

P. [227]: like the other examples in appendix C, here Handel's bass figuring has been marked on Chrysander's H-G edition. The H-G continuo realization for HWV 196 is editorial and not necessarily in agreement with Handel's figuring or prevailing Baroque practice.

P. [241] (appendix D [Amen, alleluja]): third system, measure 3, a sharp sign should precede the treble f.

P. 246, n. 31: add "Examples can also be found in Handel's Coronation Anthem, *My Heart Is Inditing*."

P. 251, n. 5: "for this information" should read "for the *Samson* reference."

P. 264: under "Aylesford Collection, keyboard parts in," the first entry should be pp. 56–64.

Introduction

The Importance of Continuo Figuring

Basso continuo figuring can provide valuable information concerning a composer's concept of accompanimental texture, chordal rhythm, and voice leading, along with his approach to continuo harmony in general. Sometimes the figuring merely corroborates the recommendations found in thoroughbass treatises of the time. Elsewhere it reveals a composer's individuality or personal preferences. In the present study the vocal music of George Frideric Handel will be considered with respect to continuo figuring. The primary focus will be on the operas and the oratorios, although occasionally evidence from the cantatas, the anthems, or even the instrumental music will be included as well.

    A detailed study of Handel's figuring is long overdue, especially since it can shed light on the proper performance of his works. It is surprising that modern editors of Handel's vocal works generally exclude continuo figuring not present in the primary source materials, i.e., the autographs and conducting scores. As a rule, these manuscripts were not figured sufficiently for the performer, primarily because they were composition drafts or Handel's own performance copies; they were not necessarily scores that he anticipated others would use. Handel's works have also been preserved in a variety of "secondary" manuscript sources, many of which are figured in a stylistically appropriate and illuminating way by copyists closely associated with the composer. Also, the contemporary printed editions, some of which doubtless had the participation of the composer, contain supplementary figuring that deserves serious consideration since much of it could derive from Handel himself. These manuscript and printed sources, authentic in their own right, often contribute invaluable supplements to the sporadic figuring found in most of the autographs and conducting scores.

    The eighteenth-century editions of Handel's music were usually figured, not always copiously or particularly well, but in the vast majority of cases, at least adequately. A decisive change, however, is reflected in the first really complete edition, begun in the late nineteenth century under the auspices of the Händel-Gesellschaft and primarily the work of Friedrich

Chrysander—hereafter H-G. For the most part, the only continuo figuring included for a given work was that contained in the primary source, usually the Hamburg conducting score.

Chrysander, whose pioneering work influenced generations of Handelians, had clearly marked prejudices with respect to thoroughbass figuring: not only did he feel that figuring was unnecessary for an experienced player, but also he felt it was *undesirable*.[1] And while he could not point to any eighteenth-century authority whose views were in accord with his own, he justified his opinion on the basis of the predominantly unfigured source material. He seems not to have considered that these sources were unfigured not by design, but simply as a practical expedient. He also seems to have regarded any figuring that had not survived in Handel's own hand as spurious.[2]

Later Handel editors, including those of the new complete edition, Hallische Händel-Ausgabe—hereafter HHA—generally follow the same policy regarding bass figuring. They have ignored or suppressed any figuring not present in their primary source or copy-text; not only is it not included in the score, but little or none of it is reproduced in the critical report. (Some exceptions will be noted below.) This is due partly to Chrysander's influence, partly to the desire to simplify the editorial process, and partly to an overly zealous application of the principles of textual criticism. These editorial principles, first developed for the literary texts of antiquity, need to be reconsidered drastically when applied to large concerted works of the Baroque period.

The comparative scarcity of figuring in the autographs seems to have had an inhibiting effect on editors of Handel's works and to have encouraged an unusually severe approach to bass figuring. Very few seem to have considered the possibility that the additional figuring that survives in secondary manuscript sources or printed editions could be authentic or at least worthy of inclusion in their critical reports. In the edition itself, autograph figuring could be easily distinguished from that found in secondary sources by using brackets or smaller type.

Fortunately, these predispositions are gradually changing. The HHA edition of *Alexander's Feast* by Konrad Ameln includes the figuring of the first complete printed edition published by Walsh in 1737.[3] J. Merrill Knapp's HHA edition of *Amadigi* includes editorial amplifications of the figuring in recitatives (where the exact harmonization can be especially crucial).[4] At the same time, these additions are clearly distinguished from figures found in the primary source. In the second volume of Gerald Hendrie's edition of Chandos Anthems, one movement includes supplementary figuring derived from a source in the Fitzwilliam Museum Lennard Collection.[5]

The situation with instrumental works is also more favorable due to Terence Best's and Frederick Hudson's collations of bass figuring from various manuscript and printed sources in their editions for the HHA.[6] Their critical reports extensively discuss figuring discrepancies among the various sources. Best also considers the possibility that variants from secondary sources could be later revisions by the composer.[7]

The Source Materials: Preliminary Clarifications

Handel did not, as a rule, make fair copies of his compositions. In most cases, the only extant copy of a vocal work in the composer's hand is the original composition score, hereafter referred to as the autograph. However, an abundance of manuscript copies was prepared by John Christopher Smith, Sr., and various other scribes, mostly anonymous, working under him.[8] As Winton Dean has recently shown, Smith served as principal copyist from 1720; before that, the position was held by a Mr. Linike.[9] The actual performing scores, the *Handexemplare* or conducting scores, were mostly the work of Smith Sr., often in collaboration with his assistants.[10] With very few exceptions, the vocal and instrumental parts used in the original performances, probably copied primarily by Smith Sr., S1, and S2, have not survived. The Smith circle was also responsible for producing library copies commissioned by wealthy patrons of the composer. These "presentation copies" fall into five major collections: Aylesford, Granville, Lennard, Malmesbury, and Shaftesbury. The Aylesford Collection, copied for Handel's friend and librettist Charles Jennens, is unique in that it contains a large quantity of vocal and instrumental parts; these, however, seem not to have been used in performance.

The autographs are seldom extensively figured throughout. The figuring is either thin and scattered, or else ample quantities are concentrated in small sections of a work. The conducting scores, since they were usually copied directly from the autographs, naturally follow the figuring of the latter very closely. The Granville and Lennard collections contain some additional figuring, but, again, it is the Aylesford collection that contains an inordinately large amount of additional figuring in scores of the major vocal works, keyboard continuo parts, and volumes of shorter compositions and excerpts (the so-called mixed volumes.) The other presentation sets, Malmesbury and Shaftesbury, are still privately owned and consequently were unavailable to me.

The scarcity of figuring in Handel's autographs and conducting scores should not surprise us; nor should we conclude that Handel felt that figuring was unnecessary for a good accompanist, or that he was generally uninterested in problems of continuo harmonization. With large vocal works, it was common practice among composers of the late Baroque period to reserve figuring for the keyboard continuo part. Numerous examples of an unfigured full score and an extensively figured continuo part for the same work can be found in cantatas and passions of J. S. Bach,[11] as well

4   Introduction

as cantatas by G. P. Telemann.[12] Handel's vocal works offer further examples. However, so few of his original keyboard continuo parts have survived that one cannot base a definitive conclusion on them.

There are other reasons for the relative lack of figuring in Handel's composition scores. Many were written at an astonishing pace. They often represent merely the first draft of a work, which was revised considerably for performance. And since Handel himself directed the initial productions of the operas and oratorios from the keyboard, details of continuo harmonization could be worked out in rehearsal. The presence of a carefully planned and painstakingly figured series of thoroughbass exercises in the Fitzwilliam Museum certainly indicates that the composer was not disinterested in these problems.

Problems Confronting the Performer of Figured Bass

Continuo figuring was not primarily intended (as some believe) for the inexperienced player. There are many reasons for this: 1) a "normal" or straightforward continuo progression may not always have been intended by the composer; 2) figuring may indicate intervals other than those implied by the composed parts; 3) figuring may suggest either a thinner or a fuller texture than the one utilized in the composed parts; 4) a composer may decide that the realization should clash with a *concertante* part;[13] 5) figuring may demand a harmonized accompaniment in situations that ostensibly require an unharmonized accompaniment: e.g., unison passages, bass rests, pedal points; 6) basso continuo parts published in the eighteenth century typically included only the figured bass; 7) very often Baroque choral and instrumental music was originally accompanied from a bass part only. In the last case the figuring would be indispensable, since even an experienced accompanist would need the figures as a guide in large, complex concerted pieces. To the best of my knowledge, unfigured basses were never actually *advocated* by anyone after the first half of the seventeenth century.

Authentic continuo figuring is usually an invaluable guide to the harmonic framework intended by the composer. But it can do more than merely show the simple harmonic progressions. It can indicate where the chords should be enlivened or enriched through the addition of suspensions or retardations that are not implied by the composed parts. The most common examples of suspensions are 4 to 3 and 7 to 6; less common, but still encountered frequently, are 9 to 8 and double suspensions, such as $^9_7$ to $^8_6$ and $^9_4$ to $^8_3$. A figuring such as $^7_5$ is frequently very helpful in that it demands that an interval (the fifth), which is usually considered optional in a seventh chord, be included in the realization. Unusually precise figurings, such as $^7_5_3$, $^6_4_2$, $^6_4_3$, $^9_7_5$, show all the intervals that should be played above the bass. Very full figuring can also imply a specific voice-leading or disposition of chord tones. Occasionally, figuring is so complete that it shows single and double passing tones, short ornamental motifs, and other melodic refinements that add elegance to the accompaniment.[14] Admittedly, a good deal of continuo figuring cannot be taken literally, e.g., when long dissonances in the obbligato parts are not accounted for, but there are many other aspects of Baroque notation that also cannot be interpreted literally.

If the musical texture was full, i.e. harmonically complete without a chordal realization of the bass, the accompanist's task was simplified considerably. He merely doubled the progressions executed by the obbligato parts, perhaps in a somewhat simplified form. Here continuo figuring by the composer was not absolutely essential; any competent musician could, if necessary, figure the bass adequately by studying the full score, although even in fully harmonized textures, a composer's figuring could prove useful in clarifying the basic progressions, especially in florid polyphony.

Continuo figures were invaluable, however, in delicately scored passages, i. e. one to three composed parts, for in these sections the continuo player was normally required to give a complete statement of the implied harmony. Frequently, this was not obvious without the aid of continuo figures, as many eighteenth-century composer-theorists, including Werckmeister, Mattheson, Geminiani, and C. P. E. Bach, have attested. The following passage from Andreas Werckmeister's *Harmonologia musica* is indicative:

> Those, too, who say that the "signatures" over the notes in a Thorough-Bass are quite useless and unnecessary, display no slight ignorance or folly; for it is clearly impossible for even an adept [accompanist], who understands the natural course of harmony and composition, to play everything correctly *in accordance with the ideas of another*, for the progressions and resolutions may take place in many different ways.[15]

This admonition is even more relevant today than when it was first written, for the modern continuo player is called upon to provide realizations for compositions written within a span of two hundred years. It is obviously impossible for a single player to be thoroughly familiar with the wide range of harmonic styles represented by Caccini, Schütz, Purcell, Couperin, Rameau, and C. P. E. Bach, not to mention Hadyn and Mozart, so that he is able to realize their basses without the aid of continuo figuring.

Previous Studies on Thoroughbass Accompaniment

Frank Thomas Arnold's *The Art of Accompaniment from a Thorough-Bass*[16] remains the most comprehensive treatment of the subject to date. Arnold's handling of individual topics can occasionally be faulted and his harmonic vocabulary is definitely post-Rameau, but his overall grasp of Baroque accompaniment has not been equalled. Not all thoroughbass treatises receive the coverage they deserve, and frequently one feels that the selection of material from the treatises is rather arbitrary. Also, Arnold made no attempt to study the many continuo realizations which survive from the seventeenth and eighteenth centuries. And even though some very significant material has come to light since its publication, the book remains a remarkable achievement.

George Buelow's *Thorough-Bass Accompaniment according to Johann David Heinichen*,[17] based on his dissertation completed at New York University in 1961, is an excellent study of Heinichen's extensive treatise, *Der General-Bass in der Composition* (1728). Most of the important sections of the original text are translated, while other portions are paraphrased or summarized. The book contains valuable supplementary material to Arnold's work, and Heinichen's treatment of *Vollstimmigkeit* and harmonization of recitatives are particularly applicable to Handel's vocal music. A complete translation, with all of Heinichen's sample realizations, would obviously be more useful for the serious performer who is attempting to recapture the art of continuo extemporization. The only problematic portion of the book is the appended realization of Alessandro Scarlatti's cantata *Lascia, deh lascia al fine*, which at times deviates from Heinichen's directives.

Peter Williams's *Figured Bass Accompaniment*[18] is perhaps the most comprehensive of all modern practical manuals. Exercises and quotations have been gathered from an unusually wide range of sources, but unfortunately these are not always identified properly and passages from treatises are often paraphrased too freely. Williams gives little of the original context that surrounds these quotations, a deficiency that can be highly misleading to the unsuspecting performer. Much of the second volume is a mere reproduction of vocal and instrumental solos readily available elsewhere; these are laced with a few brief hints of possible realization. Some questionable, but authoritatively stated, assertions lack substantiation. Nevertheless Williams, as demonstrated by this book and several articles on various aspects of continuo playing, may have the best total grasp of the subject since Arnold; his writings on thoroughbass are a lively blend of erudition and practical savvy.

Robert Donington's *The Interpretation of Early Music*[19] is a comprehensive guide to all aspects of performance practice; only a small portion is devoted to accompaniment. The format is a series of quotations with commentary; this has some obvious disadvantages. The context can be crucial to the proper understanding of excerpts from thoroughbass treatises. But within these self-imposed limits, Donington does remarkably well. His translations and paraphrases are frequently more reliable than Williams's, and his quotations generally longer. Donington's commentary contains some excellent practical insights. However, the selection of treatises and excerpts is not extensive enough to treat adequately certain aspects of continuo playing.

Previous Scholarship on Handel's Figured Bass

Previous scholars have dealt only sporadically, and never intensively, with the questions surrounding Handel's figured bass.

Both Friedrich Chrysander and Winton Dean have made perceptive comments, treated in the following chapter, on the role of figured bass in Handel's creative process. However, they have provided only general guidance.

Watkins Shaw, in *A Textual and Historical Companion to Handel's "Messiah,"*[20] states that he attempted to reconstruct the figuring of the earliest printed edition of *Messiah* excerpts, *Songs in "Messiah."* He concluded that the figuring of this edition had no special authority. But he gave no examples of it, other than two brief illustrations that were intended to show that the figuring, if interpreted literally, would generate an accompaniment that would clash with a *concertante* part.

John Tobin's book, *Handel's "Messiah,"*[21] includes a chapter and a large appendix on the subject of bass figuring. As a preparation for his study, Tobin compared the figuring of the autograph composition score, the Tenbury conducting score, three printed editions of *Messiah* "Songs" (the first two of which he dates ca. 1749 and ca. 1769), and the first published full score by Randall and Abel. The chapter introduces some intriguing performance problems, several of which are discussed at greater length in part 2 of the present book. Unfortunately, Tobin's treatment of these problems just skims the surface. Also, he does not consider the possibility that some of Handel's "errors" in figuring might be first thoughts rejected during the composition process. The appendix, "Variations in Figuring," gives the total number of figurings present in the autograph, the Tenbury score, and the Randall-Abel full score movement by movement. Variants between these two MSS and the four prints mentioned above are summarized, and interesting examples are occasionally cited, but he draws no general conclusions from this information. Nor is any indication given of the possible authenticity of the figurings in any of the printed sources. Tobin also harbors some misconceptions concerning common thoroughbass abbreviations and Handel's own figuring habits. In sum, Tobin's material is useful, but the masses of detail do not form a convincing whole and several crucial questions are left unanswered.

John Mayo, in his dissertation "Handel's Italian Cantatas,"[22] discussed some isolated figuring problems in these works. He also presented the theory that a group of continuo cantatas were revised by the composer and provided with extensive figurings for the purpose of teaching figured bass realization.²³ The idea is certainly plausible and has been accepted by most Handel scholars. But perhaps Mayo's suggestion does misplace the emphasis slightly. Another interpretation, not necessarily inconsistent with Mayo's view, would be that Handel developed, perhaps over the course of several years, richly harmonized accompaniments for these cantatas. Teaching duties may have provided the necessary impetus that made him record these harmonizations. Or it is just possible that the cantatas were revised and figured at the request of a professional singer.

Barry Cooper's article²⁴ on the organ continuo part for *Alexander's Feast* contains some inaccurate comments on bass figuring in sources for that work and, regarding the possible authenticity of the Walsh figuring, he relies too heavily on Chrysander's assumptions.

Alfred Mann's superb work on the Fitzwilliam thoroughbass and composition studies, published in the HHA Supplement/1 and related articles,²⁵ has helped to clarify Handel's attitude regarding figured bass, and has also provided some interesting hypotheses regarding his approach to teaching composition and accompaniment. Mann's commentary, as well as his decision to publish these autographs in facsimile, are to be commended. The exercises include a carefully planned, graduated course of study in the realization of bass figuring. Some of Mann's conclusions may need to be revised in light of recent evidence regarding the dating of these autographs.²⁶

Design of the Present Study

The first part of this volume provides an overview of thoroughbass figuring in manuscript and early printed sources of Handel's operas and oratorios. Primary as well as selected secondary sources will be discussed. Since certain sources are unavailable at present, this survey is necessarily incomplete. Nevertheless, it does provide a substantial and representative range of materials, sufficient to give a picture of the main problems related to figured bass in Handel sources.

Much of the figuring in the primary sources (autographs and conducting scores) originally served a compositional function; the first chapter will attempt to distinguish this type from figurings added for purely accompanimental purposes. Previous Handelians have provided little guidance in this difficult area. Figuring in the secondary sources will be described and, as much as possible, evaluated. This is a virtually unexplored area of Handel studies.

The second half of the book is devoted to several aspects of continuo accompaniment that have been superficially treated by scholars and remain problematic in modern performances. An attempt is made to provide specific guidelines for thoroughbass realization in Handel's music, but many are applicable to other composers of the period. Excerpts from eighteenth-century treatises are drawn upon to corroborate and amplify the direct evidence of Handel's own bass figuring. These performance topics are treated elsewhere, but the theoretical evidence presented is generally incomplete, and the conclusions are sometimes misleading. Also, the implications of the figuring — Handel's or otherwise — are generally ignored by scholars. The final chapter treats continuo harmonization in detail by isolating the recurring Handelian thoroughbass formulas and applying them to compositions that the composer left unfigured.

Part One

Bass Figuring in Handel Source Materials

1

Bass Figuring in Handel's Autographs

Handel's holograph composition scores consist of nearly 17,000 pages of music.[1] Originally unbound, they were probably loosely tied with thread and stacked horizontally during the composer's lifetime. Presently they are grouped into 112 bound volumes of which 97 are part of the Royal Music Library collection, British Library, and the remaining 15 are in the Fitzwilliam Museum, Cambridge. In addition, about a dozen miscellaneous pieces are scattered in various British, American, and German collections. The British Library collection, as Alexander Hyatt King observed, "is by far the largest of the autographs of any of the great musicians of the past now preserved in a single institution."[2] Certainly, the autographs form the primary source material for any serious investigation of Handel's creative process.

The autographs also afford a great deal of information on various aspects of continuo accompaniment in his music. At the same time, it must be kept in mind that his use of continuo figuring in these manuscripts was quite inconsistent. Some scores are replete with figuring, others lack it entirely. Roughly speaking, no more than half of the pages contain any figuring at all. Document 1 shows the figures that Handel used most frequently; document 2 offers a preliminary list of those autographs with significant amounts of bass figuring.

The following remarks are made with reference to the works listed in document 2. The solo sonatas and continuo cantatas are some of the most important sources of Handel's figuring extant; many of these were done with considerable care. The thoroughbass teaching material will be discussed later in the chapter. The Concerti Grossi, Op. 6, were fully figured throughout, except for the concertino sections. *Riccardo Primo* is unique among the opera autographs: it is figured fully until the middle of the last act; thereafter the figuring is sporadic. In *Siroe, Athalia,* and *L'Allegro* the figuring is incomplete, but each has a substantial amount that is spread out over the entire work. The figuring of the Coronation Anthems is complete throughout.

Document 1. Continuo Figures in Handel's Music

FREQUENTLY USED FIGURES

Single Figures

Standard Usage	6 , 7 , 2 , 4
Normally Used to Indicate Resolutions Only	3 , 8 , 5

Double Figures

Most Common	6 6 4 5 , 4 , 2
Less Common	7 9 9 5 , 7 , 4
Normally Used to Indicate Resolutions Only	5 8 8 3 , 6 , 3

Triple Figures

7 6
4 4
2 , 2

COMMON PROGRESSIONS OVER A SINGLE PITCH

Single Figures	4 3 , 7 6 , 9 8 , 5 6
Double Figures	6 5 6 4 9 8 9 8 4 3 ,(3) 2 , 7 6 , 4 3
Triple Figures	7 (8) 4 5 2 3

Within each category, figures are listed in order of frequency, starting with the most common figures.

The choral works, such as oratorios and anthems, generally contain more figuring than the operas. Exceptions include, on the one hand, the Italian oratorios, the Chandos Anthems, *Acis and Galatea*, and *Esther*, all of which have little or no figuring. Also, many of the later oratorios, including *Messiah*, have comparatively little figuring. And although *Riccardo Primo* is elaborately figured, the autographs of the Royal Academy operas preceding it are practically unfigured. Often what little figuring we find in the operas is mostly in the recitatives, rather than the arias; e.g., *Agrippina* and *Poro*. The situation is to some extent similar in *Samson*, which contains a great deal of figuring in recitatives and choruses.

Document 2. Handel Autographs
with Substantial Figuring

Complete Works

L'Allegro
Anthem, "As Pants the Hart," HWV 251d
Athaliah
Concerti Grossi, Op. 6
Coronation Anthems
Duets: "No, di voi non vuo' fidarmi," "Quel fior che all' alba ride," "Tacete, ohime"
Funeral Anthem, "The Ways of Zion Do Mourn"
Israel in Egypt
Ode for St. Cecilia's Day
Riccardo Primo
Samson
Siroe
"Pedagogical" Cantatas
Fitzwilliam Thoroughbass and Composition Studies (HHA Supplement/1)
Also various solo sonatas, continuo cantatas, and solo songs.

Excerpts

Alcestis: "Tune Your Harps"
Atalanta: "Riportai gloriosa la palma"
Imeneo: "La mia bella"
Muzio Scevola: "Vivo senza alma"
Ottone: "Falsa imagine," "Diresti poi cosi"
Rinaldo: Ouverture
Semele: Recitative and arioso, "Daughter, Obey"
Trionfo (1737): "Son larve di dolor"
Also, many English oratorio choruses.

There seems to be a concentration of large vocal works with extensive authentic figuring during the period 1724–40. Perhaps the composer became more interested in problems of continuo harmonization at this time; it is also possible that he was obliged to indicate his intentions more precisely to assist his continuo players. This trend could be said to begin with *Giulio Cesare* and *Tamerlano*, since the Cluer printed editions of these operas contain figuring which is reputedly by Handel.[3] In any case, the trend definitely begins with *Rodelinda* (1725),[4] for which Handel provided ample figuring in the conducting copy, and continues with the autograph of *Riccardo Primo* (1727) and the Fitzwilliam thoroughbass exercises, which probably date from the mid-1720s.[5] The autograph and conducting score of *Admeto* (also 1727) are lost, but the interesting figuring found in most manuscript copies could derive from the composer. From the 1730s on, Handel's interest in bass figuring seems to have transferred to the oratorios: the best examples are probably *Athalia* (1733) and *L'Allegro* (1740), but a fair amount of figuring exists in *Deborah* (1733), *Saul* (1739), *Israel in Egypt* (1739), and *Joseph* (1744) as well.

Functions of Bass Figuring in Handel's Autographs

Thoroughbass figuring was a basic element of Handel's compositional technique and served him in a variety of ways. While writing down the first draft of an opera or oratorio, he could quickly record with a few cryptic figures any details of harmony that occurred to him in passing. In a densely harmonized passage, he could notate a complete progression of several bars as a figured bass without worrying about considerations of part-writing. In a sudden rush of inspiration, figures often came more quickly than pitches, especially in heavily concerted movements. If ideas came more slowly, he could bide his time by working out elaborate continuo figuring for a passage. Even details of part-writing or the basic shape of a melodic line could be conveniently outlined in figures.

Occasionally the figuring of an entire work is so complete that the composer must have had a special purpose in mind: e.g., publication of the work (*Rodelinda*),[6] teaching (several continuo cantatas with unusually abundant and precise figuring),[7] or the necessities of performance by unusually large forces (Coronation Anthems). In large concerted movements with chorus that contain two bass parts, the composer often figures both bass parts, again for performance purposes (e.g., *Israel in Egypt*, H-G: 228f; Chandos Anthem "As Pants the Hart," HWV 251b, HHA III/5: 53f).

On the other hand, other works have very few figures, and these are reserved for chromatically altered chords, other unusual sonorities, or situations in which the harmony is not obvious. Often the composer figures only the beginning of a harmonic/melodic sequence: the player is left to work out the remainder of the passage in accord with the initial indications (e.g., H-G 51: 120, 148). In arias especially the figuring can provide enough hints so that the remainder of the harmonization can be derived, more or less logically, from what is given. An example is the second aria from the cantata *Vedendo amor* (H-G 51: 160–61). The performer may have to collate the readings of all parallel passages within an aria to arrive at a sufficient set of figures; the opening ritornello of "Di cupido impiego i vanni" from *Rodelinda* is a good example (H-G: 17–19).

In the autographs, figures often appear at a change of texture. The most common instances are transitions from a lightly textured polyphony to block chords, or from simple to denser, more complex harmony. An example of the latter is an excerpt from *Saul* (ex. 1.1). The aria is unfigured up to this point. This figuring, although certainly helpful in performance, was not primarily intended for the convenience of the continuo player. It is too sporadic. The figuring most likely served Handel's compositional needs during an early stage of the creative process. Since the upper string parts are merely accompanimental, filling out the harmonic texture, the composer could defer the task of writing them until later. Occasionally figures are found when the music changes from homophonic to strict fugal writing.

Perhaps the presence or absence of figures was to some extent determined by the composer's initial conception of a passage. Handel, as any good continuo player would, intimately knew the "feel" of standard thoroughbass progressions as well as he knew the actual sound. The presence of plentiful figures could indicate that the original source of ideas was his tactile/keyboard orientation, rather than his aural/compositional concerns. Consider this excerpt from "Mi restano le lagrime" in *Alcina* (ex. 1.2). The open, delicate string textures of the A section (practically unfigured) are replaced by the compact, routine accompanimental sonorities in the B section (highly figured).

During the composition of sequential passages, or those built on repeated motifs in the bass, continuo figuring was a wonderfully efficient means of outlining the harmonic structure. In "The Clouded Scene" from *Athalia*, for example, a constantly recurring bass motif is figured in several different ways (ex. 1.3).

In complex fugal sections, and passages replete with suspensions, figured bass provided a welcome means of organizing the material, of imposing order on the flood of creative energy. In the great "Amen" chorus from *Messiah* the figuring is quite scanty until the first fortissimo outburst. This happens to be the first time in this movement that all four parts are singing together for any appreciable interval; this outburst also coincides with a restatement of the fugal theme in the bass. Suddenly in the space of three measures we find more figures than exist in any other passage of similar length in the whole chorus. Nor is this figuring, detailed as it is, a sufficient guide to the proper continuo harmony of the passage (see m. 103, third beat, and m. 104, second beat). An example involving suspensions can also be found in *Messiah*, in the chorus "Surely, He Hath Borne Our Griefs." It contains only a small amount of figuring until the passage beginning "he was wounded for our transgressions," which is full of suspensions; these are used sequentially later in the section with the text "the chastisement."

Example 1.1. *Saul*, HWV 53, no. 76

Example 1.2. *Alcina*, HWV 34, no. 35

Example 1.3. *Athalia*, HWV 52, no. 24

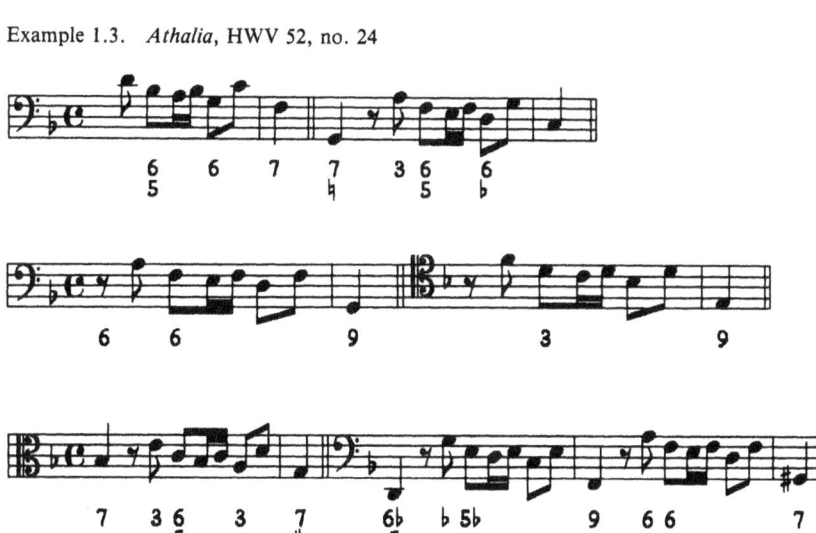

20 Handel's Autographs

Example 1.4. A Standard Recitative Progression in Handel's Music

Some Details concerning Handel's Figuring

As we study individual works more closely, and note which passages were supplied with figures, we are forced to conclude that Handel's figuring often seems to reflect his own compositional concerns rather than the needs of continuo players. This conclusion is strikingly illustrated in the oratorio holographs, where, as Winton Dean pointed out, arias of predominantly two-part texture receive little or no figuring, whereas choral movements have a great deal.[8] This is the opposite of what a capable accompanist requires. Figuring can be dispensed with in the choruses, since the vocal/orchestral parts are usually complete harmonically; any competent continuo player should be able to scan the score accurately, or figure the bass himself from the written parts. But the figuring is far from superfluous in the delicately scored arias, for here the player often has several stylistic options for the harmonization of a given passage. Dean's observation was made with specific reference to *Theodora* but is equally true of other oratorios. The continuo aria "Author of Peace" from *Saul*, for example, has only one figure, but the chorus that follows, "O Fatal Consequence of Rage," has a large amount. Continuo arias that are completely unfigured, or practically so, abound in the operas, especially *Teseo, Pastor Fido, Agrippina*, and *Rodrigo*. In *Orlando*, act 2, scene 10, there is even a continuo solo of some length which, except for the first note, is without harmonic indications.

Then, on the other hand, we often find figuring in stereotyped progressions that would have been familiar to any experienced accompanist of the period. For example, in recitative Handel repeatedly figures a particular standard progression, demonstrated in example 1.4. It is probably the most frequently used progression over a bass pedal in Italian recitative of the late Baroque period, and the accompaniment was practically standardized.[9] Yet

Handel usually figures it carefully, frequently even repeating the $^7_4$ and indicating the points of resolution with $^5_3$ or merely 3.
$_2$

There are two possible explanations for these $^7_4$ signatures in simple
$_2$
recitative. Perhaps the composer wished to indicate that a fresh chord or harmonic change was obligatory, that the accompaniment should not rest at these points. The figuring $^7_4$ seems unusually precise for Handel, but it is one
$_2$
that cannot be abbreviated: 2 implies either $^6_4$ or $^5_2$ (a bass suspension resolv-
$_2$
ing to a first inversion triad); $^4_2$ is the standard abbreviation for $^6_4$; $^7_4$ would
$_2$
imply $^7_5$ (resolving to $^7_5$); and $^7_2$, a figuring hardly ever encountered, might be
$_4$ $_3$
interpreted as $^9_7$ (normally realized as $^9_7$ resolving to $^8_6$). Thus, there is no
                                       $_3$ $_3$
other figuring for the $^7_4$ sonority. Once these dissonant intervals were shown,
$_2$
he was obliged to indicate the point of resolution as well.

But other habits of figuring are almost impossible to explain. For example, in the autograph of *Acis and Galatea*, Handel marks the phrygian cadence at the end of the Sinfonia "7 6 ♯," which is typical for this type of cadence and duplicates the orchestral parts. But the long instrumental introduction to Galatea's lament, "Must I My Acis Still Bemoan," scored only for solo oboe and continuo, is totally lacking in figuring.

Thus it would seem that the composer was seldom concerned about details of continuo harmonization, since he often provides figures where the harmony is obvious and frequently provides none where the accompanist might require some assistance. But there are exceptions, most notably Handel's thoroughbass teaching material. These manuscripts fall into two main groups: the Fitzwilliam figured bass exercises (facsimile edition, HHA Supplement/1, edited by Alfred Mann), and the "pedagogical" cantatas (found in the British Library, Royal Music Collection, RM. 20. d. 12. and RM. 20. e. 5.).

Very little can be added to Alfred Mann's work on the Fitzwilliam teaching material.[10] However, there is one important aspect of these manuscripts that reflects Handel's attitude toward continuo figuring. There is no evidence in the extant thoroughbass exercises to indicate that the composer expected the pupil to realize an unfigured bass. These manuscripts contain nothing that relates to realization of an unfigured bass as taught by contemporary theorists: no *regola dell' ottava*, no list of common bass patterns with figures, and no list of standard harmonizations of specific intervals in the bass. True, Handel was not writing a thoroughbass treatise. But he was preparing a systematic course of instruction; if the composer regarded improvisation from an unfigured bass as indispensable, or desirable, certainly some evidence of that would be present. Therefore, we cannot conclude that Handel's frequent neglect of continuo figuring in the autographs was based on a belief that it was unnecessary for the performer.

Further evidence is provided in the elaborately figured "pedagogical" cantatas. John Mayo, in his dissertation, "Handel's Italian Cantatas," first expressed the very plausible theory that certain continuo cantatas were revised by the composer as teaching material for a student of accompaniment, perhaps Princess Anne.[11] These cantatas are:

E partirai	HWV 111b
Lungi dal mio bel Nume	HWV 127c
Ninfe e pastori	HWV 139c
Sei pur bella (*La Bianca Rosa*)	HWV 160b and c
Sento la che ristretto	HWV 161c
Se pari è la tua fè	HWV 158c
Son gelsomino (*Il Gelsomino*)	HWV 164a

It should be noted that a few other cantatas, because of their unusually complete and meticulous figuring, could also have been figured for pedagogical purposes, for example, *Dolce pur d'amor*, HWV 108b, and *Mi palpita il cor*, HWV 132a.

These cantatas are indeed unique: very few others are figured so completely throughout. Also, the figuring is quite specific as regards the intervals required for a given bass note. For example, the composer seems to distinguish between $\frac{4}{2}$ and $\frac{6}{4}$, whereas in other contexts he would probably write $\frac{4}{2}$ or merely 2; he writes $\frac{6}{4}$ where he would otherwise simply write 6. The placement of figures is also very precise. The Chrysander edition of these cantatas contains several errors in the figuring alone: omission of some numbers, misplacement of others.[12] Handel has obviously taken some care with the recitatives as well as the arias. The figured harmonies can be exquisite, frequently adding single or double suspensions that are not implied in the composed parts (e.g., H-G 50: 82, last system).

The opening ritornello of the second aria of HWV 111b contains an extraordinary passage (ex. 1.5) in which the composer indicates the whole realization in notes and figures. The numerals in the first measure and a half should not be interpreted literally; they merely represent intervals above the bass. Together with the two composed parts, we have a realization (ex. 1.6) that is not only extremely effective, but also it prefigures similar passages in the body of the aria (ex. 1.7). There are other brief passages in this aria that contain two composed parts in the bass with figures; these should be realized in the same way.

These cantatas demonstrate vividly that the composer did not look upon continuo figuring as gratuitous or as unnecessary for the experienced player. On the contrary, he seems to have regarded it as a valuable tool that could be used to convey specific thematic ideas to be included in the realization. The figuring is so detailed that only an advanced player could execute

Example 1.5. *E partirai, mia vita?*, HWV 111b, no. 2

Example 1.6. Realization of Example 1.5

Example 1.7. *E partirai, mia vita?*, HWV 111b, no. 2

it adequately. If these cantatas were intended for Princess Anne, we have additional proof, since by all contemporary reports she was an excellent continuo player.[13]

Handel's Method of Composition

Friedrich Chrysander was probably the first scholar to notice that Handel's continuo figures occasionally call for chords that are not compatible with the written parts.[14] In order to explain this rather perplexing phenomenon it is necessary to outline briefly Handel's creative method in the operas and oratorios.

Five distinct stages of the composition process can be delineated:

I   Sketches
II Short score (melody and bass)
III Filling up of short score
IV Pre-performance revisions
V   Alterations for later revivals

The majority of Handel's extant sketches are housed in the Fitzwilliam Museum, Cambridge.[15] The existence of stage II can be substantiated by the fact that passages in the autographs have survived in this form; they were crossed out by the composer evidently before the completion of stage III.[16] In many holograph scores, Handel marked the end of the stage III by writing "völlig geendiget/geendet," or "ausgefüllt" (fully completed, filled in), along with the date.[17] The fourth stage involved additions, cuts, transpositions, and other changes made specifically for the initial series of performances. These were marked either in the autograph or the conducting score. Material relating to later revivals, stage V, was typically added to the conducting score only.[18]

Winton Dean describes the second and third stages with reference to the oratorios, but his remarks are applicable to the operas as well:

> In the autographs Handel's normal (though not invariable) procedure was to write first a skeleton score, comprising bass line and top part (first violin or voice) only, of a whole act and sometimes of a whole oratorio, adding dates generally at the beginning of each act and always at the end of the oratorio. The words of the recitatives would be written out in full, but without the music. After this, and without appreciable interval, he would go through the score again, filling-up the inner parts and the recitatives; adding dynamic or other marks if these had been omitted earlier . . . .
>
> As a rule Handel had in mind not only the detailed plan of the music but its orchestral lay-out before he sat down to the skeleton draft. At this stage, although he wrote only the top and bottom parts, he prepared all the staves necessary for filling up later. . . . Thus his fullest and his thinnest orchestration was meticulously planned from the start.[19]

Chrysander and Dean have suggested that the incorrect figures are a product of stage II of the creative process, that is, they were added to the autograph before the inner parts were written.[20] But since neither of these eminent Handel scholars ever cited any direct substantiation for this hypothesis, it will be examined here in some detail.

The composer could conceivably add figuring at any stage of the creative process, but the surviving evidence suggests that he did so mostly during stages II and III.

Continuo figures are missing from almost all the Fitzwilliam sketches, but some rejected fragments, "false starts" so to speak, in the British Library autograph composition scores are figured. The autograph of the *Ode for St. Cecilia's Day* provides a case in point. This manuscript contains a brief sketch (ex. 1.8) for a theme used in the first chorus. The passage was written on the bottom left corner of an otherwise blank page. It seems that the composer's first idea for setting this phrase of text had specific harmonic implications. This type of figured fragment is rare in the autographs. But many incomplete first drafts of individual arias and other sections contain figuring.

Example 1.8. Autograph of the *Ode for St. Cecilia's Day*
RM 20. f. 4., fol. 12v

[The] Di - a -pa - son clo -   sing full   in [Man]

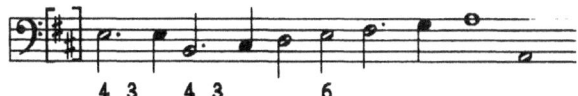

4 3   4 3   6

Reprinted by permission of the British Library

If Handel were to add figures during the fourth or fifth stages, it seems more likely that he would have put them in the performance material — conducting score and/or keyboard continuo parts — rather than the autograph, which often represents an earlier or incomplete version of a work. Admittedly a thorough examination of this aspect of the sources is yet to be done, but presently we know of only four instances in which the composer added figuring to conducting scores of operas and oratorios.[21] The few keyboard continuo parts which survive from Handel's performances contain some additional figuring, but none of this is in the composer's hand.[22] There are instances in which he added figures to scribal copies of solo cantatas.[23]

If the composer were to add bass figuring to the skeletal draft (stage II), it is possible that during the next stage he might revise some of these progressions: he might write pitches compatible with, but not implied by, the figuring (e.g., the addition of a fifth above a bass note marked merely 6), or he might alter certain sonorities drastically such that their figures would no longer be valid. The latter contingency was Chrysander's explanation for the inaccurate figures that he noticed in the scores of *Joseph* and *Jephtha*: they were put into the autograph before the filling-in process, and although Handel later refined his original harmonic conception, he neglected to cancel or rectify the obsolete figures. This is all very plausible.

Furthermore, it can be proved conclusively that Handel added figures during stage II. There exist in the autographs rejected passages in skeletal form but yet having bass figuring. An excellent example occurs in the first ritornello of "Si, che desio" from *Deidamia* (ex. 1.9). This segment, which never progressed beyond stage II, was originally intended to follow measure 14 and lead into measure 17 of the aria as printed in the H-G edition. After crossing out this passage, Handel composed two measures to replace the discarded material; the new measures were squeezed into the margin of the manuscript. As a further complication, the rejected material was itself

Example 1.9. Autograph of *Deidamia*
RM 20. a. 11., fol. 22

Example 1.9a. Original Version of *Deidamia*, First System

Reprinted by permission of the British Library

revised. The first system of the example gives the revised version; example 1.9a presents the original version. In order to alter the passage, he cancelled and wrote over the original version. (In this and the following two musical examples, notational idiosyncracies of the autograph have been reproduced.)

The sequence of compositional "events" seems fairly clear. 1) Handel wrote the treble and bass parts of the first system without figuring (ex.1.9a). 2) He continued with the top part of the next system, but immediately became dissatisfied with what he had just written. 3) He went back and revised the material in the first system, as in the first system of example 1.9. 4) At some point later, he added figuring to the skeletal passage. We cannot be sure of the exact sequence of events surrounding the placement of figures; but it is obvious that they were added to the first system after the revision, since they do not fit the original version (see the arrows in ex. 1.9a). In this case at least, the composer did not add figuring until he was to some extent satisfied with the outer parts.

The autograph of "Thou God Most High" from *Belshazzar* contains additional examples of skeletal segments with figuring, one of which is reproduced here (ex. 1.10). In all, over fifty measures of similar material were cut from this aria, but the other discarded sections were very sparsely figured; a typical specimen, for first violin, voice and continuo, is provided in example 1.11.

Example 1.10. Autograph of *Belshazzar*
RM 20. d. 10., fol. 8

Reprinted by permission of the British Library

Example 1.11. Autograph of *Belshazzar*
RM. 20. d. 10., fol. 7v

Reprinted by permission of the British Library

In Handel's autographs, deleted passages in skeletal form with figuring are hardly plentiful, however. In addition to the examples mentioned above, I have found only three others: one from *Saul* with considerable figuring,[24] and one each from *Tamerlano* and *Jephtha*, both of which have only one figure.[25] The infrequency of these passages certainly does not invalidate the Chrysander/Dean hypothesis. But until further evidence comes to light, we must conclude that Handel added figures rather infrequently or sporadically during stage II of the creative process. Rejected segments in skeletal form without bass figuring are much more common. And it should be emphasized that questionable or seemingly incorrect figures can occur in the autographs for a variety of reasons. These special cases will be defined and illustrated in the final section of this chapter. For now it must suffice to say that scholars and performers must consider each passage carefully before concluding that a questionable figure is an obsolete vestige of stage II, and, therefore, should be ignored in the realization.

Figurings That Became Obsolete during the Compositional Process

Document 3 provides a list of some of these obsolete figures. In a few cases it is difficult to determine with certainty whether a given figure is obsolete or intentional; these are marked "perhaps intentional."

The vast majority of these obsolete figures occur on isolated chords. Handel was simply altering details of his original conception. At one point in the Concerto Grosso, Op. 6, No. 6 (ex. 1.12), the $^7_5$ is at odds with the first inversion triad formed by the string parts. The figuring in this case probably does represent Handel's first impulse, being placed in the score before he composed the viola part, but after he composed the outer parts.

Occasionally, the obsolete figuring will show actual part writing that the composer rejected. The chorus "With Pious Heart" from *Solomon* contains an instance of this (ex. 1.13). The figuring implies a smoother more "normal" cadence, with a specific line implied for an inner vocal part: thus 5 4 3 ♯ corresponds to B♭ A G F♯. Handel eventually opted for a stronger cadence, which should be figured: $^{\sharp 6}_5$ $^{\sharp 6}_{4 \atop 3}$ ♯.

Another interesting example occurs in the autograph of *Imeneo*. In the B section of "Sorge nell' alma mia" (ex. 1.14), the figuring of the H-G edition has been altered to conform with the autograph. Handel originally conceived a more tense harmonization for measures 3 through 5 of the B section, with suspended fifths resolving to $^6_4$ chords. In all likelihood, the figuring was added before the upper string accompaniment was written. When he decided on these detached, disjunct quarter-note chords for the violins and violas, he probably abandoned the suspension idea as being inappropriate to the new texture. Perhaps he originally planned that the upper strings move in eighth notes—conforming to the bass—in which case the suspension idea might be more effective and more characteristic of his style. In measure 12 of the autograph the composer wrote $^4_2$, which was later crossed out, but the original bass is unclear.

Further examples occur in the famous chorus "How Dark, O Lord, Are Thy Decrees" from *Jephtha*. Chrysander states, in the preface to his edition of the work, that he suppressed the $^6_4$ $^6_3$ in the first measure (ex. 1.15) because these signatures disagree with the orchestral harmony.[26] This is not necessarily the case; they could be merely misplaced. Actually, the figuring

Document 3. Figurings Incompatible with the Composed Parts

(*Printed editions are cited wherever possible; otherwise, the British Library shelfmark is cited for the appropriate volume of autographs*)

Work	Page	System	Measure
Belshazzar (H-G)	97		4
Concerti Grossi, Op. 6 (HHA)	9		27
	63		51
	65		6
	73		10
	127		20
	150		31
	170		23^1
	256		44
Deidamia (H-G)	37	5	2
Duet, "Tacete, ohime"			22
			41
			50^2
Imeneo (H-G)	55	3	1
Jephtha[3] (H-G)	105		3
(Chrysander Autograph Facsimile)	180		1
			6
	181		3
Joseph (H-G)	108	1	2
	109	2	1^4
	136		4
	157	1	2^5
	157	1	3^6
	171		6^7
	178	2	3
	213	1	1
			3
Messiah (Chrysander Autograph Facsimile)	183		last
	263		7
(HHA)	34		21
Organ Concerto, Op. 4, No. 3 (HHA)	65		141
Riccardo Primo (H-G)	26	2	11
Rinaldo Ouverture Final Movement (RM. 20. c. 3.)[8]			13

Document 3. Continued

Work	Page	System	Measure
Rodelinda (H-G)	45	7	2
	84	1	5
	94	1	2
	99	3	3
	100	3	4
	101	2	2
	104	5	1
Serse (H-G)	42		8
Siroe (H-G)	49	2	8
	93	3	4
Tamerlano Ouverture, First Movement (RM. 20. c. 11.)[9]			2
Tolomeo (H-G)	40	4	9
(RM. 20. d. 1) "Tutto contento"			50

1. See Errata.
2. See Appendix C.
3. See also H-G: v.
4. Perhaps intentional.
5. Perhaps intentional.
6. Probably a misplacement.
7. See p. iv.
8. See Appendix C.
9. This autograph is reproduced as vol. 27 of the Garland series, *Italian Opera 1640–1770*.

Example 1.12. Concerto Grosso Op. 6, No. 6, Fifth Movement

Example 1.13. *Solomon*, HWV 67, no. 3

approximates the harmony of the fourth beat; a more accurate figuring would be $\substack{6+\\4\\2}$ $\substack{6+\\3}$. It seems most likely that Handel's figuring served as a cryptic reminder for the progression in the fourth beat; perhaps he originally intended to place it differently within the bar, as the positioning of the numbers beneath the bass implies. Two bits of supporting evidence should be noted here. First, the use of $\substack{6\\4}$ to indicate $\substack{6\\4\\2}$ is uncommon, perhaps, but not unknown: Handel himself did it in the conducting score of *Rodelinda*.[27] Also, the raised sixth, although not shown in the figuring, is practically *de rigueur* in this situation, since the following chord is a secondary dominant, V of III.[28] In any case, a literal realization of the figuring in measure 1 would not result in a characteristic Handelian progression.

Chrysander neglected to mention a more striking example of obsolete figuring which occurs in measure 6 of the same chorus: $\substack{3\\4+\\5\natural}$ (ex. 1.16). (Curiously, Chrysander retains this, although there are equally valid reasons for deleting it as there are for the obsolete figures in m. 1.) The 5♮ could be merely an error on the composer's part; perhaps he intended to write $\substack{3\\4+\\6\natural}$. It is just possible that Handel originally conceived this extraordinary dissonance—a C-minor triad with an F♯—to dramatically underscore the word "thy" in the first line of the chorus. As his concept of the passage evolved, the tense sonority may have been softened considerably to $\substack{3\\4+\\6\natural}$, and the original piercing cry of anguish made instead into an expression of resignation and awe. Another possible explanation is that Handel originally intended a $\substack{3\\4+}$ sonority (with or without a major sixth), and the 5♮ repre-

Example 1.14. *Imeneo*, HWV 41, nos. 14a and 14b

Example 1.15. *Jephtha*, HWV 70, no. 29

Example 1.16. *Jephtha*, HWV 70, no. 29

(orchestral parts omitted)

sents an anticipation that would occur just before the downbeat of the next measure.

Discarded Figurings

Handel's frequent failure to correct these obsolete figures has received considerable attention in scholarly circles.[29] But, curiously, the instances in which he did make corrections or deletions in his figuring have received little, if any, serious scrutiny. These corrections are by no means rare; document 4 offers a list of some that can be found in the British Library and Fitzwilliam Museum autographs. Other examples can be found in the Hamburg performing score of *Rodelinda*.

Corrections in figuring could arise in a number of ways. Occasionally he did correct obsolete figurings, especially if they clearly contradicted a revised bass or top part. Very often Handel would scratch out an unwanted bass along with the figures belonging to it. If both the melody and the bass were altered, the composer usually provided fresh figuring, as in the autograph of *Riccardo Primo* (ex. 1.17). The remainder of the aria contains many cancelled figures as well.

Document 4. Corrections of Figuring in Handel's
Autograph Manuscripts

British Library

		(folio)
Alcina	RM. 20. a. 4.	48, 50v
L'Allegro	RM. 20. d. 5.	22, 41, 58v
Arminio	RM. 20. a. 8.	71v
"As Pants the Hart"	RM. 20. g. 10.	26
Athalia	RM. 20. h. 1.	15, 16
Belshazzar	RM. 20. d. 10.	8
Concerti Grossi, Op. 6	RM. 20. g. 11.	19v, 20, 32, 62, 93v, 96, 96v
Coronation Anthems	RM. 20. h. 5.	12v, 14v
Deidamia	RM. 20. a. 11.	22
Funeral Anthem	RM. 20. d. 9.	5, 13v, 14v, 19, 19v, 21v, 24v
Giustino	RM. 20. b. 4.	81
Imeneo	RM. 20. b. 5.	33v
Jephtha	Chrysander facsimile	pp. 33, 39, 181, 182
Lungi dal mio bel Nume	RM. 20. d. 12.	28v, 31, 31v, 43v
Messiah	RM. 20. f. 2.	47
	Chrysander facsimile	p. 93
Poro	RM. 20. b. 13.	7v
Riccardo Primo	RM. 20. c. 2.	21, 22, 27v, 46v, 47, 47v, 48, 58
Samson	RM. 20. f. 6.	54, 65
Saul	RM. 20. g. 3.	29v
Tolomeo	RM. 20. d. 1.	8v, 77
	RM. 20. d. 19.	28v

Fitzwilliam Museum (Miscellaneous short works and fragments)

	(page)
MS 252	2, 3, 4, 5
MS 253	32
MS 258	85
MS 259	48, 63
MS 260	13, 14
MS 261	39, 53, 56, 58, 59
MS 262	9, 25

Occasionally, the corrections would occur because the composer refined his sense of the continuo harmony. The opening of the autograph of *Lungi dal mio bel Nume*, one of the pedagogical cantatas, is given in example 1.18. The $\begin{smallmatrix}7+\\6\\4\\2\end{smallmatrix}$ figuring would fit the revised vocal part, but apparently

Example 1.17. Autograph of *Riccardo Primo*
RM 20. c. 2., fol. 46v

rejected for:

Reprinted by permission of the British Library

Example 1.18. Autograph of *Lungi dal mio bel Nume*
RM 20. d. 12., fol. 31

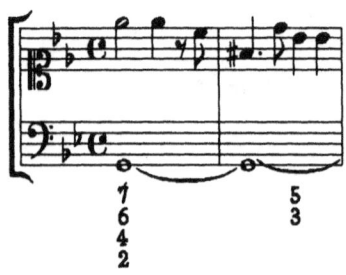

rejected for:

Reprinted by permission of the British Library

he decided to save the major seventh until the voice has it in the second measure. In the autograph of *Tolomeo* we find a correction at the end of the B section of "Cielo ingiusto" (ex. 1.19). Perhaps Handel rejected the $^6_5$ harmony because it would unnecessarily muddle the texture, and deprive the accented passing tone in the voice part of much of its expressivity. In the Fitzwilliam Museum autograph of the Sonata in B-flat for recorder, HWV 377, the second beats of the first and third full measures of the excerpt below (ex. 1.20) were originally marked $3^4_{6\natural}$. This correction is especially

Example 1.19. Autograph of *Tolomeo*
             RM 20. d. 1., fol. 8v

Reprinted by permission of the British Library

Example 1.20. Autograph of the Sonata for Recorder in B♭, HWV 377
             Fitzwilliam Museum MU MS 260, p. 13

Reprinted by permission of the Syndics of the Fitzwilliam Museum

interesting in the first measure, because the upper part has the fourth (C, held over from the first beat), which the composer obviously did not want in the continuo. This example contradicts several theorists who allow the addition of a fourth to a bass note figured 6 in certain situations, especially if the bass is moving stepwise from a first inversion tonic chord to a root position tonic chord, or vice versa.[30]

Problematic Figurings: Definitions and Examples

The autographs contain several types of problematic figuring that are not directly related to Handel's compositional concerns during the initial stages of the creative process. These types will be defined and illustrated with examples, so that scholars and performers will have some basis for distinguishing them from the obsolete figurings, which, since they represent harmonic progressions rejected by the composer, are not valid for performance. Some of the problematic figurings discussed below are valid in performance; others are valid if they are not interpreted literally.

1) Slight inaccuracies. Although the composer seldom makes an egregious mistake in bass figuring, frequently he is careless about indicating a necessary chromatic alteration: e.g., he writes simply 6 where a ♯6 or $^6_{3\flat}$ is demanded by the tonality or the composed parts.

2) Incomplete figuring. Often the figuring that is present is incomplete in itself; this can be rather misleading to the inexperienced player. Handel frequently writes 4   3 as a shorthand for $^6_4$ $^5_3$.[31] Occasionally in recitatives he writes $^4_2$ in situations where he would normally write $^7_{4}_{2}$ (e.g., *Amadigi*, HHA II/8: 14). In the vast majority of cases, he uses $^4_2$ as the standard abbreviation for $^6_{4}_{2}$. His use of 2 alone is often ambiguous; in most cases the composed parts provide a clue as to whether $^5_2$ or $^6_{4}_{2}$ is needed. The single figure 2 often means $^5_2$, possibly $^7_{4}_{2}$, but never $^2_{4}_{2}$. Sometimes the figuring even fails to indicate necessary resolutions of discords (e.g., H-G 50: 2).

3) Retrospective figurings,[32] in which intervals are reckoned from the previous bass note. Although these retrospective figurings frequently might have been inadvertent, it is also possible that they were used intentionally for ease of figuring, to clarify voice leading, or to relate the required chords to common continuo progressions. Retrospective figurings frequently appear when there is a normal resolution occurring over an ornamented bass or one which descends by step. An instance can be found in the "Hallelujah!" chorus from *Messiah* (ex. 1.21). Obviously, the figuring on the asterisked beat should be $^6_{4+}_{2}$, as Handel himself marked the same progression four measures earlier. Other examples occur in Handel's *Belshazzar* (H-

Example 1.21. Autograph of *Messiah*
From Da Capo Press reprint, 1969, p. 199

Example 1.22. *Susanna*, HWV 66, no. 1

Realization:

Example 1.23. Concerto Grosso Op. 6, No. 3, Fourth Movement

G: 97) and J. S. Bach's cantata *Schwingt freudig euch empor*, second movement, measure 7.

4) Complementary figures. These amplify the existing harmony by adding intervals, often dissonances such as sevenths or ninths, that are not present in the concerted parts. At the conclusion of the first chorus in *Susanna* (ex. 1.22), Handel's figuring $^\sharp_9$ 8 does not imply an added suspension in the first violin as the editor of the HHA edition supposed; rather, the figuring indicates an expressive enrichment of the continuo harmony. Complementary figures can imply a full chordal accompaniment in passages that are written only in two or three parts (e.g., *Joseph*, H-G: 109). They also occur in pedal points.[33]

5) Intentionally incompatible figures. Certain kinds of temporary clashes between continuo and concerted parts may have been intended by the composer. The obvious example is a short appoggiatura or accented passing tone; typically, no adjustment was made for these in the accompaniment. Sometimes the incompatible figuring is so consistent with the composer's style that it must be regarded as intentional. The fourth movement of Concerto Grosso, Op. 6, No. 3 may have a figuring of this type (ex. 1.23). The figured progression is very typical of Handel's pedal points. If the harpsichord, rather than the organ, is the continuo instrument, many of these clashes are less arresting.

2

Bass Figuring in Handel's Conducting Scores

The bulk of Handel's conducting scores are housed in the Staats- und Universitäts-Bibliothek Carl von Ossietzky, Hamburg. The remainder, along with some fragments from the set of conducting scores, can be found in the British Library, the Fitzwilliam Museum, St. Michael's College in Tenbury, and the Deutsche Staatsbibliothek in Berlin.[1] These *Handexemplare,* or performing scores, were generally copied by Smith Sr. directly from the autograph; so, for the most part, the figuring of the conducting scores accurately reflects the autograph. Friedrich Chrysander, who normally based his edition of a given work on the Hamburg performing scores, was reasonably faithful in reproducing the figuring contained therein. Thus, the H-G editions usually contain only figuring that is present in the autograph. Exceptions include *Admeto,* for which Chrysander included the figuring of an unidentified manuscript (probably British Library MS. RM. 19. c. 2.) since no autograph or conducting score exists, *Alexander's Feast,* and several arias from *Ottone*; for the last two works, Chrysander took figuring from the early printed editions.[2] Other exceptions are instances in which the composer himself put additional figuring into the performing score; these additional figurings are the topic of this chapter.

Handel frequently made annotations and corrections in the performing scores. Aside from the names of singers, directions for transposition, and alterations of vocal tessitura, one occasionally finds added figurings. Chrysander noticed these figurings in the conducting scores of *Rodelinda* and *Jephtha*.[3] Figurings in the composer's hand also occur in the Fitzwilliam fragments of the conducting score for *Scipione*.[4] Hans Dieter Clausen, in his excellent monograph on these performing scores, notes that Handel "sometimes corrected or enlarged the bass figuring," and later cites the *Cembalopartitur* for *Serse* as well as the figurings for *Rodelinda* noticed by Chrysander.[5] A thorough study of this aspect of the conducting scores may yield further examples. A summary of Handel's additional figurings in the conducting scores is contained in document 5.

Document 5. Autograph Figuring in Handel's Conducting Scores

(*Other examples may exist*)

Jephtha, accompagnato "Deeper and Deeper Still" — considerable additional figuring.

Rodelinda — extensive figuring throughout, except for the recitatives.

Scipione — slight additional figuring in a recitative.

Serse — a small amount of additional figuring, mostly in recitatives.

The figures added to the scores for *Serse* and *Scipione* are to be sure very few and are confined to simple recitative. And in *Jephtha*, Chrysander mentions autograph figuring for one movement only: the accompanied recitative, "Deeper and Deeper Still."[6] For the most part, the figuring for *Jephtha* merely duplicates the orchestral string parts.[7]

The figuring added to the conducting score for *Rodelinda*, on the other hand, is quite extensive. The present chapter will deal primarily with this work.

Handel's Figuring of *Rodelinda*

Handel completed the opera *Rodelinda* on 20 January 1725. The first performance took place under the auspices of the Royal Academy of Music at the King's Theatre on 13 February of that year. The Hamburg performing score (MA/1047) was copied by Smith Sr., presumably before the first performance. Sometime before December 1725, Handel added continuo figuring for the arias, duet, *coro*, and instrumental movements, but not for the plain or accompanied recitatives.[8] The composer used the score in performance until 1731,[9] but he did not figure additions to the opera for later revivals. These "additional songs" were copied by Smith and Clausen's H4 on smaller paper and inserted into the manuscript.

The heavy figuring that Handel placed into the conducting score for *Rodelinda* is unparalleled. Why did he take the trouble in this particular case?

Chrysander recognized the importance of the figuring and included it in the H-G edition of 1876. However, his transcription of the figuring was unreliable, possibly because of the large amount of it: there are over fifty errors of various kinds (see document 6). In the very brief preface, Chrysander offers an explanation for the composer's unusually ample figuring:

> The remarkably full figuring is a later addition to the conducting score only, in which it was inserted by Handel himself, being evidently intended to serve as a guide to an unskilled accompanist whom he had to employ at the production of this opera.[10]

Chrysander's theory was no doubt influenced by his own perceptions about figuring, which were not firmly grounded in eighteenth-century principles. He believed that continuo figuring was unnecessary, even undesirable, for a competent accompanist, and that it was only intended for those "inexperienced in harmony."[11] It is difficult to find any theoretical justification for this position, as we saw in the introduction. But even if we accept Chrysander's flawed premise, his conclusion about the figuring for *Rodelinda* is still incorrect.

His theory is untenable for these reasons: 1) An unskilled accompanist would require just as much help in some of the recitatives — especially those involving abrupt modulations, difficult keys, and so forth — as in the arias. Handel added not a single figure to any of the recitatives, which are not figured sufficiently; the only figuring contained therein is in Smith's hand. 2) Although the figuring for *Rodelinda* is much fuller than that found in most of Handel's large vocal works, it still leaves many problems of continuo harmonization unsolved. Figures are missing in places where an inexperienced player would require assistance (several instances occur in the B section of "Sono i colpi della sorte"), and can be incomplete when they are present: the composer uses some rather misleading abbreviations in the basso continuo, notably 4 3 for $^6_4$ $^5_3$, and also frequently neglects necessary accidentals in minor-key cadences and simple recitative (ex. 2.1). The figuring, useful as it is, is often not ample enough to guard against the ineptness of an "unkundigen Begleiter;" a fair amount of skill and taste, as well as a constant awareness of the composed parts, would still be required of the cembalist. 3) The figuring does not resemble that found in Handel's thoroughbass teaching material: the Fitzwilliam exercises and the pedagogical cantatas. Double figures are used less frequently in *Rodelinda* and triple figures are practically nonexistent because the composer does not explicitly spell out many chords that might call for triple figures: he uses $^6_4$ for $^6_4_2$ (ex. 2.2). His use of 6 can be ambiguous: this figure can be found where the composed parts have a fourth (implying $^6_3$) or a fifth (implying $^6_5$) above the bass; it can also occur on beats that seem to require a $^6_4_2$ chord (ex. 2.3). Despite the relative completeness of the figuring, an inexperienced player would need to supplement it considerably for performance. Also, Handel's alignment of figures with the bass is not as consistently precise as it is in the teaching material.

Document 6. Figuring Mistakes in the H-G Edition of *Rodelinda*

Page	System	Measure	Beat	H-G	Conducting Score
4	1	2	3		possibly 6
5	4	2	1	6	6
7	1	2	1	♯	7♯
8	9	9	1		6
9	3	10	1		♯
9	7	8	1		♯
10	5	9	1	(♮)	
14	3	1	3	4	♮
15	5	4	4		6
17	7	7	1	6	probably 5
18	5	4	1		7
19	1	10	1		♭7
19	1	12	2		♭
19	2	1	1		6
19	4	10	1	6	
26	3	5	1,3		4 ♯
26	4	8	2		♯
29	4	4	3	6	6
29	5	5	1½	6	6
29	7	3	1	6	6
30	1	6	1	6	
31	6	3	1	6/4	6/5
34	5	3,4	2	3/(6)	3
36	1	3	3,4		7 ♯
37	5	8	1		7
37	7	1	3	♯	5♯
37	7	8	1		6
46	4	2	4		7 6
53	7	2	2		6
54	2	4	3	6/5	♮/6/5
58	4	3	2		3
58	5	1	3,4		5/3 6/4
59	2	3	1	5/3	5/♮
60	3	3	3	7♮	♮/7

Document 6. Continued

Page	System	Measure	Beat	H-G	Conducting Score
60	4	first full	3		♮
60	4	second full		6 6 6	♭ ♭ ♭
63	7	2	3½	6♭	$^{♭}_{6}$
64	2	1	4½	6♭	6♮
64	3	2	2	6♭	probably 6♮
69	1	4	1	$^{4}_{2}$	probably $^{4♮}_{2}$
69	2	4	1	6	
69	3	4	3		6
70	1	4	1	$^{4}_{2}$	$^{4♮}_{2}$
79	1	second full	1	5	♯
83	7	5	2		♯
84	1	5	2½	6	♯
85	6	2	3	6♭	6
92	4	3	2½		♭
96	3	4	1		$^{6}_{5}$
100	1	3	4	7 6	7 6 6
105	2	1	1		6

Since it seems highly unlikely that Handel figured the opera to assist such a player, what was his intention? One explanation is that the composer was adding the figuring for inclusion in the printed edition of Cluer and Creake. This would explain why the recitatives received no additional figuring by the composer: it was assumed from the outset that the recitatives would not be printed.[12] The portions of the opera figured by Handel are identical to the contents of the print; the only exception is the short sinfonia that leads into the accompanied recitative "Pompe vane di morte." Although this movement was figured by Handel, it is missing from the print. Perhaps it was originally intended to be included since similar short instrumental movements preceding *accompagnati* were included in the Cluer prints of other Handel operas of this period, for example, *Giulio Cesare* and *Alessandro*.

Rodelinda was the first work of Handel's to be published by subscription and "in Score with all the [orchestral] Parts";[13] it would be only natural

Example 2.1. *Rodelinda*, HWV 19, Ouverture, no. 1

Example 2.2. *Rodelinda*, HWV 19, no. 20

for the composer to take a keen interest in the venture. Under these circumstances, it seems rather implausible that he would entrust the important and difficult task of figuring the work to an assistant. Also, advertisements for the original edition state that the composer provided the figuring; in this case, there seems little reason to dismiss this claim as extravagant or untrue.[14]

Furthermore, it is clear that the Cluer figuring was derived from the conducting score. A comparison of the *basso continuo* in these two sources reveals a remarkable similarity. This is true of lighter textures as well as fully harmonized passages in which the figuring is more obvious, since it

Example 2.3. *Rodelinda*, HWV 19, nos. 34a and 20

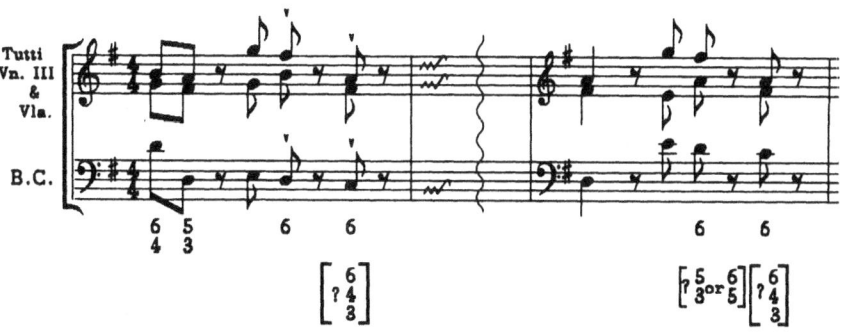

normally follows the harmony of the composed parts. Also, the print reproduces some very idiosyncratic figurings by the composer; e.g., the ritornelli of "Ritorna, oh caro" and "Tra i sospetti."

The results of a thorough comparison of these sources is given in document 7. The document follows the numbering system of Bernd Baselt's *Händel-Handbuch*. For the purposes of the chart, "figure" will denote all the symbols that apply to a single sonority: for example, ♯3 will be reckoned as one figure, as will ♮. The second column from the left gives the total figures present in the conducting score, but not in the Cluer print. The next row gives the number in Cluer but not in the Hamburg score. The last gives first the number of variants between the two sources, then details the actual variants with Handel's figuring in the conducting score first, and then, after the slash, the Cluer reading. Slight deviations in the placement of figures between the two sources have not been taken into account; examples of this are almost nonexistent in any case.

Document 7. Figuring Discrepancies between the Cluer Printed Edition (CL) and the Hamburg Conducting Score (H) of *Rodelinda*

Movement	Number in H but not in CL	Number in CL but not in H	Variants H/CL
Ouverture	1	0	1: ♯/6
1. Aria	5	0	3: 4/♮ $\begin{smallmatrix}6\\4\end{smallmatrix}/\begin{smallmatrix}6\\5\end{smallmatrix}$ $\begin{smallmatrix}5\\♯\end{smallmatrix}/\begin{smallmatrix}4\\♯\end{smallmatrix}$
2. Aria	3	0	3: all ♯/6
3. Aria	5	0	0
4. Aria	6	0	0
5. Aria	6	0	2: 6(?)/5 3/9
7a. Aria	3 — parts of 3 others	0	0
8. Aria	3 — part of 1	1	2: $\begin{smallmatrix}7\\5\\3\end{smallmatrix}/\begin{smallmatrix}7\\9\\3\end{smallmatrix}$ 8/♭
10. Aria	1	0	0
11. Aria	2	0	1: ♯/6
12a. Aria	8	1	0
14. Aria	4	0	2: ♯/6 $\begin{smallmatrix}6\\8\end{smallmatrix}/\begin{smallmatrix}6\\♯\end{smallmatrix}$
15. Aria	9	0	1: 6♮/6
16. Aria	6	0	0
17a. Aria	2	0	0
18. Aria	6	0	0
19. Aria	1	0	1: $\begin{smallmatrix}6\\5\end{smallmatrix}/\begin{smallmatrix}6\\♯\end{smallmatrix}$
20. Aria	5 — parts of 2	0	1: $\begin{smallmatrix}5\\6\end{smallmatrix}/\begin{smallmatrix}6\\♮\end{smallmatrix}$
21. Aria	12 — part of 1	0	0
22. Aria	2	0	0
23a. Aria	7	0	1: $\begin{smallmatrix}5\\♯\end{smallmatrix}/\begin{smallmatrix}5\\♯\end{smallmatrix}$
24a. Duetto	4 — part of 1	1	1: $\begin{smallmatrix}5\\♯\end{smallmatrix}/\begin{smallmatrix}(?)5\\4\end{smallmatrix}$
25. Aria	4 — 1 misplaced	0	2: 3/5 $\begin{smallmatrix}4+\\2\end{smallmatrix}/\begin{smallmatrix}4\\2\end{smallmatrix}$
26. Aria	5	0	1: $\begin{smallmatrix}4+\\6\end{smallmatrix}$ 5/$\begin{smallmatrix}4+\\6\end{smallmatrix}$ 6
27. Aria	7 — part of 1	0	1: ⁺3/7

Document 7. Continued

Movement	Number in H but not in CL	Number in CL but not in H	Variants H/CL	
28. Arioso	6 – part of 1	0	2:	$^{6\flat}_4 / ^{6\natural}_4$ $^{7\flat}_\flat / \flat 7$
30a. Aria	0	0	0	
31. Aria	7	0	0	
33a. Aria	3	1	1:	6/6
34a. Aria	7 – part of 1	0	0	
35. Coro	1	0	1:	$^{5\natural}_4 / ^{6\natural}_4$

At first glance it would seem that quite a large number of figures are missing from the Cluer edition, but the average is roughly five per movement. The engravers often had difficulty fitting in all of them within predetermined limitations of space. It is noteworthy that only four figures were added to the text by Cluer, and at least two of these are obvious engraving errors. This is true of many of the variants as well, of which there are 27; and one-fourth of these are merely the result of the engraver's failure to add a slash to indicate a raised sixth. Omissions aside, Cluer's edition, especially considering its time and the haste with which it was prepared, compares favorably with Chrysander's. Also, the Cluer edition generally follows Handel's vertical sequence of figures and alignment with the bass more closely than does Chrysander.

3

Bass Figuring in Opera and Oratorio Continuo Parts

Very few of the original vocal and instrumental parts used in Handel's performances have survived. It is generally assumed that they were destroyed in various London theater fires during the late eighteenth century. Thus, a rich resource of information on Handelian performance practice has probably been lost forever. Handel bequeathed a set of parts for *Messiah* to the Foundling Hospital, but these do not include a keyboard part. The Aylesford Collection, originally owned by Charles Jennens, contained a large quantity of vocal and instumental parts, including a large number of keyboard continuo parts, but these were probably not used in performance. Both sets were prepared by copyists of the Smith circle.[1]

This chapter will focus on opera and oratorio keyboard continuo parts which were either used in performance under the composer's direction, and/or were originally part of the Aylesford collection. The harpsichord part for *Alexander's Feast* is the prime example; this MS was actually used by continuo players in the first and subsequent performances of the work under the composer's direction. Surviving organ continuo parts for the same work may have been copied from Handel's performance material. The Hamburg *Cembalopartituren* were probably used as continuo parts in the original performances. Aylesford keyboard continuo parts in Manchester and Washington, D.C., by far the largest group, will also be discussed.

The Hamburg *Cembalopartituren*

The collection of conducting scores in the Staats- und Universitäts-Bibliothek Carl von Ossietsky, Hamburg, includes sixteen *Cembalopartituren* (harpsichord scores), all of which were evidently originally part of the composer's working collection. Chrysander believed that they were used by Handel's continuo players in the original performances, and this assumption has never been seriously questioned. (They may have been primarily

Document 8. Hamburg *Cembalopartituren*
(*With dates of use*)

Alessandro Severo	1737/38
Arianna	1733–35
Ariodante	1734–36
Ezio	1731/32
Faramondo	1737/38
Lucio Papiro	1731/32
Oreste	1734/35
Ormisda	1729–31
Il Parnasso in Festa	1733–41
Partenope	1729–31
Il Pastor Fido	1733–35
Poro	1730–37
Rinaldo	1730/31
Serse	1737/38
Sosarme	1731–34
Venceslao	1730/31

Hamburg *Cembalopartituren* in Continuo Format
(*Mostly basso continuo and solo voice*)

OPERAS BY HANDEL

Il Parnasso in Festa	MA/1038a
Il Pastor Fido	MA/1057

PASTICCI PERFORMED BY HANDEL

Oreste	MA/1034a
Ormisda	MA/1036
Venceslao	MA/189

rehearsal scores, but there seems no way to test this hypothesis.) As a rule, the *Cembalopartituren* were updated with insertions, deletions, and other alterations relating to various revivals, and were certainly used in conjunction with the conducting scores. However, only five of the *Cembalopartituren* actually have the format of continuo parts (document 8). The others are in the form of full scores, either complete or incomplete. They date from 1729 to 1738, and they relate to Handel's opera and pasticcio performances, mostly at the King's Theatre.[2]

Chrysander's contention that the *Cembalopartituren* for *Il Pastor Fido* and *Rinaldo* were partly copied by Handel's cembalist, and represented what he needed to know from the score to accompany properly, is incorrect,

Document 9. Hamburg Manuscripts with Excerpts in
Continuo Format

	CONDUCTING SCORES	
Joseph	MA/1025	H-G: v-vii
Judas Maccabeus	MA/1026	H-G: ii-iii
Occasional Oratorio	MA/1033	H-G: 188-91
Poro	MA/1042	H-G: 102, 107, 110, 115, 119
	CEMBALOPARTITUREN	
Arianna	MA/1005a	
Ariodante	MA/1006a	
Poro	MA/1042a	

as Clausen has pointed out. The contents and copyists of these MSS clearly contradict this hypothesis. The copyists were the same as those involved in the preparation of the conducting scores and other copies.[3]

The *Cembalopartituren* for Handel's operas do not contain any substantial supplementary figuring, although both *Il Pastor Fido* and *Parnasso in Festa* are sporadically figured. The contents, dating, and copyists of the *Cembalopartituren* have been thoroughly discussed in Clausen's excellent catalog. The *Cembalopartituren* for *Il Pastor Fido* and *Rinaldo* were published by Chrysander (H-G, vols. 84, 58). The preparation of the manuscript for *Rinaldo* is treated in detail in the recent study by Dean and Knapp of Handel's operas.[4] Some of the Hamburg manuscripts contain excerpts in continuo format; examples from the conducting scores were also published by Chrysander (document 9).

RCM 900

The harpsichord part for *Alexander's Feast* (London: Royal College of Music MS 900) was copied by Smith Sr. for Handel's first series of performances in 1736. Interestingly enough, it predates the conducting score. This can be ascertained by the fact that the composer made a final set of revisions to the autograph; these were incorporated into the conducting score, but were not originally present in the harpsichord part. The revisions had to be entered into the part by pasting pieces of paper—either blank or containing new music—over unwanted material. Additional music was also inserted into the part for later revivals, but this can be distinguished from the rest through an examination of paper types.[5] The contents and figuring of RCM 900 are listed below (document 10).

Some movements of the harpsichord part for *Alexander's Feast* are extensively figured, but most contain only a few figures. Only seven movements are figured to any useful extent: the Ouverture, 1, 5, 6, 12, 20, and 21 (document 10). Perhaps these are the only movements in which a second harpsichord was required, since we assume that Handel used a full score to direct performances of *Alexander's Feast* from the first harpsichord. The lack of sufficient figuring in most movements does not necessarily indicate that the second harpsichord was not called for in these cases. A competent continuo player of the period was expected to cope with a sparsely figured bass part if, as in RCM 900, the solo part was also present. Heinichen implies that such parts are common, especially in opera.[6] It is more difficult to justify the lack of figures in the choruses of RCM 900, for in these no vocal parts are given. Perhaps the continuo in these movements was provided by organ and first harpsichord (Handel). The figuring present in RCM 900 is very similar to the fuller figuring of the Walsh edition.

A curious directive is written in pencil above the Ouverture: "Don't figure it." This apparently indicates that the performer should not realize the figures in this movement. Perhaps this was Handel's intention.[7] But, on the other hand, it may not be an original marking, since the part does indeed contain extensive figurings for this movement which are not present in the autograph. Even if it does relate to the original performances, continuo chords could still have been provided by the composer.

Three names appear on the outside of the part (document 10). Sigr. Pasqualini may have been Nicolo Pasquali, keyboard player and author of *Thorough-Bass Made Easy*, or, more likely perhaps, Pasqualino de Marzis, a composer of cello sonatas published by Walsh. Caporale is certainly Andrea Caporale, a well-known cellist of the time. I have not identified a continuo player named Walsh.

RM. 19. a. 10.

The organ part for *Alexander's Feast* is preserved in two manuscripts, both originally part of the Aylesford Collection and now deposited in the British Library: RM. 19. a. 10. and RM. 19. a. 1., ff. 90–110. These parts are probably fair copies of an original that was used in Handel's performances sometime during 1736–37. The contents of these two versions are substantially the same, except that the second manuscript contains the continuo parts of two concertos which were included in Handel's performances of the work in 1736: Op. 4, No. 6 and the "Concerto in *Alexander's Feast*," HWV 318. When the parts were copied is not certain, although Donald Burrows suggests that RM. 19. a. 10. was done before 1742 on the basis of watermarks.[8] Barry Cooper believes that the part is most likely the work of

Document 10. Contents of the Harpsichord Part for *Alexander's Feast*
(Royal College of Music MS 900)
Copyist: Smith Sr.

First page (Smith Sr.): "Harpsichord./ Sigr. Pasqualini." Below, in pencil: "Mr. Walsh/ Mr. Walsh/ Mr. Walsh and Caporale."

Part I

Ouverture—Figured bass.
Recit.: Voice and figured bass.
  1. Air: Voice and figured bass.
  2. Chorus: Bass, 3 figures.
Recit.: Voice and bass, 2 figures.
  3. Accompagnato: Voice and bass, 4 figures.
  4. Chorus: Bass, 1 figure.
  5. Air: Voice and figured bass.
     (Violin cues added by another hand over rests in the vocal part.)
Recit.: Voice and bass, 5 figures.
  6. Air: Voice and bass, partially figured.
     Chorus: Bass only.
Recit.: Voice and bass, 2 figures.
  7. Accompagnato: Voice and bass, 8 figures.
  8. Air: Voice and bass, 3 figures.
     (One short cue—Vns. I and II—at the beginning.)
  9. Accompagnato: Voice and bass, partially figured.
 10. Chorus: Bass, 6 figures.
Recit.: Voice and unfigured bass.
 11. Arioso: Voice, cello, solo, and bass, 5 figures.
 12. Air: Voice and figured bass.
     (Figures present up to the beginning of measure 29, only 1 figure thereafter.)
 13. Chorus: Bass, 2 figures.
 14. Air: Bass and voice, 1 figure.

Part II

 15. Accompagnato and Chorus: Voice and bass, 3 figures.
 16. Air: Voice and bass, 6 figures (all in B section).
 17. Accompagnato: Voice and unfigured bass.
 18. Air: Voice and unfigured bass.
 19. Air: Voice and unfigured bass.
     Chorus: Bass only.

58   Opera and Oratorio Continuo Parts

Document 10.   Continued

---

20. Accompagnato: Voice and unfigured bass.
    Chorus: Figured bass.
    Recit.: Solo voices and bass, 1 figure.
21. Chorus: Bass, partially figured.
    (The Smith Sr. copy of this chorus ends at measure 26; a complete version, without any figuring, is also present in a different hand.)

Additional Movements

Recit. "Your Voices Tune:" Voice and unfigured bass.
22. Duetto: Unfigured bass.

Handel himself.[9] The contents and figuring of the organ part are given in document 11.

The organ part for *Alexander's Feast* is probably "the most valuable surviving record of Handel's treatment of the organ continuo."[10] Four different textures are found in the part: 1) bass line marked *tasto solo*; 2) bass line figured; 3) treble (usually same as the choral soprano) plus bass usually with figuring; and 4) written-out realization in 3 to 4 parts without figuring. (See document 11 for the presence of these textures in a given movement.) Textures 1 and 4 predominate; bass figuring is not present in these textures because it is unnecessary.

Figuring does appear in texture 2 as an indication of suitable harmonic filler for the outer voices notated in the part (ex. 3.1). The notation of these passages implies that the organ is being used primarily to support the choral parts, and that the exact placement of the inner voices is not crucial. The unusual nature of the figuring in this texture—frequently redundant or indicating intervals that are understood by the conventions of figured bass; for example, 3, $\frac{5}{3}$—and the fact that generally in the organ part figuring appears only when really necessary, all indicate that the figuring was added by the composer to serve the practical needs of the accompanist.

Texture 2 appears only twice in the part: the end of no. 4 (transcribed below) and the beginning of no. 23. In both cases, the use of this texture, as opposed to the more completely notated ones, may have been a practical expedient. The opening of no. 23 was one of the last revisions made to the score by Handel; perhaps he added it during or after the organ part was copied. The conclusion of no. 4 (ex. 3.2) betrays a sudden impatience in writing out full chords, which seems characteristic of the composer. The figuring idiosyncrasies also suggest the composer.

Document 11. Contents of the Organ Part for *Alexander's Feast*
(RM. 19. a. 10.)
Copyist: S2

Part I

Ouverture—Unfigured bass marked *tasto solo*.
2. Chorus: Written-out accompaniment in 2-4 parts; 15 figures, all but 3 in 2-part textures.
3. Accompagnato: Unfigured bass.
4. Chorus: Written-out accompaniment, frequently *unisono*, with 8 measures of figured bass at the end; 9 figures.
5. Air: Unfigured bass marked *tasto solo*.
6. Air: Unfigured bass marked *tasto solo*.
   Chorus: Written-out accompaniment; no figures.
7. Accompagnato: Unfigured bass marked *tasto solo*.
10. Chorus: Written-out accompaniment in 2-4 parts, only 2-part passages are figured; 17 figures.
13. Chorus: Written-out accompaniment, partially figured; only 2-part passages are figured.

Part II

15. Accompagnato and Chorus: Written-out accompaniment, frequently *unisono*, 3-4 parts; no figures.
16. Air, A section: Unfigured bass marked *tasto solo*.
    Air, B section: Written-out accompaniment in 2-3 parts, 11 figures which are mostly in 2-part passages.
18. Air: Unfigured bass marked *tasto solo*.
19. Chorus: Written-out accompaniment in 2-4 parts; the several 2-part passages are figured.
20. Chorus: Written-out accompaniment in 2-4 parts; figures mostly in 2-part passages.
21. Chorus: Written-out accompaniment in 3-4 parts, highly figured.
23. Chorus "Your voices tune:" Figured bass.
    Chorus "Let's imitate:" Written-out accompaniment in 2-3 parts, mostly 2-part; all 2-part sections figured.

Example 3.1. *Alexander's Feast*, Organ Part
RM 19. a. 10., fols. 2v and 6v

Reprinted by permission of the British Library

Example 3.2. *Alexander's Feast*, Organ Part
RM 19. a. 10., fol. 4

Reprinted by permission of the British Library

Very few passages are figured fully in both the harpsichord part and the organ part. A comparison of the figuring of these passages reveals no striking similarities.

Aylesford Keyboard Parts

The Aylesford keyboard parts, mostly in the Newman Flower Collection of the Henry Watson Music Library, Manchester, were originally owned by Handel's friend and librettist Charles Jennens. Why Jennens commissioned this large quantity of vocal and instrumental parts remains a mystery. There is no evidence that they were ever used in performance. It is certainly possible that his motivation was merely a sense of archival completeness, totally apart from any practical need for the parts. Jennens spent an enormous amount of time studying, indexing, and cross-referencing his collection of manuscript and printed sources of Handel's music. He also had a large library of Italian vocal and instrumental music. Perhaps he thought the parts would be useful for his own study purposes. It is also possible that he wanted to preserve, independent of the composer, a lasting record of Handel's achievement. He was certainly aware of the deficiencies of the printed editions; perhaps he also recognized the danger that Handel's original theater parts would eventually be scattered or destroyed.

The Newman Flower Collection contains forty-five keyboard parts for operas and oratorios; the Library of Congress houses four such parts. Some of them are marked "Organo," some "Cembalo"; both designations, interestingly enough, occur in the operas—in which an organ would be singularly inappropriate—as well as the oratorios. (In this context, "organo" refers not to the instrument but to the basso continuo part; this seems to have been common usage in eighteenth-century England.)[11] Two operas are duplicated in the collection: both *Alcina* and *Ariodante* have two cembalo parts, one copied by S2, and the other primarily by S1.

Both the opera and the oratorio parts exhibit the same kind of short score contained in the harpsichord part for *Alexander's Feast* and some of the Hamburg *Cembalopartituren*. This short score format consists of solo voice, or voices, plus basso continuo for the arias and solo vocal ensembles; bass only for the *ouverture* and *coro* movements; and usually top part plus bass for the incidental instrumental movements. The vocal parts are usually in easier clefs; in other words, treble rather than the original soprano and alto clefs. Generally speaking, the opera keyboard parts contain only the arias, accompanied recitatives, and vocal ensembles. On the other hand, the oratorio parts usually contain the overture and both types of recitative. They also include arias, choruses, and solo ensembles. As is the case with Handel's autograph scores, a few of the Flower keyboard parts are figured extensively throughout: e.g., *Scipione, Joseph, Samson, Agrippina,* and *Admeto*. Some contain partial figuring, but most contain very little.

A great deal of basic research still needs to be done on the collection as a whole, and the parts in particular, before we can form any serious hypothesis regarding the source material the copyists used to make these parts.[12] Winton Dean has suggested that the Flower parts were probably not copied from Handel's performance parts; he believes that they were derived from full scores, and that the copyist was told to use his discretion in cases where his source did not provide sufficient guidance.[13] (E.g., it is frequently difficult for the copyist to determine from Handel's score how extensively oboes and bassoon should double the written string parts.) Therefore, Dean reasons, it is unlikely that the Flower parts "incorporated Handel's corrections, or had any direct authority from him."[14] Dean's theory about the derivation of the parts may be true for the string, wind, and vocal parts of the collection. However, there are problems if we apply his theory to the keyboard parts.

Frequently one finds that the keyboard part of a given work exhibits more figuring than the full score in the same collection, even in cases where both sources were written by the same copyist. This is especially true of *Scipione*: the Flower cembalo part is heavily figured, but the Flower score has almost none.

If these keyboard parts were taken from full scores, why are they so inconsistent among themselves and with the scores? Why do the oratorio parts contain the overtures and plain recitative, while the opera parts do not? Why are the keyboard parts of some works fully figured, while the scores of the same works in the same collection are practically unfigured? Certainly these inconsistencies would be not so numerous if all the keyboard parts were derived as Dean suggests.

Another interesting aspect of the opera cembalo parts concerns the waste of staff space. The copyist S2 frequently left considerable staff space unused at the bottom right side of an opening. Sometimes this waste of space can be explained by the desire to make easier turns, for example, during continuo rests or at the end of a section. At other times no such explanation applies; the copyist seems to have made an arbitrary decision to stop writing, leaving one or more full systems blank. This suggests that the scribe was reproducing the page turns of his copy-text, perhaps some type of keyboard score, rather than extracting the part from a full score. Winton Dean noticed a similar consistency in the page turns of the Hamburg sources of *Sosarme*:

> The turnover in both copies [i.e., conducting score and *Cembalopartitur*] was always arranged at the same point, to facilitate the transference or substitution of material.[15]

Perhaps S2 faithfully copied the layout of his copy-text into the Flower parts for the same reason.

Document 12. Newman Flower Keyboard
Continuo Parts for the Oratorios

Title	Figuring
Alexander's Feast	Full
Joseph	Full
Judas Maccabeus	Partial
La Resurrezione	Partial
Samson	Full
Saul	Partial
Il Trionfo	Very little

On the whole, the oratorio parts seem to be extremely practical for accompanimental purposes. The presence of the overtures and plain recitative points to this conclusion. The form of the choruses (figured bass only) is a welcome convenience, eliminating dozens of awkward page turns. Also, all but one of the oratorio parts are at least partially figured (document 12).

The opera keyboard parts, which constitute the bulk of the collection — all of Handel's operas are represented except *Almira, Atalanta,* and *Deidamia* — do not seem to be practical continuo parts. The lack of simple recitative is perhaps the greatest difficulty. One could assume that the Flower parts were copied from the parts used by Handel's continuo assistant (Harpsichord II) in the operas. Perhaps only one cembalist, i.e., Handel, accompanied the plain recitative. The problem with this suggestion is that both Fougeroux and C. P. E. Bach imply that two harpsichords could be used in plain recitative;[16] surely the second harpsichordist was not required to switch back and forth from continuo part to full score whenever he had to accompany a recitative and adjacent aria.

Other aspects of the opera cembalo parts suggest that they were not used primarily for continuo playing. Long passages, even whole arias, clearly marked *senza cembalo*, are included. Even more curious, perhaps, is the inclusion of long sections for unaccompanied voice or voice without bass (e.g., *Rinaldo*, no. 6, and *Il Pastor Fido*, no. 18). It would seem more efficient to write rests in the part in all these instances.

All of these peculiarities lead one to the conclusion that the opera keyboard parts were not always derived from a full score. Most likely they were copied from originals that were not necessarily performance material for Handel's continuo players, although occasionally the originals may have functioned as such. Rather, they appear to have been rehearsal parts, primarily intended for the singers' study. They could also be very useful during rehearsals without orchestra. Perhaps the originals were made before the filling-up process—stage III of the composition process—so that singers could begin learning their arias as soon as possible. The recitative was not so crucial, and, in any case, was usually composed during stage III. If the opera keyboard parts were intended primarily for singers, that would explain why the overtures are consistently missing.

Appendix A gives further details regarding the figuring and contents of the Aylesford opera and oratorio keyboard parts.[17]

4

Bass Figuring in Scribal Copies of the Operas and Oratorios

The following chapter should be considered as no more than a preliminary report on an ongoing research project, which is to list all the contemporary manuscript scores of Handel's large vocal works that contain substantial supplementary figuring. Appendix B is merely a first step toward that goal; it lists all the full scores of operas and oratorios in MS that I have found to date.[1] Supplementary figuring does not normally contradict the primary sources; rather, it fills in the gaps, providing sufficient signatures in works or sections of works which would otherwise contain sporadic or incomplete figuring.

Given the scope of this book, it would be impractical to attempt even tentative evaluations of all this figuring. With regard to individual works, firm conclusions must be deferred at least until the relevant research for the HHA editions has been completed. For the present, I shall offer provisional conclusions based on some familiarity with most of the sources listed below. I would be happy if any or all of these conclusions were refined, challenged, even disproved, since this is a virtually unexplored area of Handel studies, which deserves more attention from scholars than it has hitherto received.

Of course, the figuring of these mostly secondary sources is a rather inconsequential subject if we believe that the copyists merely invented this supplementary figuring on their own initiative. But most of the evidence does not support this belief, especially in the case of the early Smith scribes. We assume that the active copyists close to Smith Sr. (S1, S2, and S5, for example) were professionals; therefore, their livelihood depended on reproducing a copy-text with a fair degree of accuracy. As Terence Best has observed, "[T]hey copied what they were told to copy. . . . [M]ostly they didn't alter or add to the music, at least not consciously."[2] We know that Smith Sr. occasionally collaborated with S1, S2, and others in the preparation of performing parts and Handel's own performing scores[3] (the "conducting scores" or *Handexemplare*; see chap. 2), so Smith and presumably

Handel must have regarded these scribes as reliable to some degree. Besides, why would a professional copyist, charged with producing masses of performable material and probably paid by the page, deliberately complicate his task by adding extra continuo figuring?

Perhaps the scribes were told by Smith or a patron to add figuring for specific copies. The problem with this theory is the nature of the figuring itself. Frequently it seems unnecessarily detailed, more than the minimum needed to clarify a progression or make the score look complete. Many of the obvious mistakes to be found in these sources seem more like copying errors than harmonic incompetencies or attempts to be daring. Besides, if they were told by Smith or a knowledgeable patron, like Jennens, to add figuring, then they must have been at least competent at it.

Also, occasionally this supplementary figuring looks rather suspicious on paper. In example 4.1, derived from the Aylesford full score of *Agrippina* in Manchester, the figuring clearly contradicts an exposed vocal solo in a manner that is hardly characteristic of the style. The clash between the F demanded by the figuring of the third beat and the soloist's high E does not seem intentional, especially in this context. It seems more likely that the $^5_4$ derived from a performance in which the singer introduced an appoggiatura beginning on F, perhaps followed by a short trill; in this case the continuo player would need the figuring to warn of the planned, but unwritten, ornamentation. If this figuring was the invention of a copyist, why would he go to the trouble of writing four signatures (5, 4, 7, ♮) on the third and fourth beats, when one (a natural, on the third beat) would have been sufficient and actually more "correct."

Furthermore, a comparison of the available figured MSS for a given work often reveals an overall consistency in the supplementary figuring, along with varying amounts of individual variation. In *Admeto*, for example, much of the figuring is unusual, occasionally even rather eccentric, yet most of the figured sources are consistently idiosyncratic in this way. Example 4.2 gives a few of these anomalies. But the sources for *Admeto* are

Example 4.1. *Agrippina*, HWV 6, no. 5
　　　　　　 MS 130 Hd4 v. 11

Figuring from this manuscript reproduced by permission of the Director of the Manchester Public Libraries

Example 4.2. *Admeto*, HWV 22, nos. 5, 23, and 25

different in another respect: some manuscripts contain fuller figuring than others. The Smith Sr. copy in the British Library and the Manchester full score are probably the most complete (see document 14). The manuscripts of *La Resurrezione* which I have been able to study are even more consistent, and in all of them listed below precisely the same portion of act 1 contains figuring.

Generally speaking, it seems most likely that the copyists of the Smith circle did not add substantially to the figuring of their copy-text, but they may have altered or enlarged it somewhat: for example, by adding necessary chromatic alterations, obvious resolutions, or figures derived from parallel passages; by changing the placement or the vertical disposition of the figures ($^9_7$ as opposed to $^7_9$, for example); and by correcting obvious errors.

It is frequently suggested that many of these scores might have been copied directly from the original printed editions,[4] which were copiously figured. In some cases it is obviously impossible because the copies date from well before the first printed editions. For example, we may consider *Agrippina* and *La Resurrezione*, not published until the mid-1790s, and *Rodrigo*, first published by Chrysander; all of these contain significant supplementary figuring that exists in manuscript copies by members of the Smith circle. But even if this kind of direct relationship between the MS and the print could be proven in certain cases, it would not necessarily invalidate the figuring; our critical estimate of the authority of the figuring in the manuscript depends, certainly, on the authority of the figuring in the printed edition from which it was taken. And all too frequently, the figuring of the early prints has been ignored or rejected summarily by Handel specialists. A direct relationship of this type would at least imply that someone — the copyist, Smith, or the person who commissioned the copy — valued the printed figurings enough to have them reproduced in a MS score.

On the other hand, it is difficult to see a direct relationship between the figuring in most of these manuscripts and that in the original prints. The MS sources frequently represent a different version of the work from that given in the print. And besides, the figured MSS usually contain the recitatives (almost always missing from the prints) and inner orchestral parts (often missing from the prints). If the figuring was directly derived from the printed edition, in most cases the copyist would have needed two or more sources: the print and at least one MS to make up for the deficiencies of the print. If a copyist were doing that kind of collating, presumably rather rare, then he would have been acting on orders — either from Handel, Smith, or the person who commissioned the copy — or else he would have been exercising a type of editorial judgment that is not normally associated with the duties of a scribe.

In most cases it seems unlikely that the figuring was derived from the print simply because of the kinds of differences that occur between the prints and the manuscripts. Figurings may be included only for selected arias in the manuscripts, whereas all arias of a print tend to be figured. Also, the manuscripts may contain many added figurings, or figurings that differ significantly from those of the print. The question then arises: why would a professional copyist, if asked to take figuring from the printed edition, do it so selectively and so inaccurately?

The Cluer edition of *Giulio Cesare*, for example, contains fairly full figuring throughout, except for the aria "Se in fiorito ameno prato" and the accompanied recitative "Alma del gran Pompeo." The Manchester cembalo part and RM. 19. c. 7. both contain figuring that is rather similar to the print, but the figuring is mostly confined to two arias in act 2 and six in act 3. (These arias are not necessarily the most complex harmonically or particularly challenging for the accompanist.) Both of these sources also contain a fair amount of figuring that is absent from the print, and usually do not contain the mistakes in figuring found in the print.

The Manchester full score of *Joseph* has figuring that could not have been copied from the print. Aside from the fact that the Manchester score contains much more music—most of which is figured—and a different version of the work than the print, the differences in figuring are striking, even in harmonically simple movements such as the Menuet of the Ouverture. Another striking example is the continuo aria "Alma mia" from *Floridante*. The Manchester cembalo part is figured quite differently than the Walsh printed edition. These differences concern placement as well as the choice of figures (see ex. 4.3).

To illustrate the kinds of consistency, as well as the kinds of differences we find in the figuring of these manuscript scores, this chapter will conclude with two general examples. The first, example 4.4, is the aria "A languir" from *Admeto* as it is figured in four manuscripts: RM. 19. c. 2., copied by S13 (ex. 4.4a); the British Library Granville Collection score, Eg. 2924, copied by S5 (ex. 4.4b); the Manchester full score, copied by S2 (ex. 4.4c); and British Library Add. 38002, copied by Smith Sr. (ex. 4.4d). The original Cluer edition (ex. 4.4e), as well as the H-G figuring (ex. 4.4f) are included for comparison. The following analysis of these four manuscript sources is not intended as a detailed stemma. The investigation will be confined to the figuring; other aspects of these sources may present a different picture.

The figuring of example 4.4a is probably closest to that of the lost autograph. This example contains several features which resemble the composer's habits, especially when he did not take the time to figure a piece thoroughly. Many measures are figured completely, but some (mm. 3-5 and m. 9) have little or none. The figuring of the first two beats of measure 6 looks like a characteristic Handelian idiosyncrasy (only one of the naturals is necessary, since the harmony does not change), and could relate in some way to the creative process. Note that in the same measure the resolution of the $^4_2$ is not indicated; Handel frequently omitted these details. Figuring is also missing in other, more problematic places; for example, measures 9 (second beat), 13 (fourth beat), and 18 (beats $3^1/_2$ and $4^1/_2$). There is a slight misplacement in measure 14: the last figure 6 should probably occur half a beat later. Such misplacements are not unknown in the Handel autographs.

The copyist of the Granville score (ex. 4.4b) added a few figures to the text. These clarified a few of the composer's presumed omissions (but not all—see mm. 4 and 5 especially); still, these additions do not solve all realization problems, nor is the misplacement in measure 14 corrected. In measure 9, a cadential trill with a long appoggiatura in the violin part would eliminate the "paper-clash" with the figuring.

Unfortunately, this aria is not contained in the Newman Flower cembalo part, but it is present in the full score of the same collection (ex.4.4c).

Example 4.3a. *Joseph*, HWV 59, Ouverture

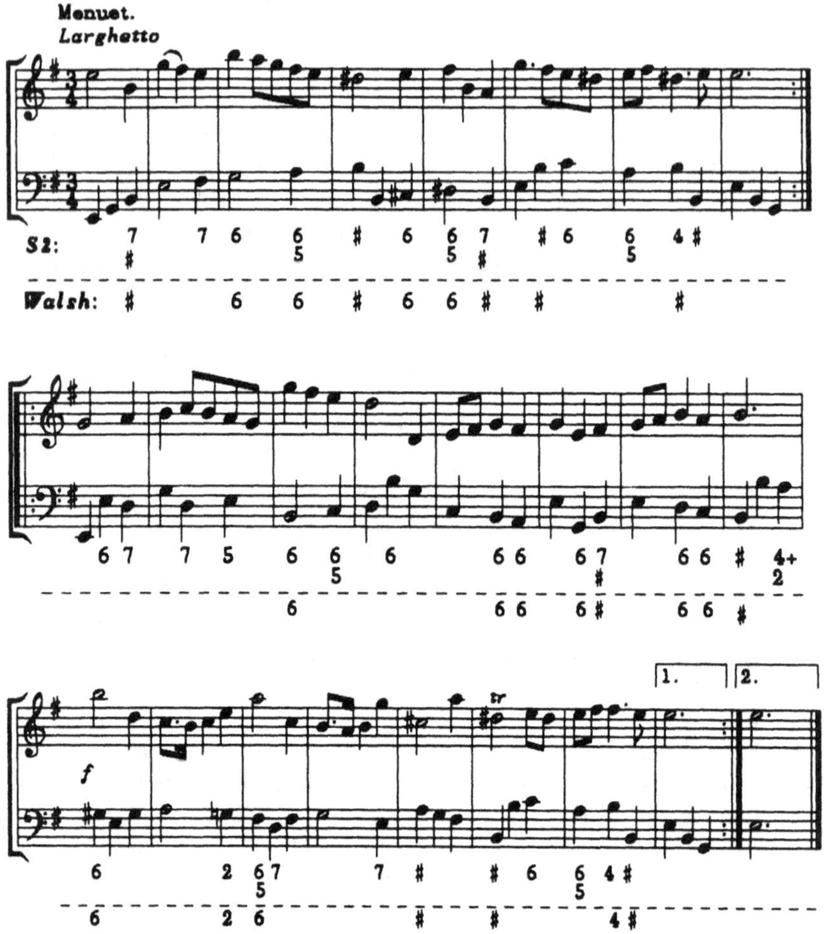

Figuring reproduced by permission of the Director of the Manchester Public Libraries

Example 4.3b. *Il Floridante*, HWV 14, no. 5

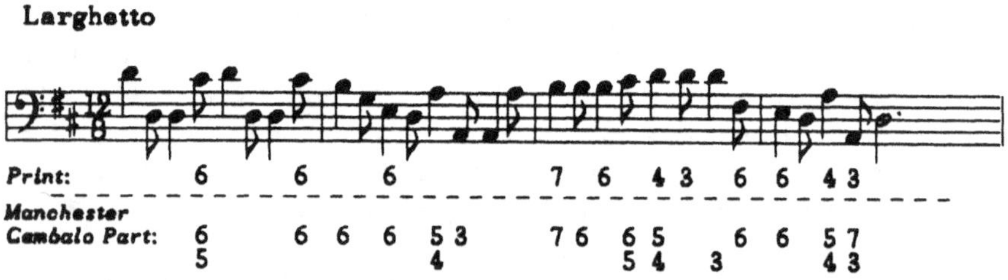

Figuring reproduced by permission of the Director of the Manchester Public Libraries

This source adds further figuring, notably in measures 3 through 5. The figuring of the second half of measure 3 is interesting primarily for three reasons: it introduces an expressive countermelody to the texture, which could derive from the composer; it is a good example of unnecessarily detailed figuring—the only figures required would be a 6 on beats 3½ and 4; and the 7　6 on beat 4 makes sense only if the violin part is executed with an appoggiatura G, so the figuring probably originated in actual performance rather than in the work of the copyist. In any case, the figuring is typical of Handel's continuo harmony (see formula IV.13, chap. 10). The only other figuring added is on the second beat of 9, a necessary indication since the chord requires a chromatic alteration. S2 fails to include two figures that are present in both examples 4.4a and 4.4b (mm. 7 and 11), and he also changes the vertical order at the beginning of measure 13. Nevertheless, the Manchester score, unlike the two sources discussed previously, contains sufficiently detailed figuring for performance.

The Smith Sr. copy (ex.4.4d) contains bass figuring that is basically the same as that of S2, but Smith includes the two figures that S2 left out, corrects the misplacement in measure 14, and turns the $^{4+}_{2}$ in measure 15 to $^{6}_{4+}_{2}$. The only figure he omits is the 6 on the first beat of measure 16. Smith neglects to show the chromatically altered sixth in bar 9; this is no doubt a simple copying slip.

All four sources share certain characteristic details. None of them indicates the diminished seventh in measure 13. The natural third on the third beat of measure 5 is not figured. They all retain the redundant natural in measure 6. None of them shows the 4　3 that occurs in the violin part at the end of measure 18. If the copyists were freely inventing or changing continuo figuring, some of these deficiencies would certainly have been corrected by one or another of them.

The Cluer version of the figuring generally follows the Smith readings, but with several omissions. As was mentioned in chapter 2 with respect to *Rodelinda*, many of these omissions could be the result of limitations on space.

The Chrysander edition was based on an unidentified manuscript, probably RM. 19. c. 2. However, since he included in parentheses the Manchester/Smith figuring in measure 3, he clearly had access to another source, perhaps the Cluer print.

Example 4.5 is an excerpt from the solo with chorus "In Sweetest Harmony," from the final scene of *Saul*. The figuring derives from the British Library manuscript RM. 18. d. 9. (Smith Sr.) and the Newman Flower full score MS 130 Hd4, v. 271 (S2).

The two sets of figures are actually rather similar, but Smith's seems closest to what Handel would have written in performance parts or wanted from his players. Smith includes some characteristically Handelian 7　6

Example 4.4. *Admeto*, HWV 22, no. 29

Example 4.4. Continued

Example 4.4 Continued

Figuring reproduced by permission of the British Library and the Director of the Manchester Public Libraries

Example 4.5. *Saul*, HWV 53, no. 83

Example 4.5. Continued

Figuring reproduced by permission of the British Library and the Director of the Manchester Public Libraries

suspensions (especially in mm. 23 and 36). S2 does not include these (although the second may have been part of his copy-text; note the suspiciously dangling 6 in m. 36) and his figuring seems unusually fussy (see mm. 22, 37, 39, and 40). Also, the 9 8 suspension that S2 puts in measure 24 does not seem Handelian in this context. The 7 6 in measure 37 is probably a copying error and should have been placed in the previous measure without the natural (which probably was intended originally to apply to the pitch of the second bass note in m. 36).

Charles Jennens's Bass Figuring

Many of the scores in the appended list, especially those now housed in the Manchester Public Library, have supplementary figuring in the hand of Charles Jennens. As we examine his markings and annotations in the Aylesford Collection, there appears a side of Jennens that has not been sufficiently considered in the scholarly literature. What we find is an enthusiastic admirer and devoted student of Handel's music. Jennens obviously spent hours studying it assiduously; the collection is full of cross-references, memoranda, additions, and corrections in his own hand. He frequently collated his full score of a given work with the keyboard part, copying markings from the one that were missing in the other. The extent to which he compared and collated various sources for a given work is astonishing, but, as it turns out, also characteristic of his methods as editor of four Shakespeare plays.

A large proportion of these additions involve continuo figuring. Judging by the amount he copied into his MSS and printed scores, he was certainly a fanatic about this aspect of Baroque notation. Our task is to assess the value and authority of his supplementary figuring.

One point that should be considered at the outset is that Jennens had direct access to at least some of the autographs. This is demonstrated by the autograph of *Saul*, wherein Jennens actually adds three notes of simple declamation at the beginning of the aria "Impious Wretch." It is also clear that he copied various markings from the autographs as part of the collation process. These markings include tempo indications, completion dates, and bass figuring. If he had access to Handel's holograph scores, then there is a good chance that he could also have consulted the performance parts or other important manuscript sources that have not survived. It is totally consistent with his habits and interests as revealed in the Aylesford Collection to suppose that he might have taken bass figuring from these sources and incorporated it into his own copies.

My research points to the conclusion that most of the time Jennens was indeed copying figuring from other sources; sometimes from the autograph, sometimes from scores or parts in his own collection. Occasionally he invented figuring himself; this can be distinguished from the rest by its

Example 4.6. *Riccardo Primo*, HWV 23, no. 17
RM 18. c. 10., fol. 167

Reprinted by permission of the British Library

Example 4.7. *Tolomeo*, HWV 25, no. 30
RM 18. c. 1.

Reprinted by permission of the British Library

needlessly detailed quality and unmusical character. But scholars and performers should not automatically dismiss figuring which has survived in Jennens's hand for that reason alone. Much of his figuring is excellent; in this and other respects he deserves to be treated as any other Handel copyist.

The following are representative examples of Jennens's habits of figuring.

In one of the British Library Aylesford "mixed" volumes, S2 copied an arietta from *Riccardo Primo*, but included only about half of Handel's figuring. Jennens added the missing figures so that the copy would conform to the autograph (ex. 4.6).

He respected the composer's figuring to such an extent that he even copied obsolete figures[5] that Handel had crossed out. Example 4.7 is taken from the final duet in *Tolomeo*, as preserved in the British Library volume RM. 18. c. 1. The figuring which Jennens added to his copy of this duet was most likely taken directly from the autograph.

Jennens frequently copied the figuring of other Handel scribes, especially S2. An example can be found in the Aylesford sources of *La Resurrezione*. Both the full score and the cembalo part were copied by S2, but the cembalo part originally contained considerably more figuring. Jennens copied all these figurings, and other markings as well, from the cembalo part into the full score. In this case at least, he added nothing of his own. Other similar examples can be found in Appendix B. Indeed, it is not unusual to find instances in which the figuring of Jennens is identical, or almost identical to that of S2. On the other hand, Jennens's fragmentary keyboard arrangement of *Messiah* contains some highly detailed figuring which is probably his own work (ex. 4.8).

Example 4.8. *Messiah*, Vocal Score (frag.) by Charles Jennens
RM 19.d. 1., fol. 19v

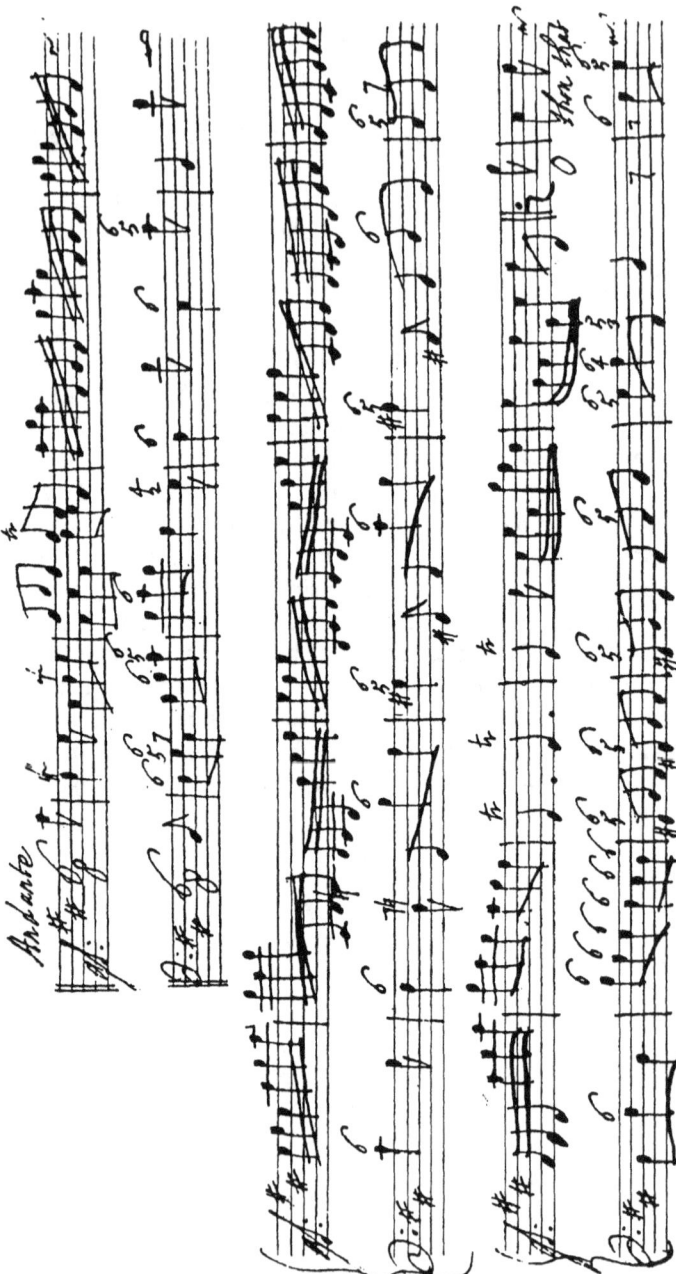

Reprinted by permission of the British Library

5

Bass Figuring in the Royal Academy Opera Editions, 1720-1728

The original printed editions of Handel's operas and oratorios, published by Walsh, Cluer, and others,[1] are usually much more extensively figured than the primary sources, that is, the autographs and conducting scores. This additional figuring is an obvious boon for the modern continuo player. But Handel scholars have been justifiably suspicious of it since the musical texts presented in the early prints are mostly incomplete and often inaccurate. Also, no real documentary evidence has survived regarding the extent of Handel's participation in these ventures. As Donald Burrows suggests, "It seems most likely that Handel's involvement in the publications extended only up to the moment when Walsh paid him for music copy."[2] This seems a reasonable working assumption for Handel's relations with his other publishers as well.

When Handel provided his publishers with opera or oratorio "copy," was it fully figured? If it was, then Handel probably had some participation in or control over the additional figuring. If the copy contained only the autograph/conducting score figuring, then probably the composer was not involved with the extra figuring. It was most likely provided by a publisher's assistant.

It seems unlikely that Handel would have made a regular practice of handing over sparsely figured copy to his publishers. He was certainly aware of the unscrupulous and often sloppy practices of the Walsh firm. Even if the full figuring provided in the publisher's copy was not completely his own, there are other possibilities that would involve active participation by the composer. He may have given the task of providing fuller figuring to one of his continuo players or other trusted musical assistants. Regardless of who was responsible, once the figuring had been added, he could have looked it over, made a few corrections, and approved it. (Busy as the composer often was, this process would not have been inordinately time consuming.) Another possibility is that the figuring provided to the publishers was collated by the copyists from full scores and performing parts.

Even if the extra figuring was provided after Handel released copy to the publisher, that does not totally invalidate the figuring. The figurer may have been a reputable, though anonymous, master, even an experienced accompanist; it is quite possible that he was thoroughly familiar with Handel's style of continuo harmonization. In any case, it seems dangerous to ignore evidence so close in time and place to the composer's regular professional sphere. Even if these additional figurings do not derive from the composer, they are still extremely valuable records of contemporary harmonization practice.

Unfortunately, at present it is not possible to test these hypotheses regarding the figuring of the publisher's copy since "no copies of Handel's music have yet come to light which can be regarded with certainty as copy texts for Walsh's editions."[3] And I am aware of none, with the possible exception of the conducting score of *Rodelinda*,[4] which might have served as copy for the original editions of Handel's vocal music. Hopefully further research into Handelian source materials will yield some examples.

The printed editions of Handel's operas and oratorios are highly deficient by twentieth-century standards. All the secco recitative and much of the accompanied recitative is usually missing. The oratorio choruses are also missing. Also frequently lacking are inner orchestral parts, especially the viola line. The abbreviated ritornelli, which Handel often uses in da capo arias to lead into the repeat of the A section, are often missing. Indications of instrumentation can be absent at the beginning of an aria. The musical texts are frequently inaccurate in detail.

Nevertheless, several factors indicate that the composer was involved in many of these publications. In 1720 Handel was granted, under the terms of the Copyright Act of 1709, a publication "Privilege" which ostensibly gave him exclusive control over publications of his music for a period of fourteen years; later this was renewed.[5] Handel's own prefaces to the 1720 Cluer edition of harpsichord suites and the Walsh edition of Concerti, Op. 4, demonstrate a desire to single out these as the only authorized versions. Many of the opera and oratorio prints were, as the title pages state, "Publish'd by the author." The exact meaning of this is unclear, but it probably indicates some form of financial involvement and control over the venture. Another factor is the involvement of J. C. Smith Sr., Handel's principal copyist, as printer and music seller for some of these editions.[6] Many of the prints contain the claim "corrected by the Author;" this may indicate some form of intervention on the part of the composer, although it seems unlikely that he checked the proofs with any great care.[7] Such claims occur suspiciously often, but the claim that the composer actually provided the figuring for a printed edition occurs only three times, for the Cluer editions of *Giulio Cesare* (1724), *Tamerlano* (1724), and *Rodelinda* (1725). In the first two cases there is evidence to substantiate the claim, and Handel certainly did provide bass figuring for the Cluer print of *Rodelinda*, as the Hamburg conducting score shows.[8] Only two large vocal works were issued complete during Handel's lifetime: *Alexander's Feast* and *Acis and Galatea*. It seems reasonable to suppose that these two publications were done with more care and that the composer was more closely involved with the preparation of them. Subscriptions for *Alexander's Feast* were taken at Handel's house, and the edition was also available for purchase there.[9] The first printing contained several corrections written by an unidentified hand, perhaps Smith Sr. or a member of the Walsh firm.

It is important to consider the time limits under which these editions were produced. Deletions, additions, transpositions, and the like could take place between the "completion" of Handel's autograph and the first performance of an opera; usually these changes were dictated by performance conditions. The printed editions incorporate many of these pre-performance revisions and were available for purchase just weeks or months after the first performance. The incompleteness of the orchestration in the prints could be related to constraints of time; perhaps in some cases the engraving started before the composer had completed stage III of the composition process. Advertisements for the Cluer print of *Rodelinda* show that it took at least ten weeks to produce that edition: six weeks or more for the engraving, about four for printing and binding.[10] After issuing *Rodelinda* the Cluer firm had to apologize to customers for neglecting other publications,[11] so the production schedule of approximately ten weeks was probably unusually short.

Many questions remain unanswered regarding Handel's relations with his publishers. However, if we consider the Royal Academy opera editions separately, as I propose to do in the remainder of this chapter, a clear progression emerges: one of growing participation by the composer and a proportionate increase in the completeness of the editions.

Document 13 summarizes this progression. Nine of the twelve Royal Academy operas are listed.[12] The dates of completion given usually derive from the composer's dating of the autograph. The seventh line lists the number of arias or duets of the original performing version, as detailed in Bernd Baselt's *Händel-Handbuch*, vol. 1, which are not contained in the print. (Question marks are included when there is some doubt regarding the first version of the work.) Missing instrumentation is treated in the next two lines: the number of arias with instrumental parts that are completely lacking in the print, followed by the number of arias with accompanimental lines that are partially missing. The statements given in quotation marks are taken from the original title pages or early advertisements, unless otherwise credited.

Document 13. Nine Royal Academy Prints

Radamisto
    Published by Subscription: Yes
    Imprint: Meares, Smith
    Opera completed: ? early 1720
    First performance: April 27, 1720
    Edition available: December 15, 1720
    Arias or duets missing: 0
    Instrumental parts lacking in whole arias: 23
    Instrumental parts lacking in parts of arias: 2
    Remarks: "Corrected" and "Publish'd by the Author."

Ottone
    Published by Subscription: No
    Imprint: Walsh, Hare
    Opera completed: August 10, 1722
    First performance: January 12, 1723
    Edition available: March 19, 1723
    Arias or duets missing: 0
    Instrumental parts lacking in whole arias: 13
    Instrumental parts lacking in parts of arias: 9
    Remarks: "Publish'd by the Author."

Flavio
    Published by Subscription: No
    Imprint: Walsh, Hare
    Opera completed: May 7, 1723
    First performance: May 14, 1723
    Edition available: June 21, 1723
    Arias or duets missing: 0
    Instrumental parts lacking in whole arias: 15
    Instrumental parts lacking in parts of arias: 1
    Remarks: "Publish'd by the Author."

Giulio Cesare
    Published by Subscription: No
    Imprint: Cluer, Creake
    Opera completed: December, 1723
    First performance: February 20, 1724
    Edition available: July 24, 1724
    Arias or duets missing: 2 (?)
    Instrumental parts lacking in whole arias: 4
    Instrumental parts lacking in parts of arias: 6
    Remarks: "Corrected and Figur'd by [Handel's] own Hand."

Document 13. Continued

Tamerlano
    Published by Subscription: No
    Imprint: Cluer
    Opera completed: July 23, 1724
    First performance: October 31, 1724
    Edition available: November 14, 1724
    Arias or duets missing: 4 (?)
    Instrumental parts lacking in whole arias: 3
    Instrumental parts lacking in parts of arias: 6
    Remarks: "Corrected and Figur'd by [Handel's] own Hand."

Rodelinda
    Published by Subscription: Yes
    Imprint: Cluer, Creake
    Opera completed: January 20, 1725
    First performance: February 13, 1725
    Edition available: May 6, 1725
    Arias or duets missing: 1 (?)
    Instrumental parts lacking in whole arias: 1
    Instrumental parts lacking in parts of arias: 0
    Remarks: ". . . figur'd and corrected by his [Handel's] Hand . . ." Figuring derived from the autograph figuring in the Hamburg conducting score. The only instrumental parts lacking are the horn parts in the Coro at the end of the work.

Scipione
    Published by Subscription: Yes
    Imprint: Cluer, Creake, Smith
    Opera completed: March 2, 1726
    First performance: March 12, 1726
    Edition available: May 27, 1726
    Arias or duets missing: 2
    Instrumental parts lacking in whole arias: 1
    Instrumental parts lacking in parts of arias: 1
    Remarks: Figuring practically the same as the Flower cembalo part.

Document 13. Continued

Alessandro
    Published by Subscription: Yes
    Imprint: Cluer, Creake
    Opera completed: April 11, 1726
    First performance: May 5, 1726
    Edition available: August 6, 1726
    Arias or duets missing: 2
    Instrumental parts lacking in whole arias: 0
    Instrumental parts lacking in parts of arias: 2
    Remarks: According to Charles Burney, this edition was "published by the Author."[13]

Admeto
    Published by Subscription: Yes
    Imprint: Cluer, Smith
    Opera completed: November 10, 1726
    First performance: January 31, 1727
    Edition available: June 24, 1727
    Arias or duets missing: 0
    Instrumental parts lacking in whole arias: 0
    Instrumental parts lacking in parts of arias: 1

The Cluer editions contain orchestral accompaniments that are substantially more complete than the Walsh or Meares editions; the last four Cluer editions listed in the table are practically complete in this respect.

The Figuring of Specific Printed Editions

This discussion is limited to those Royal Academy prints with figuring that is especially noteworthy. See chapter 4 regarding the figuring of *Admeto*.

Radamisto

On the whole, the figuring seems excellent and rather detailed. However, two factors suggest that the composer was not involved in the figuring. When the bass instruments rest for several bars, the viola part is figured. This is not Handel's normal practice, although short rests in the bass are frequently figured by the composer. Also, the printed figures often disagree with inner orchestral parts which are not included in the edition. Example 5.1 is an excerpt from "Quando mai spietata sorte." Only the outer parts of

Example 5.1. *Radamisto*, HWV 12a, no. 12

Example 5.2. *Radamisto*, HWV 12b, no. 16

the example are given in the print, and the figuring would be acceptable if these were the only parts being played. However, with the actual accompaniment written by the composer the figuring creates unsuitable clashes. On the other hand, passages like example 5.2, from "Lascia pur amica spene," are typical of Handel's figuring of pedal points.

Ottone

Most of the figuring is stylistic; even Chrysander had to admit that it was "thoroughly in his [Handel's] manner."[14] The Walsh edition was Chrysander's only source for several arias, and in these he retained the printed figurings. However, the Walsh figuring of the aria "Diresti poi cosi?" is considerably different from that contained in the autograph. This does not suggest the composer's involvement. Discrepancies of this type (i.e., figurings that actually contradict the autograph) are very unusual in both the Walsh and Cluer printed editions of the operas and oratorios. The unisono passages of the opening aria, "Pur che regni il figlio amato" (excerpted in ex. 5.3) contain extensive figuring that, again, is totally in keeping with the composer's methods.

Example 5.3. *Ottone*, HWV 15, no. 1

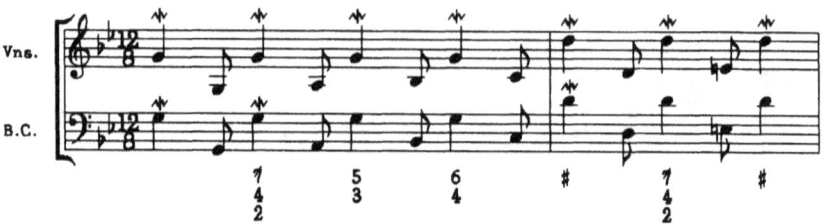

Giulio Cesare

An advertisement in the London Journal, on 6 June 1724, stated that this edition was "Figur'd by Mr. Handel's own Hands."[15] With this print, John Cluer took over from Walsh as the regular publisher of Handel's operas. It seems highly unlikely that Cluer would have jeopardized his lucrative relationship with the composer by making such a claim unless it had some basis in fact. Furthermore, as recent research into sources for *Giulio Cesare* has shown, a lost manuscript must have intervened between the autograph and the Hamburg performing score.[16] This lost source was probably either a short score or incomplete full score, like many of the Hamburg *Cembalopartituren*. It certainly contained some bass figuring in the composer's hand,[17] along with other autograph material. The composer could conceivably have added fuller figuring to this manuscript *after* Smith Sr. had used it to prepare the conducting score.

The figuring of the Cluer edition is full throughout, except for the accompanied recitative "Alma del gran Pompeo" (sporadically figured as in H-G) and the aria "Se in fiorito ameno prato" (entirely unfigured). Most likely, the former was neglected because it was originally not intended for inclusion; the figures printed by Cluer probably derive from the autograph. The lack of figuring in the aria might be an accurate reflection of the composer's intent to suppress continuo harmony.

Occasionally, the figures disagree slightly with inner orchestral parts which are present in the print (e.g., "Priva son d'ogni conforto") as well as those which are absent from the print (e.g., "Si, spietata"). It is possible that this is authentic figuring, perhaps from original continuo parts, which has been garbled in the transmission process. Example 5.4 is the opening of "Cara speme," as figured in the Cluer edition. The figuring is quite convincing and typical of Handel's practice of harmonization in this type of piece.

Example 5.4. *Giulio Cesare*, HWV 17, no. 12

Tamerlano

The figuring is quite sparse in places, but generally sufficient for the purposes of accompaniment. The title page claims that the figuring is Handel's. The style of engraved numbers is very similar to Handel's calligraphy; e.g., the connection which the composer often makes in this signature: 𝄞 . Perhaps the engraver was working from a copy, now lost, which the composer himself figured. Again, as with *Giulio Cesare*, source research suggests that an intermediate source, no longer extant, predated the conducting score.[18] This could have contained the composer's figuring.

Rodelinda

As stated above, this figuring is by the composer. It is similar to the autograph figuring in the Hamburg conducting score. All the variants between the conducting score and the Cluer print are listed in chapter 2. Chrysander's edition includes the figuring of the conducting score, but his transcription is rather inaccurate. There are over fifty errors of various kinds. For a more detailed discussion of this matter, see chapter 2.

Scipione

The figuring is full throughout and similar to the figuring of the Newman Flower cembalo part. The two sources also share some variant readings in the bass line. This suggests that the print and the Flower part are closely related. It does not seem, however, that one was copied from the other. The cembalo part has some music not contained in the print and usually lacks any upper orchestral parts. Also, the cembalo part does not contain the figuring mistakes of the print. This figuring could be the composer's work. Example 5.5 contains excerpts from the ario "Parto, fuggo," scored for voice, unison violins, and continuo; these passages demonstrate the valuable guidance that can be conveyed by the figuring of the Cluer editions.

Example 5.5. *Scipione*, HWV 20, no. 17

Riccardo Primo

These figures are practically identical to the autograph, which is fully figured except for the last two arias, "Tutta brillanti rai" and "Volgete ogni desir." The Cluer print provides full figuring for these arias.

Part Two

Realization Problems

6

Unisono Textures

The continuo accompaniment of unison passages is an especially crucial problem of Handelian performance practice. Few, if any, of Handel's contemporaries employed this texture so extensively or with such diversity. Throughout his career, and in nearly every genre, representative examples can be found. In dramatic works especially, it is one of the hallmarks of his style. Yet the composer seldom specified the type of accompaniment he desired for these passages. Should they be harmonized or not?

The modern predisposition is strongly against harmonized accompaniment of unison passages. In this chapter, I shall challenge this generally accepted belief by citing considerable theoretical and musical evidence. By attempting to reconstruct Handel's intentions in several examples, I hope to clarify the issue for other composers of the late Baroque.

The discussion will begin with a definition of the term *unisono* as it will be used herein. A brief survey of previous scholarly opinion on the subject will follow. Then the normal methods composers used to specify various types of accompaniment in unison passages will be reviewed. C. P. E. Bach's views, their importance, and their relevance to the music of Handel will be treated. Finally, Handel's continuo figuring and its implications for the accompaniment of these passages will be examined.

It is necessary to clarify one point of terminology at the outset. Several different types of texture could be included under the broad heading of "unison": continuo solos, unison treble parts without bass, a solo bass voice doubled by the continuo, written parts in unison accompanying an independent melodic line, or all parts performing an identical theme in different ranges. In this chapter, I will limit my discussion to this last type of unison, in which all performers execute the same—or virtually the same—melodic line, but in different octaves. For ease of reference, the Italian word *unisono* will be used to indicate this texture. These passages vary considerably in length: some are short motifs of one measure or less, some are complete themes or substantial sections; occasionally an entire aria is completely *all' unisono*.

Does a chordal accompaniment necessarily violate the striking and exceptional character of these *unisoni*? The problem has been oversimplified to a certain extent by modern scholars of performance practice, such as Arnold and Donington.[1] The received wisdom, which certainly has merit, can be stated generally as follows: since the composer has relinquished all harmony in the composed parts, any accompaniment—other than bare octaves—would be gratuitous. This view, it seems, is held by the vast majority of conductors and early music specialists. However, there have been dissenting opinions. Manfred Bukofzer felt that a light chordal accompaniment was possible, at least for the unison arias of Handel's *Agrippina*.[2] Friedrich Chrysander and John Tobin recommended a chordal accompaniment for the *unisono* sections of "The People That Walked in Darkness" in *Messiah*,[3] and Mozart, in his orchestration of the work, harmonized all but the first of these four sections.[4] On the other hand, the aria "Di cieca notte" from *Imeneo*, which is entirely *unisono* except for the final ritornello and similar to the above-mentioned aria from *Messiah* textually as well as musically, is marked by the composer *senza cembalo*.

Thus, the performer really has four options regarding the continuo treatment of *unisono* textures in a given movement: 1) no keyboard accompaniment, 2) harmonized accompaniment, 3) unharmonized accompaniment, and 4) a combination of 2 and 3. This chapter will show that there is historical justification for all of these solutions.

But before the evidence is presented, it is necessary to take a brief look at the methods with which a composer could specify the type of realization he wanted, and also to examine closely a popular misconception about one of these methods.

Basically, a composer had two ways of indicating his intentions regarding the keyboard continuo in *unisono* passages: with words or with numbers. The verbal directions were useful only if an accompaniment without harmony was intended. *Tasto solo* meant that only the bass line should be played, while *all' unisono* or *all' ottava* meant that the bass line should be played with both hands, i.e., in the written register by the left hand and doubled at the upper octave by the right. There was no widely used term that demanded continuo chords despite the prevailing *unisono* texture. If a composer desired a chordal realization, and wished to make his intentions clear in the score or parts, his only option was to figure the bass. It follows that bass figuring is an equally valid source of evidence for the chordal accompaniment of *unisoni* and should be given serious consideration along with the verbal directions present in the scores, the information provided by thoroughbass treatises, and other contemporary evidence.

Handel's own figuring is especially noteworthy because his use of the Italian terms was not at all comprehensive. The composer seldom if ever used *all' unisono* in this sense, and *tasto solo* is for the most part confined to choral and instrumental movements. However there are exceptions: *Organo tasto solo* markings in arias from *Alexander's Feast* and *Athalia*[5] (which fail to answer any questions about the harpsichord continuo in these movements), *tasto solo* in "Sweet Bird" and "But Oh, Sad Virgin," from *L'Allegro* and a very unusual *Cembalo tasto solo* marking in "Oft on a Plat of Rising Ground," also from *L'Allegro*. Given the relative infrequency of these Italian terms, especially in arias, the evidence provided by the figuring—or lack of it—is particularly valuable.

This should be self-evident, except for the popular notion that continuo figures have no practical significance in *unisono* textures and, therefore, should invariably be ignored by the accompanist. In my opinion, this is an erroneous view that has developed a wide following primarily because scholars have tended to simplify the issue, giving excessive prominence to isolated statements from C. P. E. Bach's *Versuch*. As Frederick Neumann observed,

> Incomplete quotations and quotations out of context are another source of error. Authors of treatises are not always paragons of either methodical thinking or precise formulation. They often make a definite statement that is later qualified or even contradicted.... The modern researcher who makes a law out of the first statement he finds misrepresents the author.[6]

Perhaps it would be unfair to imply that such eminent authorities as Arnold and Donington have made "a law out of the first statement" they found. But, in disregarding the better part of a chapter directly related to the topic, they seriously risk giving the performer a one-sided and misleading impression.

Evidence from C. P. E. Bach

A thorough examination of C. P. E. Bach's views on the accompaniment of *unisono* passages is an indispensable part of any scholarly treatment of the problem. He is perhaps the only eighteenth-century theorist who discussed the topic in any detail. For reasons to be given later, I believe his views on the subject are generally applicable to music by Handel and that of other German masters of the late Baroque period. Also, an accurate presentation of all relevant matter from his *Versuch* will serve to refute the modern prejudice against any harmonized accompaniments in this texture.

Chapter 22 of the *Versuch* is titled "Vom Einklange" (Of Unisons). After a few preliminary clarifications, Bach states:

> Yet it is surprising that some composers do not always specify a unison accompaniment in scoring the bass. Figures will be found when they are not to be realized.[7]

To elucidate this paradox, Bach presents a hypothetical situation: A composer deliberately decides to renounce harmony at a specific place for the sake of an arresting *unisono* statement. However, a mistake is made in preparing the performance material: the *unisono* theme is copied out with figuring in the continuo part. During the performance the keyboard player, with only the figured bass in front of him, naturally accompanies the passage with chords. But almost immediately he realizes that the chords are inappropriate and abandons them for a simple doubling of the melody, *all' unisono*. Bach concludes,

> When all performers play in unison it is only natural that the accompanist too should follow the unisons and give up his chords.[8]

This sentence sounds so conclusive that one is tempted to close the *Versuch* and regard the problem as solved.

Yet the following paragraph, ignored by Donington and inaccurately paraphrased by Arnold in a footnote,[9] strongly suggests that the matter is not that simple. Bach cites a closely related type of texture, the unison accompaniment supporting an independent melody or long sustained note in the principal part. He states:

> The melody of the ripieno parts must be observed carefully, whether it is so constructed that the most necessary intervals of the basic harmony, especially the dissonances and their resolutions, are touched upon by broken chord patterns. If so, the accompanist also should play in unison. But if the idea which accompanies the principal part is simple and not only tolerates harmony, but through it attains an exceptional brilliance, then one chooses a chordal accompaniment.[10]

If this last sentence could apply to a unison theme that supports no more than a single sustained note, why could it not also apply to *unisoni* scored without any other parts? Surely some of these could also attain "an exceptional brilliance" with a harmonized accompaniment.

The penultimate chapter of the *Versuch* proves conclusively that the author regarded chordal continuo realizations of *unisono* textures as mandatory in certain cases. The subject of the chapter is not unisons per se, but bass themes, which can be performed either by all parts in unison or by the bass instruments together with other melodic material. Unfortunately, Bach does not give us an example of a bass theme, but he does mention that they are expressive and have a "manly bearing;" they contain broken chord figurations and typical bass progressions at cadences and pauses. Appoggiaturas and other melodic refinements are best avoided in bass themes, so as not to disturb the "flow of the harmony." Rather,

> the foundation tones must have with them a harmonic pattern with numerous, effective suspensions [*Bindungen*] which allow for the addition of a singing principal part. Especially delightful are progressions which permit the use of many seventh, five-four, six-five, and ninth chords.[11]

To illustrate, Bach gives several short, sequential bass formulas, any one of which would provide an acceptable harmonic structure for a bass theme (ex. 6.1). We might apply, for purposes of clarification, the first of these patterns — the one containing sequential seventh chords — to an aria by Handel. Here, a portion of "Dall' occaso in oriente" in *Giustino* (ex. 6.2), contains a bass theme derived from this first progression.

Up to this point in the chapter, Bach's primary topic has been the composition of bass themes; he proceeds to discuss the accompaniment of them:

> Bass themes are performed either in unison by all instruments or by bass instruments alone. In the first case the accompanist omits chords and plays the written notes in octaves with both hands. But should the composer place signatures over the bass advisedly, they must be realized. The reason is that the suspensions [*Bindungen*] which may be thereby introduced need to be heard, for they will not only not obscure the theme but make it more lucid. Some themes are so constructed that an understanding listener is only half satisfied in the absence of an accompaniment, for in his inner comprehension the harmony is inseparable from the tones he hears. In such a case the organ provides the best accompaniment, not only because of the suspensions but also because of its pene-

Example 6.1. Sequential Progressions Recommended by C. P. E. Bach for Bass Themes

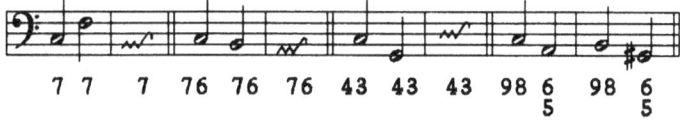

Example 6.2. *Giustino*, HWV 37, no. 35

trating volume. The second case mentioned above, which is found in vocal and instrumental pieces, requires a chordal accompaniment.[12]

C. P. E. Bach's recommendations on the accompaniment of *unisono* textures appear to be generally applicable to Handel's music for the following reasons. 1) To date no evidence has surfaced that would indicate any radical changes in the art of continuo playing during the 1740s and 1750s. 2) Bach begins this chapter by stating that J. S. Bach, G. P. Telemann and Carl Heinrich Graun all left excellent examples of bass themes. These composers flourished during Handel's lifetime, and the first two were his contemporaries. Even Graun, although he was considerably younger than Handel, died in the same year. C. P. E. Bach's statement implies, then, that he was describing a compositional technique more characteristic of the late Baroque period than of the Pre-Classical era. Thus his views on the accompaniment of bass themes are more likely to reflect the German practice of his father's generation than of a later time. 3) The recommendations represent a balanced, rational approach that recognizes the diverse nature of these themes. Some of Handel's *unisono* passages have strong harmonic implications, while others sound complete without harmony. Continuo chords would only obscure certain *unisono* ideas, but others might tolerate either a harmonized or a nonharmonized realization. The composer's intent must be respected, Bach implies, whether this is indicated by bass figuring or by verbal directions. 4) There is substantial corroborative evidence in Handel's autograph and conducting scores, as well as early printed editions and manuscript copies by Smith Sr. and his associates, that demonstrates clearly that the composer frequently intended a chordal accompaniment of his *unisono* themes.

Evidence from Handel's Autograph Figuring

Unless otherwise stated, the following examples were figured by the composer himself, and the only figuring given is that which survives in his hand. The initial set of examples will be limited to those that seem quite conclusive, especially in terms of length or amount of figuring. Examples that are sparsely figured will be discussed separately. In all cases the bass part is doubled by treble instruments at the upper octave.

The first example is an aria from the opera *Radamisto* (1720). Unfortunately, the H-G edition lacks two autograph figures, both of which occur in a *unisono* passage. These figures are restored below (ex. 6.3), where chordal accompaniment gives the material more dramatic intensity since Handel places the dissonant $^{6}_{4+2}$ on a weak beat followed by a rest. This treatment occurs in measures 8, 48, 51, and, by implication, 38.

The conducting score of *Rodelinda* (1724) is an extremely valuable source of evidence.[13] This performance copy, written by Smith Sr. with

Example 6.3. *Radamisto*, HWV 12, no. 1

extensive figuring added by the composer, contains numerous passages that call for harmonized accompaniment. Indeed, it is interesting that Handel figured *unisono* textures in *Rodelinda* in the vast majority of cases.

Example 6.4 is an excerpt from the bass aria "Di cupido impiego i vanni." Here it seems likely that Handel intended a realization in which the right hand plays in parallel thirds and tenths with the bass, along with the normal block chords at the beginning of the measure (ex. 6.5). This approach helps to alleviate the awkward progression (mm. 3-4 of ex. 6.4), which is accentuated if the right hand plays only block chords at the beginning of each measure.

The next example is taken from another bass aria in *Rodelinda*, "Tirannia gli diede il regno." The final vocal phrase of the A section (ex. 6.6), begins with a *unisono* descending scale, as a preparation for the harmonized cadence. The figuring introduces a kind of "continuo-motif," that is, chord changes in anapestic rhythm. This rhythm also appears prominently at the beginning of the B section (ex. 6.7).

The last example from *Rodelinda* is the opening ritornello of the tenor aria "Tuo drudo é mio rivale" (ex. 6.8). In this case the figured harmony clarifies the progression, enabling the listener to interpret the downbeats of the third and fourth measures as suspensions. Later in the aria, the violins play broken chord patterns over the same bass subject and harmonic progression. Also, the use of the $^6_{4\ 2}$ chord followed by a rest, which recalls the example from *Radamisto*, gives the theme more rhetorical emphasis.

In the opera *Riccardo Primo* (1727), there is an example that is considerably different from those quoted above. It is a broad, cantabile theme from the arioso "Quanto tarda il caro bene"; example 6.9 gives the opening ritornello. Like the example from *Radamisto* quoted above, the figuring derives from the holograph composition score. A chordal accompaniment expresses the affect better than would simple unisons or octaves by giving weight to the theme.

Further examples can be found in the aria "Nò, non temere" from *Ottone*.

The first version of *Il Pastor Fido* contains a very unusual, but conclusive piece of evidence that does not involve bass figuring. It occurs in the arioso "Occhi belli." The orchestration of the piece is quite unusual: violins and cellos play pizzicato, while the harpsichord, according to Handel's own marking, arpeggiates throughout. The opening ritornello is given in example 6.10. At this point the voice enters, singing an independent melody, but the instrumental texture, except for a short rest in the strings, remains unchanged.

Many *unisono* passages or motifs in Handel's music contain only a few figures. Some of these are listed in document 14. Since the passages from *Rodelinda* listed in the document contain only one figure, and the others

Example 6.4. *Rodelinda*, HWV 19, no. 5

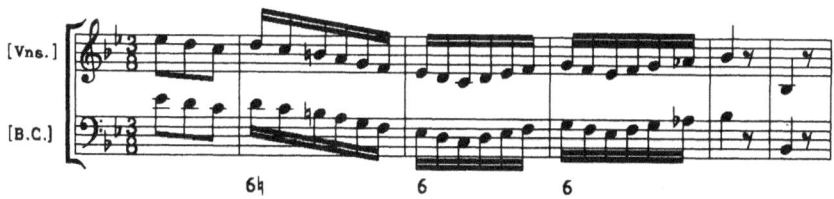

Example 6.5. Realization of Example 6.4

Example 6.6. *Rodelinda*, HWV 19, no. 18

Example 6.7. *Rodelinda*, HWV 19, no. 18

104　Unisono *Textures*

Example 6.8.　*Rodelinda*, HWV 19, no. 23a

Example 6.9.　*Riccardo Primo*, HWV 23, no. 16

Example 6.10.　*Il Pastor Fido*, HWV 8a, no. 10

have very few, it is tempting to disregard this evidence. However, sparseness of figures could indicate a predominance of root position chords. And, as we noted in the first chapter, Handel was far from meticulous or consistent in the matter of figuring; only rarely in the operas and oratorios is it complete. It is possible that he intended a chordal realization in these instances but did not bother to indicate the continuo harmony in detail; instead he relied on these sporadic hints to guide his accompanists.

The extended *unisono* themes in example 6.11, all of which occur at the beginning of an aria, have figuring only on the first note or on the first note

Document 14. Short *Unisono* Passages with Sparse Figuring

Aggrippina	"Qual piacer"	H-G: 22
Rodelinda	"Morrai, si"	H-G: 30
	"Confusa si miri"	H-G: 37–38
	"Spietati"	H-G: 45–46
	"Se fiera belva"	H-G: 93
Athaliah	Sinfonia	H-G: 1
L'Allegro	"Hence, Loathed Melancholy"	HHA: 3 (facsimile p. ix)
Samson	"Why Does the God of Israel Sleep?"	H-G: 75, 80
Judas Maccabeus		H-G: 66–67
Ah, crudel nel pianto mio		H-G 52A: 6 (same as *Agrippina* motif)
Op. 5, No. 5	First Movement	HHA IV/10/2: 49

that would require a figure. It is difficult to understand Handel's purpose in this quixotic kind of figuring. Certainly he did not intend to imply that the figured note should be harmonized, and the remainder unharmonized, especially since these themes usually begin with an anacrusis. As I have shown in the first chapter, bass figuring in Handel's autographs often functioned as a kind of *aide-mémoire* during the second stage of the creative process. Perhaps, then, these isolated figures were merely reminders? This explanation is also inadequate, since the appropriate chord is quite obvious; it is highly unlikely that Handel needed to remind himself of such routine progressions, even if he did not originally conceive of the themes *"all' unisono."* It is just possible that these isolated figures were intended as signals for the continuo player, Handel's assistant at a second harpsichord, to harmonize the whole passage or aria. Indeed, it seems the only logical reason to figure merely the first note of a piece.

Example 6.12 presents excerpts from two compositions that suggest that Handel desired both harmonized and nonharmonized accompaniment of *unisono* passages in the same movement: the B section of "Se il mio paterno amore" from *Siroe* contains both figured and unfigured *unisono* passages; in the third movement of Concerto Grosso Op. 6, No. 3, the main theme is marked *tasto solo*, but related material is figured. There is ample justification for such an approach in Mattheson's *Grosse General-Bass Schule*; see particularly the commentaries to Prob-Stück 6, Middle Class, and Prob-Stück 2, Higher Class.[14]

It is important to realize that other masters of the late Baroque period evidently used chordal accompaniments in *unisono* contexts. J. S. Bach figured the *unisono* ritornelli in the aria "Streite, siege, starker Held!" from the cantata *Nun komm, der Heiden Heiland*, BWV 62.[15] This aria, like the

Example 6.11a. *Athalia*, HWV 52, no. 19

Example 6.11b. *Orlando*, HWV 31, no. 28

Example 6.11c. *Giustino*, HWV 37, no. 35

Example 6.11d. *Scipione*, HWV 20, no. 35

Example 6.11e. *Samson*, HWV 57, no. 8

Example 6.12a. *Siroe*, HWV 24, no. 2

Example 6.12b. Concerto Grosso Op. 6, No. 3, Third Movement

movement from *Il Pastor Fido* mentioned earlier, has a *unisono* accompaniment with an independent vocal part. The first ritornello of the Bach aria is given in example 6.13. For this cantata, as with many others, Bach himself added figuring to the scribal organ continuo part. It is difficult to imagine evidence more conclusive than this, since it comes from the original performance material. G. P. Telemann figured much shorter *unisono* passages from the Paris Quartet No. 2 in D;[16] similar examples abound in the concerti of Antonio Vivaldi.

Before we conclude this chapter, a few words of warning are in order. Handel's dramatic works vary considerably in the amount and distribution of continuo figuring. Occasionally, it seems that the figuring reflects an early stage of the creative process; it records his original conception of a progression, which later might be elaborated upon or even altered. Thus it is possible that some of the *unisono* figuring could be more closely related to the act of composition than to performance. In any case, this condition would not apply to the several examples from *Rodelinda* since the figuring was added after the work was finished.

Many of the composer's most striking *unisono* themes would not benefit from a chordal realization; e.g., "Del minacciar del vento" from *Ottone*,[17] the prison scene from *Joseph*, the beginning of the "Jealousy" chorus from *Hercules*, the initial statement of the passacaglia theme before Daniel's reading of the prophecy in *Belshazzar*. Many of Handel's *unisoni*

Example 6.13. J. S. Bach, *Nun komm, der Heiden Heiland*, BWV 52, no. 4

were never figured, either by the composer or by scribes from the Smith circle. It would probably be a mistake to add harmony in these instances. Also, any passages involving an abrupt change to *unisono* texture for dramatic or pictorial effect, such as the ending of the Trio in *Acis and Galatea* or the famous instrumental depiction of Goliath in *Saul*, should be left unharmonized.

Nevertheless, it seems obvious that Handel frequently intended a chordal accompaniment for his *unisoni*. Therefore, if autograph figuring survives—and there are no authentic *tasto solo* or *senza cembalo* markings to contradict it—the figuring should be realized. Lacking any indication from the composer, the decision regarding whether or not to harmonize a given *unisono* passage should be based on musical considerations, such as those articulated by C. P. E. Bach, and the relative authenticity of any figuring that has survived in contemporary manuscript and printed sources.

7

Plain Recitative

Our understanding of stylistically appropriate thoroughbass realization in plain, or so-called secco recitative has grown substantially in recent decades.[1] But present-day performances still leave a great deal to be desired. To a large extent this is due to inadequate scholarly scrutiny of certain key issues. In this chapter I will focus on three problematic issues as they relate to Handelian recitative: whether the chords should be detached or held; the kind of melodic and harmonic support necessary; and the use and harmonization of foreshortened cadences. These aspects of recitative accompaniment need to be considered more thoroughly by scholars and performers.

The first section will treat the question of shortened accompaniment. It has become standard practice among knowledgeable continuo players to shorten the chords in simple recitative. There is certainly historical justification for this practice, but it comes almost entirely from German sources, many of which are far from categorical on the subject. Are these sources applicable to Handel's music, especially to his operas and Italian cantatas? Also, most of the German theorists speak of organ accompaniment, whereas in the plain recitative of Handel's theatrical works and chamber cantatas the harpsichord is the proper instrument. Can these recommendations regarding organ continuo apply to the harpsichord? My research has uncovered considerable evidence from German and Italian theorists, as well as Handel's autograph scores, which supports "sustained" chords on the harpsichord in plain recitative.

In the second section of this chapter I will discuss the issue of harmonic and melodic support. Modern performances, especially by members of the Amsterdam school (e.g., Gustav Leonhardt, Ton Koopman), often fail to provide sufficient support: chords are not repeated if the same harmony prevails for several bars; even if the figuring prescribes a complete change of harmony over a bass pedal tone, frequently no chord is played. As a result, the voice can be left unaccompanied much of the time; this sparse effect is particularly unfortunate when the solo part modulates or contains difficult intervals. There is to my knowledge no evidence which would justify a blithe disregard of bass figuring in plain recitative.[2] On the contrary, the accompanist is obliged to include all the harmonic inflections of the vocal part, whether or not these are shown in the figuring. The accompanist is also obliged to assist the singer "melodically," by giving prominence to the initial pitches and important intervals which he must execute. This type of generous support from the keyboard was no doubt dictated by practical necessity, especially when the recitatives had to be memorized, but it is often advantageous aesthetically as well.

In the final section of this chapter I will discuss the use and harmonization of foreshortened cadences. In contrast to the more familiar delayed cadence, the foreshortened cadence is played so that its dominant chord coincides with the last accented syllable of the text; the second chord usually comes just after the singer has finished. Should this type of cadence be applied to all of Handel's plain recitative? The theoretical sources describe it as an operatic convention, yet some prominent conductors use it in nonoperatic works; John Eliot Gardiner uses it in *Acis and Galatea*, a serenata or "masque," and Christopher Hogwood uses it in *Messiah*, a nondramatic oratorio. How should the keyboard player realize foreshortened cadences? Simple block chords, in a dominant–tonic progression, create a clash with the usual vocal appoggiatura. The theoretical and musical evidence suggests that this clash was usually not accepted; in most cases the foreshortened cadence needs to be realized with more circumspection than the delayed cadence.

Detached or Sustained Chords?

Handel's Practice

Handel's treatment of this aspect of recitative accompaniment is difficult to reconstruct. Although he was German by birth and early training, his affinity for Italian vocal and instrumental forms was strongly marked and the bulk of his creative life spent composing and performing opera seria. It is possible that initially his practice was similar to that of Francesco Gasparini, who advocated a nondetached harpsichord accompaniment in simple recitative. Later, perhaps in the late 1720s, Handel's practice became more eclectic. Very few of his original performance parts have survived, but there is no evidence in the extant parts to indicate that he consistently shortened the recitative chords in a given work, as Telemann and J. S. Bach did.

Winton Dean believes that recitative accompaniments in Handel's dramatic works should be detached, basing his conclusions on the testimony of Pierre Jacques Fougeroux, who recorded his impressions of three Royal Academy opera performances in 1728.[3] The operas he heard were *Admeto*, *Siroe*, and *Tolomeo*, all by Handel and presumably performed under his direction. Fougeroux noticed that the sound of each chord in recitative was cut off, a "mauvaise manière d'accompagner." But Fougeroux was not a professional musician, nor even a completely reliable observer, so there is no guarantee of his accuracy. He was incorrect about the instruments used in these operas: trumpets are mentioned, which the score does not call for, while oboes and violas, which the score does call for, are not mentioned. He was also incorrect regarding some of the singers he heard.[4] As for the recitative, it is likely that he remembered merely the predominant style of accompaniment; we cannot take his statement as proof positive that the chords were always detached. Actually, any amount of detached accompaniment would have made a strong impression on Fougeroux since, as Dean points out, he was accustomed to the sustained delivery of French recitative. Also, there is the possibility that he was referring to Handel's *accompagnato*, which frequently contains detached chords. There are striking examples in *Admeto*; in *Tolomeo* both the *accompagnato* "Inumano fratel" and the following arioso "Stille amare" have repeated, detached chords in varying rhythms and articulations. Fougeroux's testimony is of considerable but not overriding importance; we cannot afford to ignore conflicting evidence from other sources.

Autograph markings of "sostenuto" or "sostentato" over the bass in plain recitative sections of Handel's scores demonstrate that he did demand sustained chords on occasion: *La Lucrezia* (H-G 51: 41); *Giustino* (H-G: 63, 100); *Ode for St. Cecilia's Day* (H-G: 6); and *Samson* (H-G: 217).[5] The first is an autograph marking on a scribal copy in British Library manuscript RM. 19. e. 7.; the others occur in British Library autograph scores. The examples from *Giustino*, which also include rests in the bass, are especially significant because they show clearly how the two styles—sustained and detached—can be juxtaposed in order to highlight contrasting emotions in the text. This same contrast is indicated with rhythmic values alone in the following brief recitative from *Susanna* (ex. 7.1). The autograph shows that Handel began writing the bass in the conventional way but soon changed his mind, blackened the first two notes, and added rests.

Example 7.1. *Susanna*, HWV 66; HHA I/28: 121

The Hamburg conducting score of *Samson*, mostly copied by Smith Sr., is marked "sostenuto" by Smith three additional times in simple recitative, during Delila's attempts at reconciliation with Samson in act 2. The first two markings are cancelled a few measures later by the directive "staccato."[6] In the space of slightly more than two pages, the continuo execution changes frequently from detached to sustained chords.

An interesting piece of secondary evidence can be found in the volumes of Handel autographs in the Fitzwilliam Museum, Cambridge. This is a cello continuo part, again written by Smith Sr., for the opening of an unpublished version of the cantata *Mi palpita il cor* (ex. 7.2).[7] This is obviously not a normal recitative, but rather a lyrical, highly ornamented type. (Two other versions are given in H-G 50: 153 and 161). Presumably, the harpsichordist would fill in during the long bass rests in the first and third systems of the Fitzwilliam version, but this is only conjectural. In any case, it seems that the composer intended both styles of execution: predominantly detached cello part for the first section—probably with keyboard chords of the same length—and an almost completely sustained accompaniment for the second section.

Along with the passages mentioned above, there are other examples in which Handel writes rests in the bass of plain recitative: *Poro* (H-G: 29); *Deidamia* (H-G: 19); *La Lucrezia* (H-G 51: 42); and *Israel in Egypt* (H-G: 17). (Other examples no doubt exist.) Admittedly, the passages from *Poro* and *Deidamia* are rather unusual, a kind of a middle ground between arioso and recitative. But the other two passages, together with the excerpts from *Giustino* and *Susanna* listed above, are normal recitative.

Since the composer frequently did not have the time or inclination to mark the basso continuo execution carefully, these examples should not be regarded as isolated phenomena, not as mere exceptions to the rule, but as models that can be applied with discretion to similar passages in other vocal works. We must also keep in mind that his intentions could have been communicated verbally or written down in performance material that is no longer extant. The surviving evidence may not be representative of the extent to which he used nondetached styles of accompaniment and juxtaposed contrasting styles within the same recitative.

It should also be noted that the issue of melodic and harmonic support in plain recitative, treated below, is closely related to the duration of the chords. Handel's habit of repeating identical figuring over the same bass note, frequently at small intervals, strongly implies a nondetached, and normally arpeggiated, realization.

Theoretical Evidence for Sustained Chords

There is ample theoretical justification for sustained, or rather nondetached harpsichord accompaniment of plain recitative. This includes

Example 7.2. *Mi palpita il cor*
Fitzwilliam Museum MU MS 265, p. 61

Reprinted by permission of the Syndics of the Fitzwilliam Museum

excerpts from the thoroughbass treatises of Gasparini, Heinichen, Pasquali, and C. P. E. Bach.

Francesco Gasparini's *L'Armonico pratico al cimbalo* (1708) was a practical guide to continuo accompaniment used throughout the eighteenth-century and one of the most influential of all thoroughbass treatises. Chapter 9, "Dissonances in the Recitatives and How to Play Acciaccaturas," begins:

> In recitatives pay particular attention to the composed part, that is, to the part that is sung. Often above a sustained bass note the composed part will be dissonant, and after proceeding through new and different dissonances becomes consonant again, without the bass having moved. Thus when the composed part begins with a consonance and moves to a second above the bass, harmonize the bass note by playing simultaneously the second, fourth, and major seventh. Similarly, if the composed part goes to any other of these dissonances, that is to the fourth or major seventh, do not play one without the others. *Sustain these dissonances until the composed part resolves to a consonance*, that is, to a third, fifth, or octave. Adding a fifth to these dissonant notes, next to the fourth, is effective.[8]

The author is describing a very common recitative progression; Handel used it hundreds of times, invariably with the figuring $\frac{7}{4}$ $\frac{5}{3}$.[9] Gasparini refers to passages of this type as the "cantilene of recitatives,"[10] which implies that they should be performed lyrically. This by itself would suggest that a detached accompaniment is probably inappropriate. The desired effect is one of consonance–dissonance–consonance: the common chord changes to the richly dissonant $\frac{7}{4}$, possibly with doublings, which resolves to the initial chord—all over the same bass note. It is impossible to achieve this result without sustaining or re-striking the bass, since the intervals of the $\frac{7}{4}$ sonority are dissonant only with respect to the bass.

Gasparini's description is clarified at the end of the chapter; here he notates an unusually full accompaniment for one of these "cantilena" passages:

> I discovered, in the course of practice, that one can play a certain dissonance (a doubled acciaccatura of fourteen notes) all at one stroke. This occurs, as in the example, when the interval of a major seventh is found in recitative (ex. 7.3). . . . This, however, is an oddity, rather than an example or general rule; its occasional use would be qualified by considerations of time, place, and company. These and similar dissonances, or harsh harmonies, would seem to allow the good singer scope for better expression of the affections and spirit of compositions.[11]

The first part of example 7.3 is a segment of recitative as normally written; the remaining three measures, a continuo realization of that segment. As Gasparini tells us earlier in the chapter, "all the notes placed between the barlines are played together at a single stroke,"[12] that is, slightly

Example 7.3. Francesco Gasparini: Sample Recitative with Realization

spread. Note that the bass G is repeated at the end of the second chord, intensifying the dissonant effect.

At this point it might be argued that Gasparini is recommending sustained execution only for the dissonant chords of these "cantilena" passages. The third paragraph of this chapter shows that this is not the case:

> In order to perform the accompaniments of recitatives with some degree of good taste, the consonances must be deployed almost like an arpeggio, though not continuously so. Once the harmony of a note has been heard, *hold the keys fast* and permit the singer to take the lead, singing at his discretion and in accord with the expression of the words.[13]

The command "hold the keys fast" could not be more explicit as a description of sustained execution.

Peter Williams suggests that Gasparini is describing the style used predominantly in opera seria, as opposed to the lighter, highly detached opera buffa style popular later in the century.[14] This is certainly plausible, although it is difficult to believe that the distinction was so simple and clearcut. In any case, Gasparini's recommendations deserve considerable weight and are especially applicable to Handel's early operas and cantatas. The treatise was probably the most widely used Italian continuo method of the eighteenth century. To my knowledge, the statements quoted herein were never contradicted by any Italian author. The book appeared during Handel's first sojourn in Italy; perhaps he read it to further his mastery of Italian style and practice. The two men may even have met in Venice during 1708. We do know that Gasparini's operas, especially *Tamerlano*, *Bajazet*, and *Faramondo*, greatly influenced Handel.[15] And all the evidence suggests that Johann David Heinichen, another German opera composer who was very successful in Italy, agreed with Gasparini, at least with respect to *recitativo semplice* accompanied on the harpsichord.

116   Plain Recitative

In his 1711 treatise, *Neu erfundene Anweisung*, Heinichen mentions that both sustained and detached recitative accompaniment are acceptable on the organ.[16] However, it seems that this statement was not repeated in his 1728 treatise, *Der General-Bass in der Composition*, which is an enlarged and revised version of the earlier work and deals extensively with realization of accompaniments for recitative. Heinichen's treatment of the acciaccatura (part I, chap. 6: "Of Embellished Thoroughbass") is largely derived from *L'Armonico pratico*.[17] He repeats Gasparini's recommendation that the consonances of chords which contain acciaccaturas be sustained.[18] Admittedly, Heinichen's topic at this point is not recitative specifically but the ornaments that can be used in continuo realizations. He does mention, however, that the acciaccatura can be very effective in recitative accompaniments.[19]

Later in the treatise, Heinichen gives detailed instructions on realizing an unfigured cantata for voice and continuo by Alessandro Scarlatti, *Lascia, deh lascia al fine*. The instructions for the two sections of simple recitative fail to inform the reader of any necessary shortening of chords.[20]

An indirect reference in the Supplementa of *Der General-Bass* provides further evidence. Heinichen attempts to rationalize the "5ten-Fehler" which must result in the realization of example 7.4.

> Even though the chord . . . is also used by great masters in the recitative, still one would not suggest that it was completely correct, because the diminished fifth over the first bass must resolve over the following, forming two forbidden fifths. As an excuse for this error the following can serve: these fifths (1) do not appear in the two composed parts; (2) are not too prominent in a recitative with a stable bass and the rapidly disappearing harpsichord tone; and (3) can easily be covered up by a full-voiced chord in the accompaniment.[21]

The implied description of recitative accompaniment—"einem stillstehenden Basse und verschwindenden Clavicimbal-Tone"—does not suggest detached chords; German writers normally refer to shortened accompaniment in unequivocal terms.

Example 7.4.   Johann David Heinichen:
              Sample Recitative Progression

Similarly, the brief example of recitative realization from the *Versuch* (1752) of Johann Joachim Quantz, which will be quoted and discussed in the next section of this chapter, in no way implies detached execution.

Nicolo Pasquali's *Thorough-Bass Made Easy* (1757) gives realizations for two complete recitatives; these are notated in the conventional way with "the manner of accompanying" underneath on separate staves. One of these realizations is given in example 7.5.[22] Except at cadences, the chords are arpeggiated and held; there is nothing in Pasquali's verbal text that implies detached continuo chords.[23]

Pasquali's little tutor was intended primarily for *dilettanti*, but that is no reason to discredit his testimony on this particular question. It is just as easy for the amateur to release a chord as it is to hold one. Also, it is clear that Pasquali has attempted to indicate some of the refinements that a good accompanist would use, for example, the varying amounts and directions of arpeggiation, the careful alignment of the realization with the normal notation (especially in the third and fifth measures), the short rest at the beginning of the second measure, which allows the appoggiatura in the solo part to stand out, and the completion of the G major chord in measure 3, slightly before the soloist's appoggiatura. The other recitative realization from Pasquali's manual, quoted later in this chapter, is written in the same style.

Unlike Pasquali, C. P. E. Bach was an innovative composer at the forefront of musical development during the middle of the eighteenth century. Part 2 of his *Versuch*, published in 1762, deals with figured bass and accompaniment. If, as Peter Williams has plausibly suggested, the practice of shortened accompaniment became more common as the century progressed,[24] one might expect that Bach would recommend the practice exclusively.

However, this is not the case. Chapter 38 of the *Versuch* treats all kinds of recitative—simple, accompagnato, buffo, sacred—but it is evident from the context that the following remarks from paragraphs 3 and 4 apply primarily to simple recitative,[25] and they do not imply that detached execution was a universally practiced performance convention.

3. When the declamation is rapid, the chords must be ready instantly, especially at pauses in the principal part where the chord precedes a following entrance. At the termination of a chord, its successor must be struck with dispatch. Thus the singer will not be hampered in his affects or their requisite fast execution, for he will always know in good time the course and construction of the harmony. Were it necessary to choose between two evils, it would be preferable to hasten rather than to delay. Indeed, the former is always better. Arpeggiation must be withheld from rapid declamation, especially when there are frequent chordal changes. For one thing, there is no time for it, and even if there were, it might very easily lead accompanist, singer, and audience into confusion. Furthermore, arpeggiation is not required here, for it finds its natural employment in quite different situations, in slow recitatives and long lasting harmonies. In such cases it serves to remind the singer that he is to remain in a given chord, and prevents him from losing the pitch

Example 7.5. Nicolo Pasquali, *Thorough-Bass Made Easy*

because of the length of the chord, or from assuming that the chord has changed. . . .

4. The pace with which a chord is arpeggiated depends on the tempo and content of a recitative. The slower and more affetuoso the latter is, the slower the arpeggiation. But as soon as the accompaniment shifts from sustained to short, detached notes, the accompanist must play detached, resolute chords, unarpeggiated, and fully grasped by both hands. Even if the score expresses tied white notes, the sharply detached execution is retained.[26]

Here we see a striking contrast between two divergent styles of playing: crisp, short chords for fast or resolute declamation, and slowly arpeggiated chords for sustained affetuoso singing. Since the arpeggiation "prevents" the singer "from losing the pitch because of the length of the chord," it must be continuous to some extent or repeated at intervals. It is difficult to imagine an arpeggiated, detached accompaniment that would help the singer stay on pitch; the chords would have to be repeated frequently and obtrusively. Also, it must be remembered that slow arpeggiation on the harpsichord is a means of achieving sostenuto; to play a slow arpeggio and then immediately release all the notes is to work at cross purposes. Certainly it seems likely that the second style of recitative accompaniment described by C. P. E. Bach would encompass little, if any, detached execution.

Evidence for Detached Chords

There is a large body of evidence that supports detached chords, especially in German recitative accompanied on the organ. Much of the theoretical evidence was brought to the fore by Arthur Mendel in the preface to his vocal score of J. S. Bach's *St. John Passion*. Mendel also emphasized that although the autograph score of Bach's *St. Matthew Passion* has the conventional long notes in recitatives, the original continuo parts have quarters with rests. This notation is also found in the cantatas, for example, no. 94, no. 95, and no. 97.[27] Laurence Dreyfus has included a comprehensive survey of eighteenth-century sources that refer to and describe shortened accompaniment in his recent book on continuo practice in the music of J. S. Bach.[28] After a thorough study of performance material for vocal works of the Leipzig master, Laurence Dreyfus concluded that "the convention of 'shortened accompaniment' emerges as the prevailing practice in Northern Europe throughout the 18th Century."[29]

This conclusion is certainly valid, but there is evidence that the practice of recitative accompaniment, even in Germany, was hardly uniform. Three early eighteenth-century theorists—Kellner, Krause, and Lustig—qualify their preference for shortened accompaniment, and Heinichen leaves the matter to the discretion of the organist, who should decide according to the musical textures and the length of the particular chord. So far, I have been able to uncover only four German sources, dating from 1754 or earlier, which unequivocally recommend detached chords in recitative: Neidt, Stölzel, Voigt, and G. P. Telemann.

Telemann's practice deserves to be singled out for comment, partly because of the plethora of source material, but also because there seems to be some confusion among modern scholars regarding the recommendations in his *Singe-, Spiel- und Generalbass-Übungen*. The work is a song collection, as well as a thoroughbass tutor; it consists of 42 short lieder, each of which is provided with a figured bass and a realization for the right hand. Telemann's concise and pithy commentary offers advice on problematic aspects of continuo accompaniment. The work contains one recitative, excerpted in example 7.6, in which the bass is written in conventional long notes, while the realization has quarter note chords with rests.[30] Some scholars, notably Dreyfus and Peter Williams, have implied that this notation should be taken literally: detached chordal realization above a sustained bass.[31]

However, there is considerable evidence which suggests that Telemann's notation should not be interpreted literally. As part of the commentary to this example, Telemann illustrates the arpeggiation appropriate in recitative (ex. 7.7).[32] Note that here the bass is consistently written as quarters with rests, even though the rest is metrically incorrect in the first three arpeggiated chords. It is also significant that in the fourth chord the bass rhythm is notated precisely—in sharp contrast to the remainder of the chord. Why did Telemann write the bass in long notes in the actual recitative? Because any practical tutor must familiarize the student with standard notational practices. Thus, it seems more likely that Telemann preferred a detached bass, together with similarly detached right-hand chords, in simple recitative. This interpretation is confirmed by manuscript scores and original continuo parts of at least four Telemann cantatas[33] — *Wer mich liebet, Christus ist um, Ein ungefärbt Gemüte, Jesu, wirst du* — as well as the cello part of his opera *Der geduldige Sokrates*.[34]

But even Telemann and J. S. Bach, who favored the extensive use of shortened accompaniment in their works, occasionally specified sustained chords in simple recitative, for example, the anguished cry of Christ on the cross, "Eli, eli . . ." from the *St. Matthew Passion*,[35] and example 7.8 from Telemann's *Der Messias*.[36] Also, as Peter Williams has correctly pointed out: "J. S. Bach frequently varied recitatives within a work by writing long held notes at some points, short notes (with rests) at others; surely, therefore, the composer did not expect chords in all recitatives to be shortened uniformly."[37]

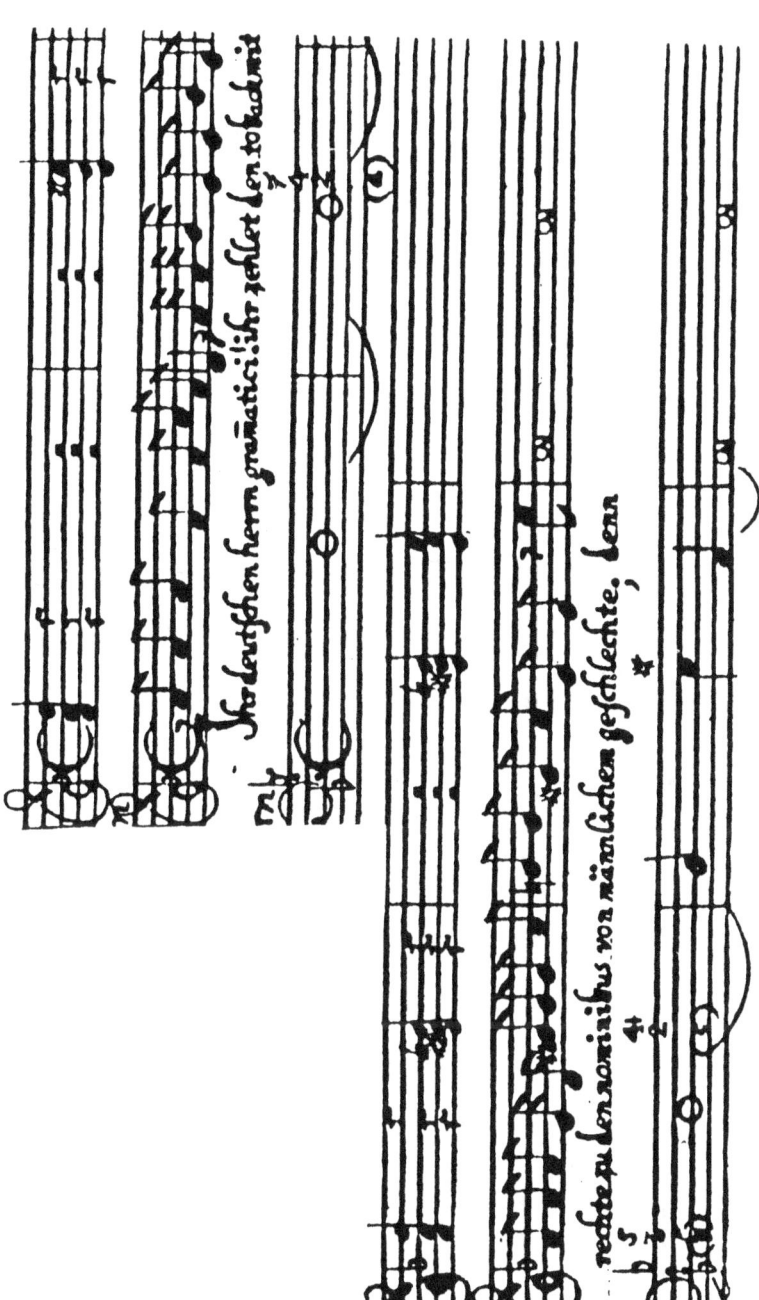

Example 7.6. Georg Philipp Telemann, *Singe-, Spiel- und Generalbass-Übungen*

Example 7.7. Georg Philipp Telemann: Samples of Recitative Arpeggiation

Example 7.8. Georg Philipp Telemann, *Der Messias*

Melodic and Harmonic Support

In plain recitative the accompanist must provide the soloist with sufficient support, regardless of whether detached or sustained execution has been chosen. Indeed, generous support is perhaps more necessary in a detached accompaniment. There is no historical justification for the extremely discreet style of many continuo players, for whom the guiding principle seems to be: play as few chords as possible. Some practitioners of this approach never play more than one chord per bass pitch, regardless of the harmonic implications of the voice part or the figuring. This, together with a highly detached execution of the chords, gives an almost monophonic cast to simple recitative; this effect was certainly not intended in most cases, and seems especially inappropriate for Italianate recitative.

This support will most often take the form of chords, but frequently the accompanist should give melodic support as well. What should this melodic support consist of? It should not consist of scales, running passages, or melodic embellishments. The extent of agreement on this rule among the eighteenth-century authorities is striking.

> Do not annoy or disturb him [the singer] with a continuous arpeggio, or with ascending or descending scale passages, as some do.
>
> Gasparini (1708)[38]

> All scales and runs and all the little *Manieren* must be omitted when playing recitatives.
>
> G. P. Telemann (1734)[39]

> ... keyboard instruments do not use ornaments or refinements, aside from arpeggiation, in the accompaniments to recitatives.
>
> C. P. E. Bach (1762)[40]

The recommended type of melodic support consists of anticipating initial pitches and important intervals from the vocal part. Thus, the accompanist does not invent additional melodic material; he merely takes these fragments from the solo part, playing them just before the singer must execute them. The theoretical justification for this practice in Handelian recitative comes from the writings of Quantz and Macfarren (discussed below).

The amount of harmonic support required is extensive. Once the initial chord has been played, there are many excellent reasons for supplying additional chords or chord tones over the same bass. First, there are purely practical reasons: the singer may need to be reminded of the underlying harmony, or he may require help with a difficult interval or complex harmonic progression.[41] Next, there are several musical considerations. The solo part may imply a change of chord, which may or may not be indicated in the figuring. The solo part may introduce a dissonance that does not resolve normally; in this case the accompanist should include the dissonance and resolve it at an appropriate point in the harmonic structure. Occasionally, the figuring indicates an harmonic change not implied in the vocal line, usually to provide a smoother or more expressive progression. Lastly, there are the dramatic reasons: rhetorical emphasis, the entrance of a character, and noisy stage action that obliterates the accompaniment.[42] Also, the mood of the text may suggest additional sonority for any number of reasons.

To illustrate and justify the proposed musical considerations for ample harmonic and melodic support, excerpts from the theoretical literature will be presented to corroborate the evidence which is directly relevant to Handel's recitative.

Johann Joachim Quantz realized four measures of recitative accompaniment (ex. 7.9) in his famous flute treatise of 1752.[43] The difficulty with this example is that Quantz has included both the conventional notation of the continuo as well as written-out realization on the same system, similar to Telemann's recitative from the *Generalbass-Übungen*. For clarity, it is necessary to separate the two layers that have been superimposed upon each other; the conventional notation is example 7.10, and an interpretation of Quantz's accompaniment is example 7.11. Note how extensively the harmony is filled in; this type of passage is frequently realized with four chords only, one at each of the asterisked points. Notice also the chord repetition in the first measure; many players would regard that as unnecessary. Quantz's realization actually anticipates important intervals of the solo part: the minor seventh in measure 2 and the fourth in measure 3. The increased harmonic movement in the third measure helps to prepare the cadence. The chord change on the second beat of this measure is extremely interesting; it is implied by the upper part (but not strongly — the E could be considered as an anticipation of the following chord) and further prepares the singer for the upcoming leap of a fourth. Also, without this harmonic change the progression would be as in example 7.12; perhaps Quantz felt that would be awkward.

The prominence in the accompaniment of crucial intervals from the voice part is a conscious effort to assist the singer's memory. Quantz states in the text that accompanies his realization:

> In a recitative sung from memory it is much easier for the singer if the accompanist anticipates the singer's first notes at each caesura, and, so to speak, puts them into his mouth for him by striking the chord with a quick arpeggiation, in such fashion that, where possible, the singer's first note lies in the upper part; immediately afterwards he should strike separately several of the following intervals that appear in the vocal part. This is most helpful both to the memory and to the intonation of the singer.[44]

Example 7.9. Johann Joachim Quantz: Sample Recitative with Realization

Example 7.10. The Quantz Example in Conventional Notation

Example 7.11. An Interpretation of the Quantz Realization

Example 7.12. The Progression Quantz Avoided

These directives sound very similar to the only extant description of Handel's recitative accompaniment. This is the recollection of Joah Bates, transmitted by Sir George Smart to Sir George Macfarren, and reported by Macfarren in 1885:

> [Handel's] accompaniment for recitative was made interesting by the "sprinkling" ... of harmony, or spreading it in arpeggio across a large part of the compass of the instrument, and so confirming the voice with the note which was to be prominent in the succeeding phrase; never being struck together with the voice, [but rather] succeeding vocal closes [i.e., after cadences], and anticipating the frontal notes of new phrases.
>
> It had always been the custom to accompany in the opera, as much as in the oratorio, recitative in this manner.[45]

In his youth, Joah Bates reputedly heard some of Handel's performances, so despite the fact that this is a recollection twice removed, it is probably accurate. Unfortunately, Macfarren's syntax is rather muddled. Presumably, the intended meaning is that the accompaniment consisted of full chords, arpeggiated in such a way that the beginnings of phrases and other prominent tones in the vocal part were played just before the soloist had to sing them. This description leads one to the conclusion that Quantz and Handel had remarkably similar approaches to recitative accompaniment.

Example 7.13 is the second realization of a recitative from Pasquali's *Thorough-Bass Made Easy*.[46] This exhibits many of the same features we noticed in the other example of recitative realization from Pasquali's tutor, quoted earlier in this chapter (ex. 7.5). The reader should note that in measure 2 the chord is reiterated with the addition of the diminished fifth from the voice, even though the figuring does not indicate this interval. In measures 4 and 12, the harmonic change over the bass pedal is realized in accordance with the figuring.

Pasquali's book is clearly an extremely important source for the performance of Handel's music, for, as John Churchill states in his introduction to the facsimile edition of the treatise, "Pasquali was a man in daily contact with the musical world of Handel, Greene, Stanley, Geminiani. . . . [Pasquali] himself prepared countless works for public performance, and he remains a very reliable guide to anyone preparing such music two centuries later."[47]

Heinichen's treatise, *Der General-Bass in der Composition*, includes dozens of examples which illustrate the kind of firm harmonic support required in recitative accompaniments. However, only a representative sample will be discussed here. In the examples which follow, the premise is that these segments of *recitativo semplice* lack any bass figuring; Heinichen's commentary gives detailed instructions on the proper harmonization of them.[48] In example 7.14, one must play a root position

Example 7.13. Nicolo Pasquali, *Thorough-Bass Made Easy*

128 Plain Recitative

Example 7.14. Johann David Heinichen:
Sample Recitative Progression

triad for the first half of the measure, and a $\genfrac{}{}{0pt}{}{7}{\genfrac{}{}{0pt}{}{4}{2}}$ for the second half; one should not treat the B as a passing tone and play a C-major chord for the entire measure. This is the common "cantilena" progression described by Gasparini in the first section of this chapter. In example 7.15, the seventh on the third beat of the solo part does not resolve; the accompanist must play 7 6 in the last half of the measure. In example 7.16, the accompanist must execute a progression of four chords over the bass note C: first a root position triad, then a $\genfrac{}{}{0pt}{}{6}{4}$ chord for the second half of the first measure, at the beginning of the second measure a $\genfrac{}{}{0pt}{}{7}{\genfrac{}{}{0pt}{}{4}{2}}$ chord, which resolves to the original root position G major triad on the third beat. In example 7.17, according to Heinichen, the harmony should be: a root position triad at the beginning, changing to a first inversion chord on the third beat, and then a $\genfrac{}{}{0pt}{}{6}{\genfrac{}{}{0pt}{}{4}{2}}$ at the beginning of the next measure. Heinichen's instructions imply that the D in the vocal part should not be regarded as an anticipation. Aesthetic as well as practical considerations justify this approach: the recommended harmonization is smoother and more elegant than $\genfrac{}{}{0pt}{}{5}{3}$ $\genfrac{}{}{0pt}{}{6}{\genfrac{}{}{0pt}{}{4}{2}}$; it also prepares the singer for the leap at the end of the first measure. (The same situation is found in the third measure of the Quantz realization, exx. 7.9 and 7.11.)

All four of these progressions, as well as others similar to them, can be found in Handel's plain recitative with original figuring which is in accord with Heinichen's recommendations. The cantilena progression $\genfrac{}{}{0pt}{}{5}{3}$ $\genfrac{}{}{0pt}{}{7}{\genfrac{}{}{0pt}{}{4}{2}}$ $\genfrac{}{}{0pt}{}{5}{3}$ occurs hundreds of times; it is the most common chord change over a bass pedal in Handel's recitative. Instances of the other three progressions are illustrated in examples 7.18, 7.19, and 7.20. As examples 7.18c and d demonstrate, Handel even indicated the 7 6 progression when the seventh is not present in the vocal part, to provide for a smoother or more expressive accompaniment.

Handel's figuring in plain recitative, as in all forms, is often incomplete. But when he takes the trouble, his recitative figuring is almost

Plain Recitative   129

Example 7.15.   Johann David Heinichen:
                Sample Recitative Progression

Example 7.16.   Johann David Heinichen:
                Sample Recitative Progression

Example 7.17.   Johann David Heinichen:
                Sample Recitative Progression

always in agreement with Heinichen's precepts as given in *Der General-Bass*. This treatise is certainly the best guide for any problems of harmonization in Handel's plain recitative.

Handel's preference for rich, sonorous support is demonstrated by an interesting idiosyncrasy of his recitative figuring. He frequently repeats a figure over a long, tied note in the bass. This repetition, which is found only seldom in other forms, is unnecessary according to the conventions of figured bass, since no harmonic change is involved. It seems obvious that he intended that the chord be re-struck or the arpeggiation be continuous or resumed. Example 7.21, from *Messiah*, is perhaps the best known instance. Here the best solution is probably a simple repetition of the $\frac{7}{4}$ chord, slightly spread, thus providing a brief moment

Example 7.18a. *Semele*, H-G: 138

Example 7.18b. *Amadigi*, HHA: 14

Example 7.18c. *Orlando*, HHA: 37

Example 7.18d. *E partirai, mia vita?*, H-G 50: 84

Example 7.19a. *Poro*, H-G: 8

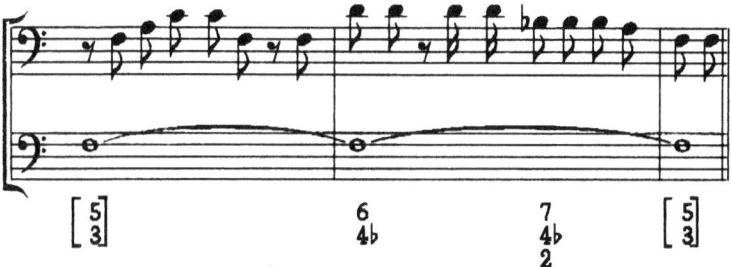

Example 7.19b. *Deborah*, H-G: 44

of reflection to underscore the mystery of the biblical prophecy. This solution is also recommended for example 7.22, an excerpt from *Siroe*. Examples 7.23 and 7.24 require repeated arpeggios, ascending and descending: bold, dramatic arpeggios for *Lucrezia*, and slower, lyrical ones for *Ninfe e pastori*. If one accepts John Mayo's theory that the figuring of the last example was added by the composer for the purpose of teaching continuo realization,[49] then it is even more convincing proof that Handel intended the additional sonority. Further examples of this type of repetition can be found in document 15.

All of this evidence demonstrates that the accompanist should provide ample support throughout Handel's plain recitative, not merely at the beginnings and ends of harmonic units. Often the situation will require that more than one chord, if not several chords, be played over the same bass note. The accompanist is normally obliged to play all the harmonies implied by the solo part as well as the figuring. He must also include and resolve any dissonances that are not resolved normally in the solo part. Chordal repetition can be desirable for aesthetic as well as practical reasons. Arpeggiation must not be excessive, but continuous arpeggiation for a few measures is justifiable in highly dramatic pieces. In lyrical recitatives slow and discreet arpeggiation, repeated at inter-

Example 7.20a. *Sento là che ristretto*, H-G 51: 99

Example 7.20b. *Orlando*, HHA: 43

Example 7.20c. *Samson*, H-G: 56

vals, can greatly enhance the affect (amorous, pathetic, and so forth). In addition, a certain amount of melodic support is required of the accompanist, especially if the recitatives are memorized: the beginnings of phrases and other crucial intervals from the vocal part should be underscored prominently just before the soloist must sing them.

The application of these principles need not result in an obtrusive accompaniment that hampers the singer, but at times it may be difficult to strike the ideal balance between too much and too little support.

Example 7.21. *Messiah*, HHA: 39

Example 7.22. *Siroe*, H-G: 26

Example 7.23. *La Lucrezia*, H-G 51: 32

Example 7.24. *Ninfe e pastori*, H-G 51: 16

Document 15. Repetition of Figuring during
Long Bass Notes in Handel's Plain Recitative

Arminio	H-G: 68
Atalanta	H-G: 67
Berenice	RM. 20. a. 10., fol. 40
Deborah	H-G: 72, 160
E partirai, mia vita?	H-G 50: 81
Ezio	HHA: 96, 183
Flavio	H-G: 62
Joseph	H-G: 178
Messiah	HHA: 39
Ninfe e pastori	H-G 51: 16
O numi eterni	H-G 51: 32, 38
Poro	H-G: 17, 19, 30, 34
Samson	H-G: 118, 163
Scipione	H-G: 58
Sento la che ristretto	H-G 51: 93
Siroe	H-G: 26
Tamerlano	H-G: 71

Nevertheless, modern players should attempt to find this balance; an extremely discreet realization is perhaps as undesirable as one that overwhelms singers and audience alike with arpeggios, scales, and ornaments. In his *Versuch*, C. P. E. Bach asserted regarding recitatives that "neither too little nor too much unfilled space should be allowed in the accompaniment."[50]

Foreshortened Cadences

It would be impractical to give a comprehensive treatment of the issue of delayed versus foreshortened cadences in this chapter. The question is quite complicated, especially if one considers different genres, national styles, and time periods. Until fairly recently, all standard recitative cadences were generally "delayed," i. e., the dominant-tonic progression was played after the singer had completed his phrase. This traditional practice was seriously questioned by Jack Westrup, who suggested that foreshortened cadences were generally more appropriate for music from the first half of the eighteenth century.[51] Sven Hansell noted that Hasse, in his opera *Artaserse*, wrote the same cadence in two different ways: foreshortened in 1730, and delayed in 1762.[52] It seems that a considerable amount of research still needs to be done with Italian opera of this period; this research should focus on the text as well as the music. For now, the conclusions offered herein are in some respects tentative. I would like to begin with a few preliminary remarks, or problems, regarding foreshortened cadences in Handel's music, followed by a discussion of their harmonization.

All the evidence indicates that the foreshortened cadence was an operatic prerogative. Recitatives in opera are often quite long, some containing several cadences. As Heinichen points out, the cumulative effect of so many delayed cadences would be disastrous to the animation and flow of a dramatic performance.[53] Also, occasionally it may be desirable to rush through a cadence as quickly as possible to keep the action moving. The foreshortened cadence in Handel's music should therefore probably be restricted to the operas, and probably the dramatic oratorios as well. Works with recitatives that are mostly quite short, such as *Alexander's Feast* and *Acis and Galatea*, do not urgently require foreshortened cadences. This reasoning could also apply to non-dramatic oratorios, such as *Messiah* and *Israel in Egypt*.

Modern scholars often cite Quantz to justify the extensive use of foreshortened cadences.[54] Actually, Quantz recommends that the cadence should begin on the last note of the vocal phrase, a practice which could be described as "semi-delayed":

> In general the bass in all cadences of theatrical recitatives, whether accompanied with violins or plain, must begin its two notes, usually forming a descending leap of a fifth, during the last syllable; these notes must be performed in a lively manner, and must not be too slow.[55]

This recommendation is in fact a compromise between the foreshortened cadence (which begins with the penultimate or last accented syllable) and the delayed cadence (which begins just after the singer has completed his phrase). Furthermore, we must assume that Quantz wrote precisely what he meant, since throughout this paragraph a logical distinction is made between the last syllable and the preceding or penultimate note of the vocal part. Occasionally, in English or German recitative, the final syllable will be sung to the last two notes of the vocal part, but in Italian recitative, which is the only style Quantz mentioned here, the final syllable inevitably coincides with the last note. Elsewhere in this paragraph there are two rather misleading references to beginning a cadence with the penultimate syllable, but most likely these were meant to apply only to *recitativo accompagnato*.[56]

It is difficult to agree completely with Winton Dean's assertion that "when Handel wrote a foreshortened cadence he meant it."[57] That is, whenever the composer aligned the first cadential chord with the penulti-

Document 16. Delayed or Semidelayed Cadences in Handel's Plain Recitative

L'Allegro	HHA: 34
E partirai, mia vita?	H-G 50: 78, 79
Hercules	H-G: 113
Joseph	H-G: 235
La bianca rosa	H-G 51: 82
Messiah	HHA: 233
Parti, l'idolo mio	H-G 51: 43
Poichè giuraro Amore	H-G 51: 48
Samson	H-G: 108
Se per fatal destino	H-G 51: 111
Siroe	H-G: 79
Susanna	HHA: 155, 174

mate syllable, he intended a foreshortened cadence. And since Handel almost always wrote his recitative cadences in this manner, therefore, Dean reasons, all of them should be foreshortened in performance unless he indicated otherwise by placing a rest under the last syllables of the vocal part. The problem with this line of reasoning is that there is so much theoretical evidence that supports delayed cadences in cantatas.[58] Perhaps Dean intended this remark to apply only to the dramatic works, in which case it is more defensible. Also, we must be careful not to assign too much importance to the mere alignment of parts in the autographs; the operas were often written in haste, some completed just weeks before the premiere. A firm conclusion must be deferred until there is a comprehensive study of recitative cadences in Handel's autograph scores.

Although it is usually best to keep the action moving in Baroque opera, theatrical values do not always suggest foreshortened cadences. In some situations a delayed cadence can be more suitable, especially if hesitation, languor, or pathos are involved. Foreshortened cadences can obscure the text; if the final word is forceful or unexpected, a delayed cadence may be preferable to insure audibility and rhetorical effectiveness. Evidently, these or other similar considerations prompted Handel to write delayed or semi-delayed cadences on occasion. Some of these are listed in document 16. In a few instances, Handel ends an operatic recitative with two or more soloists singing simultaneously. The delayed cadence seems the only satisfactory solution in these cases; otherwise, the vocal parts would clash rather raucously with the continuo, and these endings, one of which is example 7.25, would lose most of their beauty and charm.

Harmonization

Example 7.26 shows the two standard phrase endings for the voice in plain recitative, one conjunct, the other disjunct. If a foreshortened cadence is applied to both, the results, harmonically speaking, are quite different. The first looks like a dissonance on paper, but is not so in performance (see ex. 7.27). In Handel's music, this ending is occasionally figured 4 3.[59] If this is followed, and the cadence foreshortened, the resulting clash just before the tonic can be stylistic and effective. The second ending looks consonant, but in practice the addition of the usual vocal appoggiatura creates a clash that is hardly stylistic, often ineffective, and, as Robert Donington aptly phrased it, "ungrammatical" (see ex. 7.28). Nevertheless, should this dissonance — 4 in the voice against 3 in the accompaniment — be accepted for the sake of the speed and animation that it provides?

Historical evidence suggests that in most cases the clash should not be accepted. The solution preferred by Heinichen was that the keyboard harmony should be adjusted to accommodate the nonharmonic tone by using either a $\smash{{}^6_4}$ $\smash{{}^5_3}$ or a $\smash{{}^5_4}$ $\smash{{}^5_3}$ progression over the dominant bass tone, as

Example 7.25. *Siroe*, H-G: 97

Example 7.26. Normal Vocal Cadences in Simple Recitative

Example 7.27. Recitative Cadences

Example 7.28. Recitative Cadences

in example 7.29. Heinichen seems to have been the only eighteenth-century theorist to address this problem. But even if we lacked his recommendations, certain basic assumptions and rules of thoroughbass accompaniment would be sufficient justification for this approach. To begin with, these progressions are the most common continuo formulas used to embellish the dominant in a normal cadence. The second — $^5_4$ $^5_3$ — is so common that it is practically implicit whenever it is compatible with the composed parts. It was generally assumed that a good accompanist would adjust the realization, if necessary departing from the figures, to accommodate appoggiaturas added by the soloist; this is particularly true of long appoggiaturas at cadences.[60] And, as we have seen in the previous section of this chapter, it was also assumed that the accompanist would include and resolve any dissonances that do not resolve normally in the solo part. The conditions surrounding these two assumptions are met exactly if the disjunct ending with appoggiatura is accompanied with a foreshortened cadence: the nonharmonic tone is usually unwritten (and therefore not accounted for in the figuring), at least moderately long, and does not resolve normally.

As mentioned earlier, Heinichen was the only theorist to discuss the harmonization of foreshortened cadences. He highly recommends the progressions $^6_4$ $^5_3$ and $^5_4$ $^5_3$, referring to them together as "the well-known" or "usual cadence" ("die bekandte/die gewöhnliche Cadenz"), and applies them to arias as well as recitatives. He finds the first prefera-

Example 7.29. Recommended Harmonizations
of Foreshortened Cadences

Example 7.30. Sven Hansell's Realization of the
Foreshortened Cadence

ble in recitative if, as is often the case, the previous chord is a $\genfrac{}{}{0pt}{}{6}{4+}$ on the subdominant, but he acknowledges that there is not always enough time to articulate the progession clearly. A simple dominant seventh chord is also possible on the first chord of a foreshortened cadence, but it is mentioned only once in the course of the treatise and is not one of the "usual" cadences.[61] The only fully written-out recitative cadence in the book uses the $\smash{{}^6_4}\ \smash{{}^5_3}$ formula in minor mode ($\smash{{}^6_4}\ \smash{{}^5_\sharp}$).[62] The detailed instructions for realizing the unfigured bass of Alessandro Scarlatti's cantata *Lascia, deh lascia al fine* state that the accompanist should employ the "usual recitative cadence" in the first recitative. Later, at the end of the second recitative, the proper harmonization is indicated precisely: "die Cadenz 4 ♯."[63]

Sven Hansell, in a thought-provoking article on foreshortened cadences, proposes another solution: accompany this appoggiatura with a dominant seventh chord that contains an added fourth, i. e., a $\begin{smallmatrix}7\\5\\4\\3\end{smallmatrix}$ chord.[64] In the article, Hansell illustrates his proposed solution (ex. 7.30). This accompaniment is actually not as outrageous as it may seem; it is very similar to an example in Gasparini's chapter on recitative. In fact, Hansell's first chord is identical to one of two dominant chords specifically marked "Cadenza" in that chapter.[65]

Unfortunately, Hansell's article is weakened by some serious flaws. He refuses to believe Gasparini intended:1) that the chords be arpeggiated or spread, and 2) that the dissonant acciaccaturas, in this case the two As, should be released immediately, leaving the consonances sounding.[66] Hansell's refusal to accept these beliefs is contrary to the opinion of Baroque theorists, such as Heinichen, and most modern scholars.[67] There is an additional problem in Hansell's interpretation of the figuring $\begin{smallmatrix}4\\3\end{smallmatrix}$ as simultaneously sounding intervals. He suggests that since the numbers are so close together and made with a single stroke of the pen, the figuring "could have served to remind the eighteenth-century musician of the option of using acciaccaturas."[68] I would suggest the opposite. It seems unlikely that there is any significance in the proximity of the figures; it was understood as one of the fundamental conventions of figured bass that 4 and 3, when placed together over a single note, each get half of the value of that note. Such an extreme proximity is very common in printed as well as manuscript figuring, especially in common sequential progressions, such as 7 6 7 6, and so forth. It seems more plausible that the performer should feel inclined to add acciaccaturas in cadences that do not specify a $\begin{smallmatrix}5\\4\end{smallmatrix}$ $\begin{smallmatrix}5\\3\end{smallmatrix}$ or a $\begin{smallmatrix}6\\4\end{smallmatrix}$ $\begin{smallmatrix}5\\3\end{smallmatrix}$ harmonization. These reservations aside, his solution has some merit and could be quite effective in highly declamatory cadences. If the dissonant tones are released quickly, as they should be, a dissonance-to-resolution effect is achieved, which is very similar to that of a $\begin{smallmatrix}5\\4\end{smallmatrix}$ $\begin{smallmatrix}5\\3\end{smallmatrix}$ realization.

In exceptional circumstances the piquant, arresting effect of a plain dominant or dominant seventh, clashing with the vocal appoggiatura, may be desirable, for example, in dramatic situations which require extraordinary speed, but these instances are relatively infrequent.

8

Short Rests in the Bass

Short rests that occur on the beat in basso continuo parts offer an interesting challenge to students of Baroque accompaniment. Should chords or chord tones be played on these rests? Does a rest for the left hand necessarily imply a rest for the right? There are no easy answers, and no general rule or convention of thoroughbass performance that pertains to these situations. But if the composer has placed continuo figures on these rests, as Handel often did, common sense would dictate that the figures should be realized.

Unfortunately, even this guidance is not regarded as totally reliable. Scholars of performance practice, not to mention performers, are frequently suspicious of continuo figures in these contexts. Robert Donington has written: "A rest in the continuo line implies, normally, a rest in the accompaniment, unless the rest is short and bears figures to an upper part."[1] This is a reasonable statement, as far as it goes, but the second half is rather puzzling. Does "upper part" refer to the accompaniment or to a composed part? Is Donington implying that chords can be played on rests only when they are figured? Peter Williams, perhaps the foremost contemporary authority on continuo playing, has stated: "[I]n most cases where a figure is written above a rest . . . no note at all is required, and the previous chord should be taken off before the beat."[2] Williams gives no substantiation. Elsewhere, in a discussion of a C. P. E. Bach recitative, he wrote:

> [U]nfortunately he [Türk] does not tell us what to do at those points where a new chord is figured above a rest in the bass: [there follows a musical example from C. P. E. Bach's *Die Israeliten in der Wüste*]. The answer, as with similar situations in other music of that time is: nothing. It was a guide to the director-accompanist, like the figures Corelli put above notes expressly marked *tasto solo*.[3]

Again, no theoretical evidence is given, nor any attempt made to reconcile this assertion with unequivocal statements to the contrary from C. P. E. Bach's own *Versuch*.[4] And although both scholars are careful to qualify their statements to some degree, they present, at best, an extreme oversimplification of the problem.

If these figures are not intended to be realized, why are they present in the score? Williams, in the last quotation above, offers one explanation: they served as "a guide to the director-accompanist." A guide to what, for what purpose? Williams does not elaborate. Perhaps he meant that the figuring in these instances was merely a shorthand representation of the upper parts, a kind of concise overview of the harmonic movement. In fully orchestrated pieces, this figured bass shorthand would be very useful since the director would not have to scan the full score to determine the harmonic structure. If this is Williams's meaning, then he has chosen a poor example. Why would the director need some kind of "guidance" during bass rests in plain recitative, when a quick glance at the vocal part would be just as easy and more reliable? And what of pieces which do not require a director-accompanist? Why do we find figures over rests in chamber works, solo sonatas and continuo cantatas, even in passages for continuo alone?

Perhaps a more likely explanation, especially for Handel's music, is that figures over rests might have served a compositional function. As we have seen in the first chapter, bass figuring was often used as an *aide-memoire* during the initial stages of the creative process. It served to remind the composer of a specific chord or progression, to be written out later; occasionally long sections would be notated in short score (melody and figured bass), to which he would subsequently add the inner parts. It is therefore possible that the composer may have figured a rest merely to remind himself that the concerted parts—as yet unwritten—would play at that point. In that case, the figures would not necessarily reflect Handel's conception of the continuo realization.

This brings up a closely related topic: the vertical alignment of figures with the bass. In Handel's autographs, the intended alignment is not always obvious, and the composer could be rather careless in this regard. Perhaps a figure on a short rest was actually intended for the following note? This is also possible; however, in some autograph manuscripts (fair copies, teaching material, and the like) his vertical alignment was clear and precise. Each context must be examined closely; we cannot automatically assume in doubtful cases that the composer's placement is faulty. Friedrich Chrysander in the H-G editions made this assumption all too often; he silently transferred figures—ones that Handel had clearly placed on rests—to the following note.[5]

Handel's Practice

A series of musical examples has been chosen which should eliminate all doubts regarding the validity of these figures for accompanimental purposes. The examples are derived from a set of continuo cantatas which were most likely used by the composer to teach thoroughbass realization.[6] These "pedagogical cantatas" are for the most part revisions of earlier works; in the process of reworking them, Handel added unusually elaborate bass figuring. And not only is it complete, it is accurately aligned with the bass part—as one would expect with copies prepared for teaching purposes. The examples are limited to passages that were not altered for the new versions, except possibly to be transposed; thus in these examples the figuring could not possibly have any compositional function. The autograph manuscripts have been consulted to eliminate the inaccuracies of Chrysander's figuring; page citations to his edition have been included merely for reference.

My purpose in scrutinizing these examples is threefold: first, to establish that Handel did, in fact, intend that figures over short rests be realized; second, to offer suggestions as to the composer's reasons for figuring the rests; these reasons will provide guidelines for performers who must deal with rests in other Handelian basso continuo parts; and third, to show how the figuring should be interpreted, that is, whether the intervals should be reckoned from the preceding or the succeeding bass note. The rule of thumb, as stated by C. P. E. Bach, is generally valid for Handel: "Figures over short rests . . . apply to the following note," but "figures over long rests . . . pertain to the preceding note."[7]

In *Ninfe e pastori* (ex. 8.1), the figuring demands that the right hand maintain a steady harmonic sequence: five descending first inversion chords, each played at the beginning of the measure. This is not altered by the temporary deviation in the rhythm of the composed parts in measure 3. Chrysander suppressed the figure 6 in this measure, perhaps because it contradicts the written parts. At any rate, this excerpt demonstrates an important characteristic of Handel's figuring: the continuo harmony relentlessly preserves the established pattern, even though the solo part may alter it in places. Here it is obvious that the 6 in the third measure should be read as a first inversion chord of E♭.

The next examples are excerpted from the cantata *Lungi dal mio bel Nume*. The opening ritornello of the first aria illustrates a very common reason for figuring a rest (ex. 8.2): it coincides with the most appropriate point for the resolution of a discord. Here again, the figuring indicates a steady harmonic pattern, which allows the bass motifs to stand out in bold relief. Example 8.3 involves the addition of a vocal part above the same material. The first 6 is necessary as a preparation for the dissonant 7 on the following beat. Note that the regular continuo pattern of dissonance-to-resolution is present here as well, despite the ornamental resolution of each seventh in the voice. The last 6 in the second measure of example 8.3, contrary to the general rule, refers to the previous note, B♭, rather than to the following. The final illustrations from this cantata, examples 8.4 and 8.5, demonstrate another reason for Handel's figuring of rests: firm support of a difficult leap in the solo part. This support is given, as the excerpts

Example 8.1. *Ninfe e pastori*, HWV 138c, Second Aria

demonstrate, not only when the voice ascends diatonically, but also when the voice leaps down to a modulatory tone. In this case, the continuo-reinforcement of the soloist may also be dictated by the proper expression of the text, which is more declamatory than languishing in Handel's setting, especially in the phrase "struggo l'amante cor." In example 8.5, the figures are placed on quarter rests, in contrast to the shorter rests of the other examples, so they apply to the preceding bass note.

The next example demonstrates that Handel was influenced by considerations of vocal tessitura. The same bass pattern is treated differently in these excerpts from *E partirai, mia vita?* At the beginning of example 8.6, the voice dips quite low, so the continuo chord is delayed until the fourth beat; when this material is repeated later the triad comes on the third beat to support the repeated Bs in the middle range. The placement of figures in the H-G edition for both excerpts is faulty: in both cases, the sharp is placed on the first eighth-note, a total misrepresentation of the meticulous placement in the autograph.[8]

Example 8.7, from *Se pari è la tua fè*, illustrates another reason for playing chords over rests: to emphasize the meter in quick passages which, in the interest of rhythmic precision, require a firm beat. It also shows that chords, as well as individual chord tones, can be resolved on a rest.

There are several additional examples from other cantatas, not to mention many from other genres, but these suffice to show that Handel frequently intended continuo chords during short bass rests in order to: resolve a dissonant note or chord, support the voice in passages involving difficult leaps or modulation, maintain a firm rhythmic pulse in the interest of good ensemble playing, and persist with a regular harmonic sequence regardless of temporary deviations in the composed parts. If any further evidence is required to prove that the composer recommended this practice, there are figured rests in the autograph thoroughbass exercises in the Fitzwilliam Museum; these are available in facsimile as part of the Hallische-Händel Ausgabe Supplement/1.[9] Also, there is an extremely interesting, possibly unique passage in the Coronation Anthem II, "Let Thy Hand Be Strengthened" (ex. 8.8). On the downbeat of the second and third measures, the composer specifically indicates a rest for all bass instruments, except the

Example 8.2. *Lungi dal mio bel Nume*, HWV 127c, First Aria

Example 8.3. *Lungi dal mio bel Nume*, HWV 127c, First Aria

Example 8.4. *Lungi dal mio bel Nume*, HWV 127c, First Aria

Example 8.5. *Lungi dal mio bel Nume*, HWV 127c, First Aria

Example 8.6. *E partirai, mia vita?*, HWV 111b, Second Aria

Example 8.7. *Se pari è la tua fè*, HWV 138c, First Aria

Example 8.8. Coronation Anthem II, "Let Thy Hand Be Strengthened," HWV 259, Final Movement

organ continuo, which sustains its bass note over the bar-line and executes the harmonic change to support the upper choral and instrumental parts. Handel was seldom so precise with his bass parts, especially when the discrepancy between keyboard continuo and other bass instruments might involve only a fraction of a measure; it seems safe to assume that this effect could have been intended for similar passages that the composer did not take the trouble to mark so carefully.

In conclusion, there is one type of Handelian bass line that probably should not be performed with chords over short rests. This is the fragmented, cantabile bass, usually marked Larghetto in common time, which appears often at the beginning of continuo arias; e.g., "Falsa imagine" from *Ottone*, "Cara sposa" from *Radamisto*, and the first aria of *Cecilia*, "Volgi un sguardo," HWV 89. Short bass rests in these contexts hardly ever bear figures. If the rests were to be realized with chords, the essential quality of this type of bass would be destroyed. Most significantly, the Aylesford keyboard arrangement of "Cara sposa," very likely the work of Handel himself, contains no chords during bass rests in the sections of continuo realization (see Appendix D).

Theoretical References

> *It is often necessary to strike chords over short rests in advance of their bass notes, as a means of retaining order and winning variety.*
>
> C. P. E. Bach, *Versuch* (1762)

Eighteenth-century manuals on continuo accompaniment recommend playing chords over bass rests in a variety of situations, whether the rest is figured or not.[10] Johann Mattheson even allows the player to harmonize a short rest when the following note is figured and the rest is not. There is, to my knowledge, no theoretical evidence to justify a total disregard of figuring that a composer has deliberately placed on a rest.

Chapter 4 of Gasparini's *L'Armonico practico* deals with ascending motion. In the section devoted to sixteenth-note motion, the author remarks: "When there is a sixteenth rest, it is effective to play the consonances of the first note of the beat while the left hand rests."[11] For purposes of illustration, Gasparini appends a bass (ex. 8.9). The figuring in brackets is mine, based on other musical examples in the treatise. It has been added merely to clarify the intended harmonic structure. This example is unusual among the theoretical sources since it implies that chords may be played on rests that appear at the beginning of the second half of the beat, as well as on the beat. As example 8.10 demonstrates, Gasparini's advice results in an effective interplay between bass and realization, especially in the second and third measures. His advice also confirms C. P. E. Bach's rule: chords over short rests contain the harmony of the following bass note.

Johann David Heinichen's *Der General-Bass in der Composition* includes a long "General Exempel" of thoroughbass realization in which several versions of the same exercise are given in various keys and meters. Each version contains several figured rests. In all cases, these are realized as right-hand chords.[12]

With the possible exception of C. P. E. Bach's *Versuch*, the largest number of references to chord playing over rests comes from Mattheson's *Grosse General-Bass Schule*. The main body of the treatise consists of 48 exercises in thoroughbass realization, divided into two classes: Middle and Higher. Extensive instructional commentary follows each exercise. Mattheson suggests four possible reasons for realizing short rests in the basso continuo part:

1) "The empty space offends the ear." In the commentary to the Ninth Test-Piece of the Middle Class, Mattheson states:

Example 8.9. Francesco Gasparini, *L'Armonico practico al cimbalo*

Example 8.10. Realization of Example 8.9

> Next, it must be observed that the right hand must necessarily sound first when a sixteenth rest occurs in the measure in the fifth line, because the empty space offends the ear, which wishes most of all that everything be orderly and continuous, complete, and not broken up. Striking first with the right hand can be used with such rests throughout in accompanying, except for a few instances where the composer's intentions must be regarded.*
>
> *Here and in harmony the word *Vorschlag* means something quite different than in melody, as everyone can see from the above description.[13]

The passage in question (ex. 8.11) contains a common type of bass; it is very similar to the example from Handel's *Se pari è la tua fè,* which was discussed in the previous section of this chapter. The quick rest gives an energetic rhythmic impetus to the bass part, which is not hampered by a forceful chord on the downbeat. Chords in such situations help the keyboard player to control the tempo and enhance the rhythmic precision of the whole ensemble. Notice that Mattheson implies that chords can be played on sixteenth rests even if the rest bears no figure and the note following does.

2) To highlight a bass syncopation. With reference to the Fifteenth Test-Piece of the Middle Class—a slow *alla breve* replete with ties, syncopations, and suspensions—Mattheson remarks:

> [W]e must point out that since this style always demands ties and syncopations, the right hand must be on the alert for these; for example, it plays the 5 above the first note, or chord, not at the same time as the note, but on the rest before it, so that the following

bass note, B-flat, is first played by itself and then held through the 6 and 4; in short, the hands play alternately in all places where the figures do not stand exactly above the notes.[14]

To clarify Mattheson's commentary, example 8.12 gives the first measure and subsequent excerpts from this Test-Piece.

3) To develop a desirable interplay between the two hands in certain types of bass figuration which contain rests at the beginnings of the beats. Regarding the Third Test-Piece of the Higher Class, Mattheson comments:

> In the tenth measure and those following, the right hand always plays first on the beat, where the rest occurs, which makes for a rather nice breaking.[15]

This measure (ex. 8.13) contains the same rhythmic pattern as is predominant in the Gasparini example quoted earlier in this section. By "breaking" or "Brechung" Mattheson means "any form of harmony in which the respective intervals are not struck simultaneously," including arpeggio.[16]

4) For a simple, clear statement of an energetic opening theme in the bass. In the commentary to the Seventeenth Test-Piece of the Higher Class, the student is instructed to play example 8.14

> quite simply so that the main subject can be stated strongly in accordance with the dictum established by nature and reason that "any beginning must be plain, simple, and clear." By simple playing we mean principally that the right hand plays only one chord to each group of six notes, noting that the first of these chords sounds over a rest.[17]

Earlier we noticed that Mattheson condoned chord playing over unfigured sixteenth rests in the bass; he also recommends chords over unfigured eighth-note rests. At the end of the "Erläuterung" for the Thirteenth Test-Piece of the Middle Class, the only Test-Piece for two keyboards, the author recommends:

> But, when in the last two lines of this example, or elsewhere, when an eighth-note rest appears, those chords or signatures which belong to the next note must be played in advance of it with the right hand, this during the rest.[18]

Relevant motifs from the last two lines of the Test-Piece are given in example 8.15.

Why would Mattheson place a figure over a note, when he actually desired the chord on the preceding rest? To answer this question we must first realize that one of the stated objectives of the treatise is to prepare the student for all the vagaries of real basso continuo parts: figures missing or misplaced, unusual clefs, abrupt clef changes, difficult key signatures, and so on.[19] Mattheson slightly misplaced these figures because they are often similarly misplaced in actual music—whether advertently or inadvertently; the player must acquire the acuity to recognize this and adjust his realiza-

Example 8.11. Johann Mattheson, *Grosse General-Bass Schule*

Example 8.12. Johann Mattheson, *Grosse General-Bass Schule*

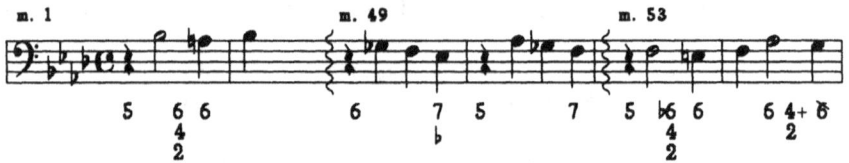

Example 8.13. Johann Mattheson, *Grosse General-Bass Schule*

Example 8.14. Johann Mattheson, *Grosse General-Bass Schule*

Example 8.15. Johann Mattheson, *Grosse General-Bass Schule*

Example 8.16. Johann Mattheson, *Grosse General-Bass Schule*

Example 8.17. Georg Philipp Telemann, *Singe-,
Spiel- und Generalbass-Übungen*

tion accordingly. Also, composers may have figured a note in preference to a rest for purely practical reasons: figures on notes are easier visually, and they can be realized more quickly. Thus, Mattheson's advice is closely related to the problems of actual continuo accompaniment.

The Second and Third Test-Pieces of the Higher Class also contain figures placed over rests, but Mattheson does not comment on them.[20] In light of all his commentary on the subject, he certainly intended that they should be realized. The excerpts in example 8.16 are representative of the Test-Pieces that contain figured rests.

Mattheson's importance as a source of information on Handelian performance can hardly be exaggerated: the two men were close friends in early life, had very similar backgrounds, and must have exchanged ideas on thoroughbass and other aspects of performance throughout their years together in Hamburg.

G. P. Telemann's *Singe-, Spiel- und Generalbass-Übungen* combines an anthology of songs with instruction on thoroughbass: it consists of 48 short songs for voice and figured bass, each of which is provided with a written-out continuo accompaniment and brief comments on some problematic aspects of realization. Figured rests, with chords at the corresponding points in the realizations, are found in six songs: nos. 6, 12, 21, and 45 through 47. In the commentary to three of these—nos. 12, 21, and 47—Telemann suggests his own reasons for a right-hand accompaniment during short bass rests: to support the metric pulses and to enhance the "sweet expression" of a soloist. The following discussion will focus on these pieces.

With reference to example 8.17, taken from the twelfth song, Telemann writes:

> The chord repetition over rests is then very good, when, as here, the purpose is to support the stress of the meter.[21]

In the song no. 21 the same rhythmic pattern in the bass is accompanied in two different ways (ex. 8.18). Telemann explains:

152   Short Rests in the Bass

Example 8.18. Georg Philipp Telemann, *Singe-, Spiel- und Generalbass-Übungen*

In the first part of this aria one finds above [i.e., in the right hand], with the rests, the same rhythm as the bass, at (a), on the other hand, another [rhythm]; the latter is best with sweet expressions and for maintenance of the meter.[22]

But the author urges caution in the explanatory material for song no. 47, which is excerpted in example 8.19, writing:

That also on rests [chords] will be struck, (d) (e) (f) show; however it is prudent to proceed with caution when they are not figured: for sometimes the rest is connected with the previous note (d); often, however, it belongs to the harmony of the following (e) (f).[23]

In songs no. 45 and no. 46, Telemann places figures on rests to indicate the resolution of a note or chord.[24] His use of figured rests for this purpose is very similar to Handel's.

Telemann's recommendations on this topic are certainly valuable; and the realizations are especially crucial because they demonstrate without a doubt that chords were played over rests in actual accompaniments. We should also note that the realizations contain no figured rests which are not realized with chords.

The evidence from C. P. E. Bach's *Versuch* is adequately treated in Arnold,[25] so only a summary of this information will be given here. Bach especially recommends the practice of striking chords "in advance of their bass notes" in the following situations: in fast tempos, as a method of establishing a firm pulse, with syncopated bass lines, and just before very fast scale passages. The first echoes Telemann's advice, the second Matthe-

Example 8.19. Georg Philipp Telemann, *Singe-, Spiel- und Generalbass-Übungen*

son's. The third recalls examples, but not actual recommendations, from Mattheson's book. Bach also cites several examples in which chords on rests would be inappropriate: resolute, "bombastic basses in the French manner," or in cases where the solo part has soft, modulatory tones to execute. But Bach does not condone ignoring any figuring that a composer has deliberately placed over a rest; the guidelines he proposes are only intended to cover passages which lack "proper signs," i.e., precise, full figuring, together with any other necessary markings, by the composer.[26]

9

Pedal Points

Most modern authorities on continuo accompaniment give the player the liberty to disregard the figuring of pedal points. Robert Donington writes:

> Pedal points may always be treated *tasto solo* or *all' unisono*. . . . When, however, the harmony is simple and changes not too frequently or rapidly, it may often be desirable to accompany with full chords . . . *at the accompanist's discretion*.[1]

Peter Williams seems to imply that the harpsichordist needs to play chords only in the absence of other accompanimental parts:

> Pedal points, like all held notes, should be restruck on the harpsichord at convenient moments. . . . In full instrumental pieces, the harpsichord-player will often find that he is most effective in repeating the bass note on the beats, perhaps with [a] mordent. But if the harpsichord is the only accompanying instrument (with cello), the player must play chords and interpret the figures.[2]

The only substantiation given by both writers is a brief quote from the chapter on organ points in C. P. E. Bach's *Versuch*:

> It is not easy to figure pedal points, and they are therefore generally handled *tasto solo*. Those who do figure them must put up with their being performed *tasto solo* just the same.[3]

This statement, in itself, does not constitute a strong recommendation for the *tasto solo* execution of figured pedal points. In any case, no substantiation of any kind is presented for the following parenthetical remark by Williams: "[T]he pedal point harmonies of the opening [of J. S. Bach's sacred recitatives require] few or even no supporting chords."[4] This should come as a surprise, for J. S. Bach's recitatives are some of the most richly harmonized and carefully figured of the entire literature. Arnold is more circumspect in his approach: he cites Türk (who allows a *tasto solo* accompaniment only if the player lacks the skill to execute the figured harmony) as well as C. P. E. Bach, and notes that J. S. Bach hardly would have added the towering masses of figures to the pedal points in the opening chorus of the *St. John Passion* if they were not to be realized.[5] Nevertheless, the general consensus is that the player may accompany any pedal point *tasto solo*.

Before we proceed to discuss C. P. E. Bach's chapter on pedal points, and whether it is applicable to Handel's music, it is necessary to mention one obvious, but important exception. The performer is *always* obliged to harmonize figured pedal points if internal evidence suggests that the figuring represents the composer's intentions. Perhaps some examples will clarify this. If a composer has taken the trouble to mark the bass carefully, with all of the necessary directives for performance, including figured pedal points, then it stands to reason that he probably desired a chordal accompaniment; for if he did not, it would have been so much easier to mark the bass *tasto solo* or even *senza cembalo*. Or if the *tasto solo* marking is found over pedal points elsewhere in the same piece, then we can safely assume that figured pedal points should be supported with chords. In some compositions by Handel, one of which is excerpted in example 9.1, we find some pedal points marked *tasto solo* and others figured within the same movement. This chorus also occurs in *Deborah* with identical markings on the bass part.[6] Other examples can be found in *Athalia*[7] and Concerto Grosso, Op. 6, No. 5 (second movement). J. S. Bach left a superb example of this varied continuo treatment of pedal points in the aria "Ach, mein Sinn" from the *St. John Passion*.

This leads us to the conclusion, which is substantiated by statements from Heinichen, G. P. Telemann, and even C. P. E. Bach, that figured pedal points were generally intended to be harmonized, whereas unfigured pedal points, or those marked *tasto solo*, were not. Consider Telemann's comment on a pedal point from his *Singe-, Spiel- und Generalbass-Übungen*:

> [T]he reposing bass, while the upper part modulates, sometimes proceeding in all directions through the harmonic circles, will seldom be figured; and then one does best when one lets the right hand rest entirely, and with the left hand now and then sound the low tone, consequently the full support is sometimes abandoned to the cello. Here, however, with a score, we have the aim first of all to support the strong beats, so we strike above [in the right hand] always on the upbeats and downbeats, which also is allowed in the bass when it is not played on the organ, which can sustain it. With such a purpose as mentioned above we leave a few subsidiary beats [*neben-Figuren*] untouched, as with (a), (b) (c) and (d).[8]

Example 9.2 is the "score" that Telemann mentions; it happens to be heavily figured.

Heinichen's *General Exempel* of thoroughbass accompaniment contains a richly figured pedal point at the end of each version;[9] example 9.3 is

Example 9.1. Coronation Anthem II, "Let Thy Hand Be Strengthened," HWV 259, Second Movement

a representative sample. In Heinichen's realizations, the right hand executes all the figured harmony. Regarding this passage, he comments in the supplement:

> Under the same steady, reposing bass tone, over which the upper parts thus make various *Syncopationes*, as we have done here to the useful exercise with very common progressions, one otherwise likes to write: *Tasto solo*, and lets the figures go, to show that the accompanist should hold merely the bass key, without any other accompaniment, until the harmony resumes.[10]

Even C. P. E. Bach, referring to an elaborately figured, harmonically dense pedal point in the chapter on the $\frac{7}{6}$ chord, wrote:

158 Pedal Points

Example 9.3. Johann David Heinichen, *Der General-Bass in der Composition*

> But in order to restore the confidence of those who are overwhelmed by the mass of numerals, we state that ordinarily the right hand does not play such passages. *The signatures are therefore omitted*, and *tasto solo* is written over the bass. In our present study they serve to indicate the voice leading and chord changes.[11]

Notice that Bach feels compelled to explain the presence of figures which are not to be realized; they are included as a kind of harmonic analysis of a complex passage.

The chapter on organ points provides further elucidation of Bach's views. A substantial segment is given below so that the reader can gain an understanding of the context and tone of the chapter which Williams and Donington quoted so briefly.

It is not easy to figure pedal points, so they are usually set *tasto solo*. Those who do figure them must accept the fact that they will be played *tasto solo* anyway. The reason for this can be ascribed not only to a very necessary simplification of the accompanist's tasks but often to the impossibility of reading the figures. Assuming that the right hand could accompany all organ points, gratitude would never compensate for the expended anxiety and trouble.

To play the organ point *tasto solo* removes the necessity of scanning unusual signatures and successions of towering figures. Parts are often constructed in such a manner that one crosses the other. This might oblige the accompanist to cross parts, which is not allowed in thorough bass, since many errors might thereby be excused without satisfying the ear. In such a case, therefore, the entire organ point must be played in divided accompaniment to ensure correct preparation and resolution, and prevent the right hand from descending too far. This is an excessive demand. Sometimes chord changes are so rapid that they can scarcely be brought out even when the accompanist tries to realize them.[12]

By way of illustration, Bach appends several pedal points, of which example 9.4 is representative. Here again Bach feels the need to explain the presence of figures that are not to be realized by the continuo player: "Figures have been included in order to provide an understanding of the chords."[13]

It should be noted in passing that the tone of the chapter seems argumentative and rather heated. In the original, bold enlarged type is used twice for special emphasis: "a *very necessary* simplification," "the *impossibility* of reading the figures." Bach does not take the kind of balanced, circumspect approach to the topic that characterizes the chapters on recitative and unisons.

But what of pedal points that do not present the difficulties Bach describes? His remarks do not seem to be applicable to these and consequently do not provide sufficient guidance for the performance of Handel's pedal points. From the description Bach gives, as well as the musical examples appended to the chapter, it is clear that he is speaking of very densely harmonized examples, with many suspensions, in which the complex figuring practically duplicates the composed parts. He is not speaking of more lightly harmonized types in which the figuring merely shows the simple underlying progression of the composed parts or thinly textured, slower pedal points in which the upper parts are not complete harmonically. In the latter case, the figuring actually provides an enrichment or necessary com-

Example 9.4. C. P. E. Bach, *Versuch über die wahre Art das Klavier zu spielen*

160 *Pedal Points*

pletion of the harmony. Both of these types are very common in Handel's choral and instrumental music.

The first type can be illustrated by example 9.5, an excerpt from the final chorus of the *Ode for St. Cecilia's Day*. Here the figures represent very simple triadic support that does not duplicate the counterpoint of the upper choral and string parts. It seems most probable that Handel's figuring indicates the desired accompaniment: a simple chordal background that contrasts effectively with the gently flowing movement above. Other excellent examples can be found in *Deborah* (H-G: 221) and *Athalia* (H-G: 94).

The second type, in which the figuring provides a completion of the harmony, usually involves treble parts moving conjunctly in thirds over the pedal; sometimes a middle voice is added, which may double an upper part an octave lower or may be an independent part. Example 9.6 is a classic instance from Coronation Anthem IV. The composed parts frequently do not state the full chord. The figuring represents a desirable complement, enriching the harmonic texture. This type of pedal point will be discussed with further examples in the next chapter.

Many of Handel's pedal points are so precisely figured that they give the accompanist all the guidance he needs in forming a satisfactory realization. It seems unlikely that the composer would be so attentive to these needs if he did not intend that the markings be followed. There is, in these pedal points, an abnormal fullness to the figuring; more intervals are indicated than are necessary according to the conventions of figured bass.

Example 9.5. *Ode for St. Cecilia's Day*, HWV 76, no. 11

Example 9.6. Coronation Anthem IV, "My Heart Is Inditing," HWV 261, Third Movement

Example 9.7 is a passage from *Semele*, which stands out from its context because of the heavy figuring. The signatures $\begin{smallmatrix}6\\4\\8\end{smallmatrix}$ and $\begin{smallmatrix}5\\ \sharp\\7\end{smallmatrix}$ are very rare in Handel's works. Both include numerals which are superfluous. Handel usually would have marked these chords $\begin{smallmatrix}6\\4\end{smallmatrix}$ and $\begin{smallmatrix}7\\ \sharp\end{smallmatrix}$. Note also the abnormal vertical sequence of figures in this example: $\begin{smallmatrix}6\\4\end{smallmatrix}$ rather than $\begin{smallmatrix}6\\4\\6\end{smallmatrix}$, $\begin{smallmatrix}8\\4\\8\end{smallmatrix}$ instead of $\begin{smallmatrix}5\\6\\4\end{smallmatrix}$, $\begin{smallmatrix}\\ \sharp\\7\end{smallmatrix}$ for $\begin{smallmatrix}7\\5\\ \sharp\end{smallmatrix}$. The only reason to figure it as he did is to indicate the exact harmonic texture and voice leading of an accompaniment suitable for organ (ex. 9.8).

Example 9.9, from a chorus in *Samson*, contains figuring that reinforces a chain of suspensions implied, but not always stated, by the inner parts. This support is most helpful for the inner voices, which must repeatedly clash with each other at the intervals of a second. This implied two-part realization clarifies — rather than muddles — the texture. The 6 in the first full measure of the example cannot be interpreted literally; it does not indicate a first-inversion triad, but merely the resolution of the previous 7.

Finally, we turn to two excerpts from Concerto Grosso, Op. 6, No. 7. Both examples occur over a repeated, accelerating bass, which happens to be the main fugal subject of the movement. Example 9.10 derives from the exposition. Similar to the passage from *Semele*, this example begins with figuring that strongly implies specific voice leading: $\begin{smallmatrix}8\\3\end{smallmatrix}$ $\begin{smallmatrix}7\flat\\5\end{smallmatrix}$. And like the pedal point in *Semele*, it implies an accompaniment of predominantly three-part texture, illustrated in example 9.11.

The second passage from this concerto (ex. 9.12) occurs just before the final cadence of the movement. Most of the figurings in the last three

Example 9.7. *Semele*, HWV 58, no. 32

Example 9.8. Realization of Example 9.7

Example 9.9. *Samson*, HWV 57, no. 21

measures are quite unusual for Handel, especially $\smash{{}^{7}_{6},{}^{8}_{7},}$ and $\smash{{}^{7}_{5}}$. The figuring, and indeed the whole passage, are heavily amended in the autograph, so it is unlikely that the continuo signatures represent a momentary caprice of the composer. A three-part realization seems to be implied at the beginning, possibly with the bass doubled at the upper octave, which becomes thicker in the last measures (ex. 9.13). The last beat of the third measure exhibits an interesting clash between the viola part and the continuo figuring of the previous beat (presumably still in effect). This clash may be intentional, included as a means of increasing tension until the fermata chord. In actual performance, especially with harpsichord continuo, the listener will probably be unaware of the dissonance. For those who find the clash intolerable, two solutions are possible: 1) a rest for the right hand of the continuo, or 2) an adjustment of the figuring, adding a $\smash{{}^{7}_{3}}$ or $\smash{{}^{7}_{5}{}_{3}}$ chord to the last beat.

Example 9.10. Concerto Grosso Op. 6, No. 7, Second Movement

Example 9.11. Realization of Example 9.10

Example 9.12. Concerto Grosso Op. 6, No. 7, Second Movement

Example 9.13. Realization of Example 9.12

In conclusion, I have attempted to show that C. P. E. Bach's generalization on the accompaniment of pedal points cannot be applied indiscriminately to the music of Handel; many of his pedal points, and certainly those that are figured, should be harmonized. Bach's argument is based primarily on the difficulty of reading highly complex, unusual *getürmte Ziffern* and of adjusting the texture and voice leading of the accompaniment to suit the particular passage. Handel's pedal points usually do not present such problems. German theorists contemporary with Handel, including C. P. E. Bach, imply that the presence or absence of figures is a valuable clue regarding the intent of a composer. Some of Handel's pedal points are figured so completely and meticulously, with a specific voice leading and disposition of tones within a chord clearly implied, that the composer must have desired a chordal accompaniment for them.

10

Continuo Harmonization

Standard Formula Progressions

There are certain recurring patterns, or formula progressions in Handel's bass figuring, with which every serious continuo player should be familiar. This section is an attempt to define these standard progressions. To some extent, they are common to all composers of the late Baroque period; many of them can be found in the thoroughbass treatises of the period, most notably, Gasparini's *L'Armonico pratico*. On the other hand, others are not so common and seem to be especially characteristic of Handel's music, virtual touchstones of his harmonic style. Most of these frequently used patterns can be identified by the bass line only, others are more recognizable in two-part form — treble and bass.

The primary source for this investigation has been Handel's autograph figuring. After studying the vast bulk of it, which is readily available in complete editions and the major holograph collections of the British Library and the Fitzwilliam Museum, I have attempted to isolate these constantly recurring patterns, or clichés, of continuo harmony.

No attempt has been made to give a comprehensive overview of Handel's harmonization practice, for that would involve a thorough examination of fully harmonized music — figured or not — in all genres. Aside from the impracticality of such an undertaking, it seemed desirable to separate, as much as possible, Handel's continuo harmonization from his harmonic style in general. Often the separation is impossible, since thoroughbass is closely related to the art of composition, and as the Fitzwilliam thoroughbass/composition exercises demonstrate so acutely, each influenced the other. Nevertheless, some distinction can be made between them.

Therefore, in deference to this necessary separation between composition and accompaniment, the examples are derived mostly from compositions or passages in two parts— solo sonatas, continuo cantatas, and thinly-scored arias — since in these cases, the completion of the harmonic texture would be executed by the continuo player alone, guided by the figuring.

166   Continuo Harmonization

Many of the examples have been simplified or slightly altered to facilitate comparison. All of them are given in C major or A minor. The reader will notice that some very obvious clichés have been given, along with those that are not so obvious. This was done because it seemed advisable, especially with cadences, to begin with the simplest and proceed to more complex examples. For some sequential patterns, such as first inversion chords descending by step, unusually long examples have been included to indicate how far the composer would extend a single formula progression.

The following discussion will be confined to specific points raised by each group of formulas. In those given in two-part (treble and figured bass) form, the upper part represents a solo or top part, *not* a portion of the right-hand continuo realization.

Formula Progressions, Group I

Continuo Harmonization   167

Remarks on Group I Formulas

I.1   The seventh is usually not given in the figuring of this type of cadence, unless the dominant is preceded by the supertonic 7 chord (see formulas I.4 and I.22). This does not preclude the addition of a seventh, especially as a passing tone after the dominant is struck. Performers should note that Handel often uses 4   3 as a shorthand for $^6_4$ $^5_3$; examples can be found in *Rodelinda* (H-G: 14, 20, and 60). In the formulas that follow it should be understood that any dominant tone occurring before the tonic can be figured 4   3, $^6_4$ $^5_3$, or, in an appropriate context, merely 7.

I.3   On the fourth scale degree just before a V-I cadence, the *sixte ajouté*, or added sixth chord, seems to be the preferred harmonization, although a simple triad is almost as common, and the composer does occasionally figure this degree 7 or merely 6. Handel uses 7 on the subdominant primarily when a solo part forms this interval with the bass, often as a suspension figure.

I.4   See also formula V.8.

I.7   This pattern is more characteristic of half cadences (see formulas IV.1, 6-8, 11, and 12).

Formula Progressions, Group II

Remarks on Group II Formulas

II.1   This is an extremely typical Handelian pattern. The 7 on the supertonic is frequently not implied in the composed parts.

II.2   Another characteristic progression, in which the E is treated as an accented passing tone. The keyboard realization should be $^5_4$ $^5_3$, but the fifth probably should not be restruck on the harpsichord to avoid an obvious clash with the accented passing tone. On the organ, it is best to take the fifth in a different register than the part that has this accented passing tone pattern.

II.3   Perhaps the only typically Handelian harmonization for this cadence pattern.

II.4   The third beat contains a type of clash usually avoided in modern printed continuo realizations. However, it is a characteristic anticipation pattern.

Continuo Harmonization 169

Formula Progressions, Group III

Remarks on Group III Formulas

III   With these deceptive cadences, Handel's practice is generally in accord with Heinichen's precept: "The sixth degree of minor scales uses as its natural harmony a sixth chord. (Reason: because the fifth degree is only a semitone apart and requires the triad.)" And, as Heinichen stated earlier, "[O]ne does not usually place triads on adjacent semitones. . . . In major, however, one may use either a triad or a sixth chord" (Buelow, *Thorough-Bass Accompaniment*, pp. 228, 229).

Formula Progressions, Group IV

170 Continuo Harmonization

Group IV, Continued

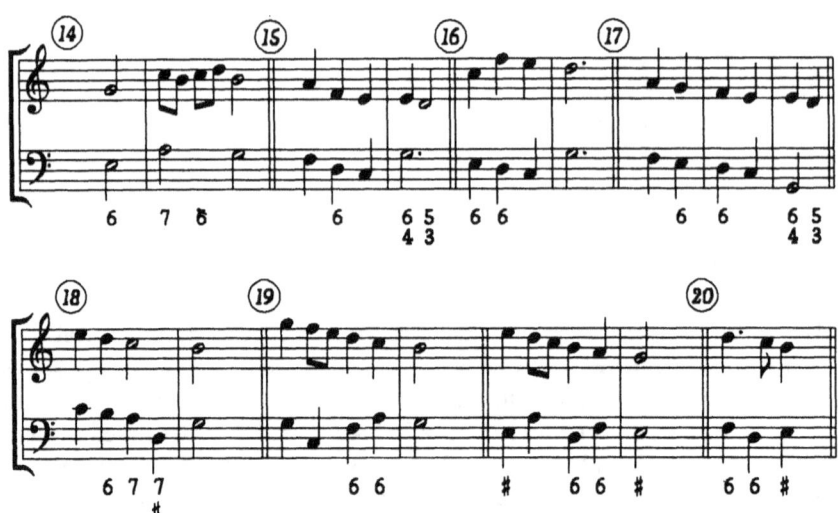

Remarks on Group IV Formulas

IV.1 When the bass descends by step to the dominant in major keys, the sixth degree invariably is figured with a raised sixth.

IV.14 See formulas IV.3 and IV.12.

IV.18 See formula IV.9.

IV.21 See formula IV.13.

Formula Progressions, Group V

Group V, Continued

Remarks on Group V Formulas

V.7 Notice that in both cases the continuo figuring indicates a steady, repeated pattern for the right hand, which the soloist states in fragmented form.

V.8 For an excellent example of Handel's use of sequential seventh chords, in root movements of fourths and fifths, see the unpublished autograph figuring of the Allegro movement of the overture to *Rinaldo* (Appendix C).

V.9 and V.10 A very common figured bass pattern, which can be found in Gasparini's treatise (*The Practical Harmonist*, p. 50) and the Kellner manuscript related to J. S. Bach's instruction (Spitta, *J. S. Bach*, 2: 346).

Formula Progressions, Group VI

Formula Progressions, Group VII: *Regole dell'ottava*

HHA Suppl./1: 81

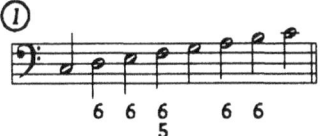

H-G 36: 237

Remarks on Group VII Formulas

VII   The *regole dell' ottava* were not written out as such by Handel, but were excerpted, as were the other formulas in this chapter, from actual compositions. These excerpts seem especially typical of his accompanimental harmonization.

176   Continuo Harmonization

Formula Progressions, Group VIII: Pedal Points

Coronation Anthem IV

Athalia

Op. 6, No. 6

Remarks on Group VIII Formulas

VIII   The pedal point examples are not formulas per se; they are short excerpts from Handel's compositions, which have not been simplified, but merely transposed to facilitate comparsion. By examining several of these excerpts it is possible to conclude the following: whenever the intervals of a second and a fourth are both stated above the pedal tone Handel figures the

La bianca rosa, HWV 160c

Athalia

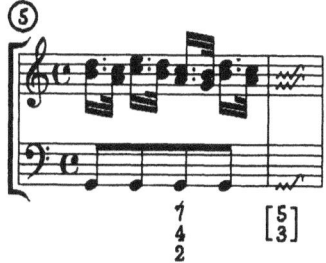

Coronation Anthem II

sonority $\begin{smallmatrix}7\\4\\2\end{smallmatrix}$; if the fourth and sixth are sounding above the pedal then, obviously, the beat is figured $^6_4$; however, if the melodic parts have a *Schleiffer*, or slide, as in excerpts VIII.1–3, the first two notes of it are treated as ornamental nonharmonic tones, and the harmony is formed by the notes at the end of the *Schleiffer*. For example, VIII.1 – first beat, VIII.2 – upbeat, VIII.3 – downbeat of the second measure.

Harmonization of Sample Excerpts

The following excerpts from Handel's operas, oratorios, and cantatas have been figured as examples of harmonization of unfigured or sparsely figured basses. I have attempted, as much as possible, to figure these passages as Handel would have done, with one exception: in order to clarify certain progressions, the horizontal line has been used to indicate retention of the previous harmony. This was a rather late development in figured bass notation, and the composer did not use it to my knowledge. However, it does appear in the printed scores published after the composer's death; for example, in Wright's edition of *Deborah* (1784) and Arnold's edition of *Sosarme* (ca. 1788). No infallibility is claimed for all the solutions offered herein; rather, a general consistency is sought with the composer's style of continuo figuring.

Giulio Cesare, First Recitative

(a) This is Handel's normal figuring for this situation in plain recitative; see chapters 1, 7, and formulas VIII.

(b) The harmony should not change until the resolution on the bass C♯ in the next measure.

(c) A 7 6 harmonization is also possible; see formula IV.5.

(d) For justification of the $\smash{\genfrac{}{}{0pt}{}{7}{\genfrac{}{}{0pt}{}{4}{2}}}$ chord with the vocal appoggiatura, see *Samson* (H-G: 55) and the original harpsichord part for *Alexander's Feast* (RCM MS 900), Recit. 5B. (The part is discussed in chap. 3.)

(e) When the composer uses the figuring 4^+, $\genfrac{}{}{0pt}{}{4}{2}$, or $\genfrac{}{}{0pt}{}{4}{2}^+$ the addition of the sixth is generally implied.

(f) The seventh might be resolved two beats later.

(g) A simple first-inversion triad is all that is really necessary since the voice does not give the diminished fifth. However, the $\genfrac{}{}{0pt}{}{6}{5}$ chord may be desirable for dramatic reasons.

(h) The 7♭ is necessary to prepare the modulation in the voice part.

Giulio Cesare, HWV 17, First Recitative

(i) A $^6_5$ chord was occasionally indicated by the composer for these cadences.

(j) The 7 is written above the bass staff to show that it is an optional addition to the figured harmony below the staff.

(k) Handel's use of the sharp here indicates a major third above D♯, i.e., F×.

(l) Another possibility is a $^6_{4♭}$ $^6_3$ realization, especially if the declamation is slow.

(m) It is not necessary to include the ninth in the accompaniment, because the voice resolves it normally at the end of the measure.

Giulio Cesare, Continued

Giulio Cesare, Continued

Agrippina, "L' alma mia," B Section

(a) The quick accented passing tone in the voice—B♭—does not affect the continuo harmony.

(b) Similarly, the ornamental chromaticism does not affect the regular progression implied by the bass.

(c) On the second beat a $^6_5$ chord would also be correct.

(d) A cadence in D major is smoother since the bass proceeds to an F♯ on the fourth beat of the measure.

(e) The seventh at the beginning of this measure—D—does not resolve normally; the accompanist should resolve it as indicated. Regarding the resolution of a dissonance over a bass rest, see chapter 9.

(f) The thoroughbass harmony continues the sequence established in the previous measure, even though the voice part does not contain the seventh.

(g) A fresh chord does not need to be struck over the bass F♯; if the first-inversion triad is retained from the previous beat, the resulting chord—F♯ A C E—provides a perfectly acceptable approach to the dominant seventh chord (see formula I.4).

Agrippina, HWV 6, "L'alma mia," B Section

Messiah, Pifa, Measures 1-11

(a) When the intervals 4 and 2 are stated simultaneously over a bass pedal, the most common Handelian figuring is $\begin{smallmatrix}7\\4\\2\end{smallmatrix}$. See formulas VII, especially 1, 2, 4, and 5.

(b) Here the upper parts do have 4 and 2 at the beginning of the beat. However, the two sixteenth notes in the violin and viola parts form a *Schleiffer* pattern and are ornamental; Handel usually figured this pattern according to the notes reached at the end of the *Schleiffer*, in this case F and A. These notes form a $^6_4$ chord with the bass, so the beat is figured accordingly. See formulas VII.1, 3.

(c) This chord could perhaps be omitted, especially with harpsichord continuo, and the $^5_3$ harmony of the previous beat held over until the third beat of this measure.

(d) Again, the two sixteenth notes of the *Schleiffer* on the fourth beat are ornamental and do not change the prevailing harmony.

(e) The figure 3 is necessary to show the resolution of the ninth—G—from the previous beat.

(f) With the signature $^9_7$ only the 3 is added. The 8 on the next beat is necessary to show the resolution of the ninth.

(g) The third is probably best omitted in this type of cadence.

(h) This is an example of the unresolving, "stationary" seventh. (See Arnold, *The Art of Accompaniment*, p. 593.) Since this seventh—C—is being sustained by all the upper parts, this seems to be the only possible harmonization, unless the bass note D is treated as an unaccompanied passing tone. But this solution is not recommended because the upcoming modulation needs to be prepared. The player need not actually strike the seventh over the bass note D; the C from the previous chord can be held over in the right hand. Indeed, the best accompaniment for the bass notes D and E is probably simple thirds with a C held from the third beat.

Messiah, HWV 56, Pifa

Cantata Se per fatal destino, Second Aria

(Cf. *Il Gelsomino*, H-G 51: 128-29.)

(a) A first inversion triad is *de rigueur* in this context, especially in a minor key. (See Buelow, *Thorough-Bass Accompaniment*, p. 229.) This harmonization is also one of the most common methods of approaching the dominant; see formula IV.4.

(b) A very common method of descending by step to the dominant; see formula IV.11. If the note values were longer, a 7 6 harmonization would be recommended on the sixth scale degree. See formula IV.13.

(c) This long suspended fourth was used by the composer over the same bass pattern in *Il Gelsomino* (H-G 51: 128).

(d) Another common approach to the dominant, see formula IV.20.

(e) See formula II.1.

(f) The B♭ in the solo part on the fourth beat does not influence the implied harmony of the previous beat.

(g) It would be easier, and perhaps less misleading, to figure this eighth-note F "retrospectively" (see Arnold, *The Art of Accompaniment*, p. 880); i.e., with reference to the previous bass note, so that the figuring for the third beat of this measure would be merely 4 3. As it is, the $\smash{\genfrac{}{}{0pt}{}{7}{\genfrac{}{}{0pt}{}{4}{2}}}$ is a clumsy way of indicating that the harmony of the preceding note continues, except for the resolution of the fourth. A fresh chord should not be struck on this eighth note.

(h) The rhythm and shape of this melodic line demand that the A♭ be treated as an appoggiatura. The progression $^6_3$ changing to $\smash{\genfrac{}{}{0pt}{}{6}{\genfrac{}{}{0pt}{}{4}{2}}}$ occurs frequently over a single bass note that subsequently descends by step. Cf. "Occhi miei che faceste?" (H-G 51: 27), where the composer uses this figuring with the same pitches and, incidentally, the same word.

(i) In cases like this the seventh does not need to be included in the realization since it is contained in the solo part, occurs on a weak part of the beat, and resolves normally.

Se per fatal destino, HWV 159, no. 2

Cantata Udite il mio consiglio, *First Aria*

(a) A slight variation on a familiar pattern in Handel's basses; see formulas V.11, 12.

(b) This pattern of four notes — F♯ G G F♯ — is obviously important thematically and challenging to the accompanist. Perhaps the best solution is a simple *tasto solo* execution; in this way the motif is likely to be heard as a "theme." The dominant chord at the beginning of the measure would be taken off before the second beat. If it must be harmonized, we have one solid piece of evidence from thoroughbass manuals: the sixth degree in minor takes a first inversion triad (see Buelow, *Thorough-Bass Accompaniment*, p. 229 and formula VII.2). This harmonization is especially applicable when the dominant precedes and follows the sixth degree. If the figuring given here is followed, the 7 chord should not contain a fifth (ibid., pp. 41–45).

(c) See formula I.14.

(d) A rather sophisticated form of another familiar progression in Handel's music; see formula V.10.

(e) See formula II.1.

(f) An alternate figuring is given above the bass staff.

(g) In this and the following system, some or perhaps all of the 6 chords that are approached by an ascending leap of a sixth could be realized as $^6_5$ chords.

Udite il mio consiglio, HWV 172, no. 1

(h) Again, the alternate harmonization is given above. The figuring above has a slight edge because it treats the B in the voice as a nonharmonic tone. In the other statements of this motif with bass, the third note is a dissonant interval (cf. the two measures marked "e").

(i) Handel's figure merely indicates that the normal third required by the key signature—F♯—is lowered one half-step to F♮. The normal figuring would be a natural sign.

(j) It is tempting to use a root position triad on the first beat of this measure, instead of the more "correct" first inversion triad (see above under "b"), especially since the text has the word "*fallace*" (false). In any case, there immediately follows a brief articulation of D major, and the whole phrase can be considered to be in that key (cf. the last measure of the preceding system).

(k) Usually Handel figures the fourth scale degree in major and minor $^6_5$, in cadence patterns especially. These measures are examples of a common exception to this rule: when the solo part has a seventh above the bass.

Udite il mio consiglio, Continued

Part Three

Appendixes

Appendix A

Aylesford Cembalo/Organo Parts for Handel's Operas and Oratorios

Location: Henry Watson Music Library, Manchester Central Library (unless otherwise indicated)

Acis and Galatea (S2)
    Library of Congress
    Shelfmark: M 2.1.H2 case v. 2, ff. 21-59
    Figuring: Very little
    Plain Recitative: Yes
    Accompanied Recitative: Yes
    Ouverture: Yes
    Other Instrumental Music: No
    Choral Parts: No
    Remarks: One-act version, lacking #9b, #9c, and #14. Occasional instrumental cues.

Acis and Galatea, "Additional Songs," 1732-6 (S2)
    Library of Congress
    Shelfmark: M 2.1.H2 case v. 2, ff. 60-92
    Figuring: Very little, except for the extensive figuring in Anh. #4 and Anh. #5 of HWV 49b.
    Plain Recitative: No
    Accompanied Recitative: Anh. #4
    Ouverture: No
    Other Instrumental Music: No
    Choral Parts: No

Remarks: A selection from HWV 49b: #'s 9, 23a, 21b, Anh. 3, 4, 28a, 11, 18, 20, 24a, 25, 29, Anh. 4, Anh. 5.

Admeto (S2)
Shelfmark: MS 130 Hd4, v. 298
Figuring: Full. The full figuring represents the original condition of the MS. Additional figures by Jennens in "Luci care" and elsewhere.
Plain Recitative: No
Accompanied Recitative: Yes
Ouverture: No
Other Instrumental Music: The opening lentement only; melody and bass.
Choral Parts: No
Remarks: "Dolce riso" in E Major.

Agrippina (S2)
Shelfmark: MS 130 Hd4, v. 18
Figuring: Mostly full, but no figures in the *unisono* aria "Col raggio placido."
Plain Recitative: No
Accompanied Recitative: No
Ouverture: No
Other Instrumental Music: No
Choral Parts: No
Remarks: Has only nineteen arias. "Vaghe fonti" in f minor!

Alcina (S2)
Shelfmark: MS 130 Hd4, v. 19
Figuring: Very little
Plain Recitative: No
Accompanied Recitative: Yes
Ouverture: No
Other Instrumental Music: Melody and bass
Choral Parts: Yes
Remarks: Has two versions of the chorus "Questo e il cielo."

Alcina (S1, S3)
Shelfmark: MS 130 Hd4, v. 64
Figuring: Very little

Plain Recitative: No
Accompanied Recitative: Yes
Ouverture: Unfigured bass
Other Instrumental Music: Unfigured bass
Choral Parts: No
Remarks: Vocal parts in original clefs. Cello obbligato given for "Credete al mio dolore."

Alessandro (S2)
Shelfmark: MS 130 Hd4, v. 298
Figuring: Very little
Plain Recitative: No
Accompanied Recitative: Yes
Ouverture: No
Other Instrumental Music: Melody and bass
Choral Parts: Yes

Alexander's Feast (S2)
Shelfmark: MS 130 Hd4, v. 28
Figuring: Full; similar to Walsh print.
Plain Recitative: Yes
Accompanied Recitative: Yes
Ouverture: Figured bass
Other Instrumental Music: No
Choral Parts: Yes
Remarks: Very different from the other surviving keyboard parts for this work. Has soloists' names at the beginning of each aria.

Amadigi (S2)
Shelfmark: MS 130 Hd4, v. 309
Figuring: Very little
Plain Recitative: No
Accompanied Recitative: Yes
Ouverture: No
Other Instrumental Music: Melody and bass
Choral Parts: Yes

Arianna (S2)
Shelfmark: MS 130 Hd4, v. 58
Figuring: Very little
Plain Recitative: No
Accompanied Recitative: Yes
Ouverture: No

Other Instrumental Music: Melody and bass
Choral Parts: Yes
Remarks: Dance movements from this opera are included in an Aylesford cembalo part in the Library of Congress; see below under *Il Pastor Fido*, 1734 Additions.

Ariodante (S2)
Shelfmark: MS 130 Hd4, v. 58
Figuring: Very little
Plain Recitative: Between #29 and #30 only.
Accompanied Recitative: Yes
Ouverture: No
Other Instrumental Music: Melody and sparsely figured bass
Choral Parts: Yes
Remarks: Some instrumental movements have detailed instrumentation indications.

Ariodante (S1, S4)
Shelfmark: MS 130 Hd4, v. 64
Figuring: Very little
Plain Recitative: No
Accompanied Recitative: Yes
Ouverture: Unfigured bass
Other Instrumental Music: Mostly unfigured bass
Choral Parts: #14 only
Remarks: Part titled "Cembalo e Violoncello;" Vocal parts in original clefs; #31 in melody plus bass format.

Arminio (S2)
Shelfmark: MS 130 Hd4, v. 73
Figuring: Virtually none
Plain Recitative: No
Accompanied Recitative: Yes
Ouverture: No
Other Instrumental Music: Melody and bass
Choral Parts: Yes

Berenice (S2)
Shelfmark: MS 130 Hd4, v. 73
Figuring: Very little

Plain Recitative: No
Accompanied Recitative: Yes
Ouverture: No
Other Instrumental Music: Melody and bass
Choral Parts: No

Esther, 1737 Additions (S2)
Library of Congress
Shelfmark: M 2.1.H2 case v. 2, ff. 93-104v
Figuring: Extensive
Plain Recitative: No
Accompanied Recitative: No
Ouverture: No
Other Instrumental Music: No
Choral Parts: No
Remarks: Contains the four arias added for the July 1737 revival (HWV 50b, Anhang).

Ezio (S2)
Shelfmark: MS 130 Hd4, v. 10
Figuring: Very little; the beginning of "Pensa a serbarmi" is figured.
Plain Recitative: No
Accompanied Recitative: Yes
Ouverture: No
Other Instrumental Music: Melody and bass
Choral Parts: Yes

Faramondo (S2)
Shelfmark: MS 130 Hd4, v. 117
Figuring: Very little
Plain Recitative: No
Accompanied Recitative: No
Ouverture: No
Other Instrumental Music: Melody and bass
Choral Parts: Yes

Flavio (S2)
Shelfmark: MS 130 Hd4, v. 231
Figuring: Very little
Plain Recitative: No
Accompanied Recitative: Yes
Ouverture: No

Other Instrumental Music: Melody and bass
Choral Parts: Yes

Floridante (S2)
Shelfmark: MS 130 Hd4, v. 212
Figuring: Very little; "Alma mia" figured.
Plain Recitative: No
Accompanied Recitative: Yes
Ouverture: No
Other Instrumental Music: No
Choral Parts: Yes
Remarks: "Fuor di periglio" has obbligato bassoon parts, as well as continuo, in the ritornelli of the A section.

Giulio Cesare (S2)
Shelfmark: MS 130 Hd4, v. 231
Figuring: Partial; similar to RM 19 c 7 and Cluer print. (See chapter 5.) "Cara speme" figured.
Otherwise, very little before "Venere bella;" full in most arias after that.
Plain Recitative: No
Accompanied Recitative: Yes
Ouverture: No
Other Instrumental Music: Arranged for keyboard; mostly melody and bass.
Choral Parts: Yes

Giustino (S2)
Shelfmark: MS 130 Hd4, v. 73
Figuring: Very little
Plain Recitative: No
Accompanied Recitative: Yes
Ouverture: No
Other Instrumental Music: Melody and bass
Choral Parts: Incomplete

Imeneo (S2)
Shelfmark: MS 130 Hd4, v. 19
Figuring: Sporadic; "Se potessero" and "Deh! m'ajutate" heavily figured.
Plain Recitative: No
Accompanied Recitative: Yes

Ouverture: No
Other Instrumental Music: No
Choral Parts: #30

Joseph (S2)
Shelfmark: MS 130 Hd4, v. 249
Figuring: Full, but six of the eight appended movements contain little figuring.
Plain Recitative: Yes
Accompanied Recitative: Yes
Ouverture: Figured bass
Other Instrumental Music: Melody and figured bass
Choral Parts: No

Judas Maccabeus (S2)
Shelfmark: MS 130 Hd4, v. 180
Figuring: Partial; mostly at the beginning of the work.
Plain Recitative: Yes
Accompanied Recitative: Yes
Ouverture: Partially figured bass
Other Instrumental Music: No
Choral Parts: No

Lotario (S2)
Shelfmark: MS 130 Hd4, v. 196
Figuring: Very little; partial figuring of #33.
Plain Recitative: No
Accompanied Recitative: Yes
Ouverture: No
Other Instrumental Music: Melody plus bass, or bass only
Choral Parts: Yes
Remarks: At the end of the part is a fragment of #31a, which stops abruptly in measure 14.

Muzio Scevola (S2)
Shelfmark: MS 130 Hd4, v. 212
Figuring: Very little; #15 is heavily figured, as in the autograph.
Plain Recitative: No
Accompanied Recitative: Yes
Ouverture: No

Other Instrumental Music: No
Choral Parts: Yes

Orlando (S2)
Shelfmark: MS 130 Hd4, v. 10
Figuring: Very little
Plain Recitative: No
Accompanied Recitative: Yes
Ouverture: No
Other Instrumental Music: Melody and bass
Choral Parts: Yes
Remarks: Jennens wrote "Da Capo" at the end of "Ritornava al suo bel viso." (!)

Ottone (S2)
Shelfmark: MS 130 Hd4, v. 231
Figuring: Partial
Plain Recitative: No
Accompanied Recitative: Yes
Ouverture: No
Other Instrumental Music: Melody and bass
Choral Parts: Yes
Remarks: #5 (Concerto in D, Op. 3 #6, first movement) given in the form of unfigured bass.

Partenope (S2)
Shelfmark: MS 130 Hd4, v. 196
Figuring: Very little, but "Seguaci di Cupido" is heavily figured by S2, "O Eurimene" figured by Jennens.
Plain Recitative: No
Accompanied Recitative: Yes
Ouverture: No
Other Instrumental Music: Melody and bass
Choral Parts: Yes

Il Pastor Fido (S2)
Shelfmark: MS 130 Hd4, v. 258
Figuring: Very little; "Lontan dal mio tesoro" partially figured.
Plain Recitative: No
Accompanied Recitative: Yes
Ouverture: No

Other Instrumental Music: Melody and bass
Choral Parts: Yes
Remarks: #10 does *not* contain the autograph directive, "Cembalo arpeggiato per tutto."

Il Pastor Fido, 1734 Additions (S2)
Library of Congress
Shelfmark: M 2.1.H2 case v. 2, ff. 105-160v
Figuring: Very little
Plain Recitative: No
Accompanied Recitative: Yes
Ouverture: No
Other Instrumental Music: Yes
Choral Parts: Yes
Remarks: Contains the new music for the two 1734 revivals of *Il Pastor Fido*: HWV 8c #'s 1a, 2a, 8, 15, 21, 35; HWV 8b #2; HWV 8c #'s 1b, 3b, 7b, 9, 10, 22-25, 36-39; HWV 8b #'s 4-13. Four dances from *Arianna*, in 2-part format, are appended: #'s 33-36.

Poro (S2)
Shelfmark: MS 130 Hd4, v. 196
Figuring: Very little
Plain Recitative: No
Accompanied Recitative: Yes
Ouverture: No
Other Instrumental Music: Melody and bass
Choral Parts: Yes

Radamisto (S2)
Shelfmark: MS 130 Hd4, v. 309
Figuring: Small amount; "Qual nave smarrita" fully figured.
Plain Recitative: No
Accompanied Recitative: No
Ouverture: No
Other Instrumental Music: Melody and bass
Choral Parts: Yes

La Resurrezione (S2)
Shelfmark: MS 130 Hd4, v. 249
Figuring: Partial, very similar to RM 19 d 4. Fully figured until "Dolci chiodi."

Plain Recitative: Yes
Accompanied Recitative: Yes
Ouverture: No
Other Instrumental Music: No
Choral Parts: Yes

Riccardo Primo (S2)
Shelfmark: MS 130 Hd4, v. 257
Figuring: Full, except for three arias, the duet, and the *Marche*. Figuring derived from the autograph. Additional figuring by Jennens in "Bella, teco, non ho."
Plain Recitative: No
Accompanied Recitative: Yes
Ouverture: No
Other Instrumental Music: Melody and bass
Choral Parts: No

Rinaldo (S2)
Shelfmark: MS 130 Hd4, v. 258
Figuring: Partial. First three arias and a portion of "Lascia ch'io pianga" fully figured; very little otherwise.
Plain Recitative: In #30 only.
Accompanied Recitative: Yes
Ouverture: No
Other Instrumental Music: Melody and bass
Choral Parts: Yes

Rodelinda (S2)
Shelfmark: MS 130 Hd4, v. 324
Figuring: Full, as in the conducting score, but with various alterations, additions, and deletions.
Plain Recitative: Only three bars at the end of #9.
Accompanied Recitative: Yes, but "Fatto inferno" is missing.
Ouverture: No
Other Instrumental Music: No
Choral Parts: No
Remarks: *Coro* not present.

Rodrigo (S2)
Shelfmark: MS 130 Hd4, v. 18

Figuring: Full through Act II, scene viii, but sporadic thereafter, as in the Aylesford full score. (See Dean and Knapp, *Handel's Operas*, pp. 112-3.)
Plain Recitative: No
Accompanied Recitative: Yes
Ouverture: No
Other Instrumental Music: No
Choral Parts: Yes

Samson (S2)
Shelfmark: MS 130 Hd4, v. 275
Figuring: Full
Plain Recitative: Yes
Accompanied Recitative: Yes
Ouverture: Figured bass
Other Instrumental Music: No
Choral Parts: in "Glorious hero" only
Remarks: Additional figuring by Jennens.

Saul (S2)
Shelfmark: MS 130 Hd4, v. 275
Figuring: Partial; extensive figuring in instrumental and choral movements. Additional figuring in the Ouverture by Jennens.
Plain Recitative: Yes
Accompanied Recitative: Yes
Ouverture: Figured bass
Other Instrumental Music: Mostly bass; treble for #20, bass and organ obbligato for #58a.
Choral Parts: No
Remarks: Contains (32.) and 32a.

Songs in *Saul* (S2)
Shelfmark: MS 130 Hd4, v. 249
Figuring: Very little
Plain Recitative: No
Accompanied Recitative: Yes
Ouverture: No
Other Instrumental Music: No
Choral Parts: Yes
Remarks: Contains six numbers in unfamiliar versions, e.g., "Author of Peace," the accompagnato setting of "O Jonathan."

Scipione (S2)
>Shelfmark: MS 130 Hd4, v. 298
>Figuring: Full, except for the 1730 tenor arias.
>Plain Recitative: No
>Accompanied Recitative: Two of the four are present.
>Ouverture: No
>Other Instrumental Music: Melody and bass
>Choral Parts: No
>Remarks: *Coro* not present.

Serse (S2)
>Shelfmark: MS 130 Hd4, v. 117
>Figuring: Very little
>Plain Recitative: No
>Accompanied Recitative: Yes
>Ouverture: No
>Other Instrumental Music: Melody and bass
>Choral Parts: Yes

Silla (S2)
>Shelfmark: MS 130 Hd4, v. 309
>Figuring: First aria heavily figured, as in H-G; very sparse otherwise.
>Plain Recitative: No
>Accompanied Recitative: No
>Ouverture: No
>Other Instrumental Music: No
>Choral Parts: Yes

Siroe (S2)
>Shelfmark: MS 130 Hd4, v. 257
>Figuring: Partial, as in the autograph.
>Plain Recitative: No
>Accompanied Recitative: Yes
>Ouverture: No
>Other Instrumental Music: Melody and bass
>Choral Parts: Yes

Sosarme (S2)
>Shelfmark: MS 130 Hd4, v. 10
>Figuring: Very little
>Plain Recitative: No
>Accompanied Recitative: Yes

Ouverture: No
Other Instrumental Music: Melody and bass
Choral Parts: Yes
Remarks: #2 missing.

Tamerlano (S2)
Shelfmark: MS 130 Hd4, v. 324
Figuring: Very little; "Bella Asteria" heavily figured by Jennens.
Plain Recitative: No
Accompanied Recitative: Yes
Ouverture: No
Other Instrumental Music: Melody and bass
Choral Parts: No
Remarks: Contains eleven appended movements under the heading "Additions." Two versions of "Non e piu tempo" are present.

Teseo (S2)
Shelfmark: MS 130 Hd4, v. 258
Figuring: Very little
Plain Recitative: Only in #9.
Accompanied Recitative: Yes
Ouverture: No
Other Instrumental Music: No
Choral Parts: Yes

Tolomeo (S2)
Shelfmark: MS 130 Hd4, v. 257
Figuring: Fair amount. Generally, figuring as in H-G, but considerably more in #17 and B section of #25.
Plain Recitative: No
Accompanied Recitative: Yes
Ouverture: No
Other Instrumental Music: No
Choral Parts: No

Il Trionfo (S2)
Shelfmark: MS 130 Hd4, v. 28
Figuring: Very little
Plain Recitative: Yes
Accompanied Recitative: Yes
Sinfonias: Unfigured bass

Other Instrumental Music: Melody and bass
Choral Parts: No
Remarks: Some solo instrumental parts included.

Appendix B

Manuscript Scores of Handel's Operas, Oratorios, and Odes with Supplementary Figuring

Admeto British Library, Department of Manuscripts: Add. 38002. Copyist: Smith Sr.
No recitatives; ouverture and other instrumental pieces transcribed for keyboard. Opening instrumental piece (Lentement, I, 1) ornamented.

Admeto Manchester Public Library, Newman Flower Collection: MS 130 Hd4, v. 2. Copyist: S2.
Fully figured by the copyist, with additional figures by Jennens in "Luci care."

Admeto British Library, Royal Music Collection: RM. 19. c. 2. Copyist: S13.
Considerable figuring, but not as much as the S2 and Smith Sr. copies listed above.

Admeto British Library, Department of Manuscripts, Granville Collection: Eg. 2924. Copyist: S5.

Agrippina Manchester Public Library, Newman Flower Collection: MS 130 Hd4, v. 11. Copyists: S2, Smith Sr., H3.
Figured fully mostly by Jennens; a few arias fig-

ured by another hand, possibly Smith's. Thirteen arias have little or no figuring.

Alexander's Feast Fitzwilliam Museum, Lennard Collection Mus. Ms. 794. Copyist: Smith Sr.
Full figuring which is quite similar to the printed edition.

Alexander's Feast Manchester Public Library, Newman Flower Collection: MS 130 Hd4, v. 27A. Copyist: S2.
Figuring similar to the Walsh print until the middle of "With ravish'd ears;" thereafter figuring exists only in a few short passages.

L'Allegro Manchester Public Library, Newman Flower Collection: MS 130 Hd4, v. 189. Copyist: S2.
Figured more fully than the autograph; some additions by Jennens.

Amadigi di Gaula British Library, Department of Manuscripts Egerton 2917. Copyist: S5.
Additional figuring in recitatives.

Amadigi di Gaula British Library, Royal Music Collection RM. 19. g. 2. Copyist: RM2.
Figuring confined to Act I.

Amadigi di Gaula British Library, Royal Music Collection RM. 19. c. 5. Copyist: S13.
Additional figuring in recitatives.

Amadigi di Gaula Library of Congress "Landon" MS. Copyists: Linike, Smith Sr.
Three arias ("S'estinto," "Ti pentirai," and the E-flat setting of "Gioje, venite il sen") fully figured.

Amadigi di Gaula Library of Congress M 1500/H 13/A 44. Copyist: RM1.
Ample figuring throughout.

Arminio Fitzwilliam Museum, Lennard Collection Mus. Ms. 815. Copyist: Smith Sr.?

Additional figuring mostly toward the end of the work.

Atalanta   Fitzwilliam Museum, Lennard Collection Mus. Ms. 791. Copyists: Smith Sr., S1.
Additional figuring in Act III and elsewhere.

Belshazzar   Fitzwilliam Museum, Lennard Collection: Mus. Ms. 841. Copyist: S9.
Considerable supplementary figuring.

Belshazzar   Princeton University, Hall Handel Collection. Copyist: Smith Sr.
Portions of the work contain fuller figuring.

Brockes Passion   Staatsbibliothek Berlin, Dahlem: Mus. ms. 9002.
Figuring not done by original copyist.

Brockes Passion   Manchester Public Library, Newman Flower Collection: MS 130 Hd4, v. 233. Copyist: S2.
Ample figuring for most movements.

Deborah   Fitzwilliam Museum, Lennard Collection Mus. Ms. 806. Copyist: Smith Sr.
Fully figured in two different hands, neither of which is Smith Sr. Used as "copy" for the Wright edition of 1784.

Esther   Royal College of Music, London: MS 895. Copyist: S5.
Fully figured until the aria "Endless Fame." Figures resume for movement borrowed from Coronation Anthem I, "Zadok the Priest."

Giulio Cesare   British Library, Royal Music Collection: RM. 19. c. 7. Copyist: RM1.
Partial figuring similar to the Aylesford cembalo part. "Cara speme" figured by Jennens.

Israel in Egypt   British Library, Royal Music Collection: RM. 18. d. 7. Copyist: Smith Sr.

Joseph Manchester Public Library, Newman Flower Collection: MS 130 Hd4, v. 151. Copyist: S2.
Fully figured, very similar to Flower Organo part.

Judas Maccabeus Fitzwilliam Museum, Lennard Collection Mus. Ms. 809. Copyist: S9.
Full figuring generally, although several choruses have little or none. Appended movements unfigured.

Judas Maccabeus Royal College of Music, London MS 250. Copyists: S5 (?) and two unidentified scribes.
Fully figured, except for "Ah wretched Israel" and "O Liberty." Many figures erased.

Messiah Manchester Public Library, Newman Flower Collection: MS 130 Hd4, v. 198–200. Copyist: S2.
Very full figuring, most notably in "The people that walked in darkness."

Messiah Fitzwilliam Museum, Barrett Lennard Collection. Mus. Ms. 844. Copyist: S5.
Some supplementary figuring; vocal ornamentation by a later hand.

Muzio Scevola Nanki Library, Tokyo. Copyists: H2, H1, RM1, an unidentified hand, and possibly Smith Sr.
Handel's contribution (Act 3) copied by H2. Figuring in several numbers from Act III. Formerly owned by W.H. Cummings.

Muzio Scevola British Library, Royal Music Collection RM. 19. c. 8. Copyists: H2, RM4, RM1, and an unidentified hand.
Figuring in several Handel arias. Act III again copied by H2.

Radamisto Berlin Staatsbibliothek Berlin Mus MS 9051.

Bass figuring throughout. Gives the version Mattheson prepared for Hamburg.

Radamisto   British Library, Department of Manuscripts: Add. 39180. Copyist: BM1.
Ample figuring, but there are many differences with and, it seems, corrections of the continuo figuring as given in the Meares print. Formerly belonged to John Stanley.

Radamisto   Collection of Gerald Coke. Copyist: Unidentified copyist of the Coke *Teseo* copy listed below. (For further details on this interesting copyist, see Dean and Knapp, *Handel's Operas*, p. 257f.)
Figurings similar to the Meares print.

Radamisto   Manchester Public Library, Newman Flower Collection: MS 130 Hd4, v. 238. Copyist: S2.
Generally unfigured, but Jennens added some for several arias, including "Cara sposa," "Qual nave," "Quando mai," "L'ingrato non amar," and "Fatemi o cieli."

Radamisto   Royal College of Music, London MS 905. Copyists: Smith Sr., Gamma, H2.
The full figuring is possibly by another eighteenth-century hand. Many figurings similar to those of the Meares printed edition. Only half of the appended movements are figured. No recitatives.

La Resurrezione   Manchester Public Library, Newman Flower Collection: MS 130 Hd4, v. 239. Copyist: S2.
Figured mostly by Jennens to make the MS conform with the Flower cembalo part.

Rodelinda   Fitzwilliam Museum, Barrett Lennard Collection. Mus. Ms. 818. Copyist: S1.
Some figuring, but not nearly as much as the Hamburg conducting score.

Rodelinda   Manchester Public Library, Newman Flower Collection: MS 130 Hd4, v. 267. Copyist: S2.
Jennens figuring in #'s 1, 6, 7, 8, and 14.

Rodrigo   Fitzwilliam Museum, Lennard Collection Mus. Ms. 855. Copyist: Lenn2.
Figured up through the A section of "Ti lascio."

Rodrigo   Manchester Public Library, Newman Flower Collection: MS 130 Hd4, v. 268(1). Copyist: S1.
Fully figured until Act II, Scene 8; after that only #25 figured. Almost all the figuring is in Jennens's hand.

Samson   British Library, Department of Manuscripts: Add. 37323-5. Copyist: BM6.
Fully figured. Inscription: "Randall 1761."

Samson   Fitzwilliam Museum, Lennard Collection Mus. Ms. 851. Copyist: S9.
Fully figured; aria figurings perhaps related to Walsh print. Unisoni in "Honor and Arms," "Presuming slave," Thy glorious deeds," and "Why Does the God of Israel Sleep?" all figured.

Saul   British Library, Royal Music Collection: RM. 18. d. 9. Copyist: Smith Sr.
Figuring is ample, but different from the Walsh and Randall prints, as well as the other MS source listed below.

Saul   Manchester Public Library, Newman Flower Collection: MS 130 Hd4, v. 269-271. Copyist: S2.
Heavily figured; some of it by Jennens.

Scipione   Manchester Public Library, Newman Flower Collection: MS 130 Hd4, v. 291. Copyist: S2.
A few arias figured by Jennens: #'s 8, 9, and 11.

Tamerlano Manchester Public Library, Newman Flower Collection: MS 130 Hd4, ♯. 317. Copyist: S2.
Figures added by Jennens for a few arias: ♯'s 3, 5, and 7.

Teseo British Library, Royal Music Collection: RM. 19. g. 4. Copyists: RM2 and two unidentified.
Many figurings in a different ink than the body of the score, probably these are later additions. Figures similar to Arnold edition.

Teseo Collection of Gerald Coke. Copyist: Unidentified (see the Coke *Radamisto*, listed above).
This manuscript, one of three copies of the work in the Coke Collection, has been designated "*Teseo* III" by Dean and Knapp.

Triumph of Time and Truth British Library, Department of Manuscripts: Add. 31568. Copyists: S4, BM3.
Some figures by original copyist, some added by another hand, perhaps BM3.

Appendix C

Unpublished Autograph Figuring

Rinaldo, HWV 7, Ouverture
RM 20. c. 3.

Rinaldo, Ouverture, Continued

Rinaldo, Ouverture, Continued

Figuring from this manuscript reproduced by permission of the British Library

Ottone, HWV 15, "Falsa imagine"

Figuring from this manuscript reproduced by permission of the British Library

"Tacete, ohimè, tacete," HWV 196
Fitzwilliam Museum MU MS 253, pp. 25-31

"Tacete, ohimè, tacete," Continued

"Tacete, ohimè, tacete," Continued

"Tacete, ohimè, tacete," Continued

"Tacete, ohimè, tacete," Continued

"Tacete, ohimè, tacete," Continued

"Tacete, ohimè, tacete," Continued

***Radamisto*, "Cara sposa"**
RM 19. c. 9., fol. 106v

Radamisto, "Cara sposa," Continued

Radamisto, "Cara sposa," Continued

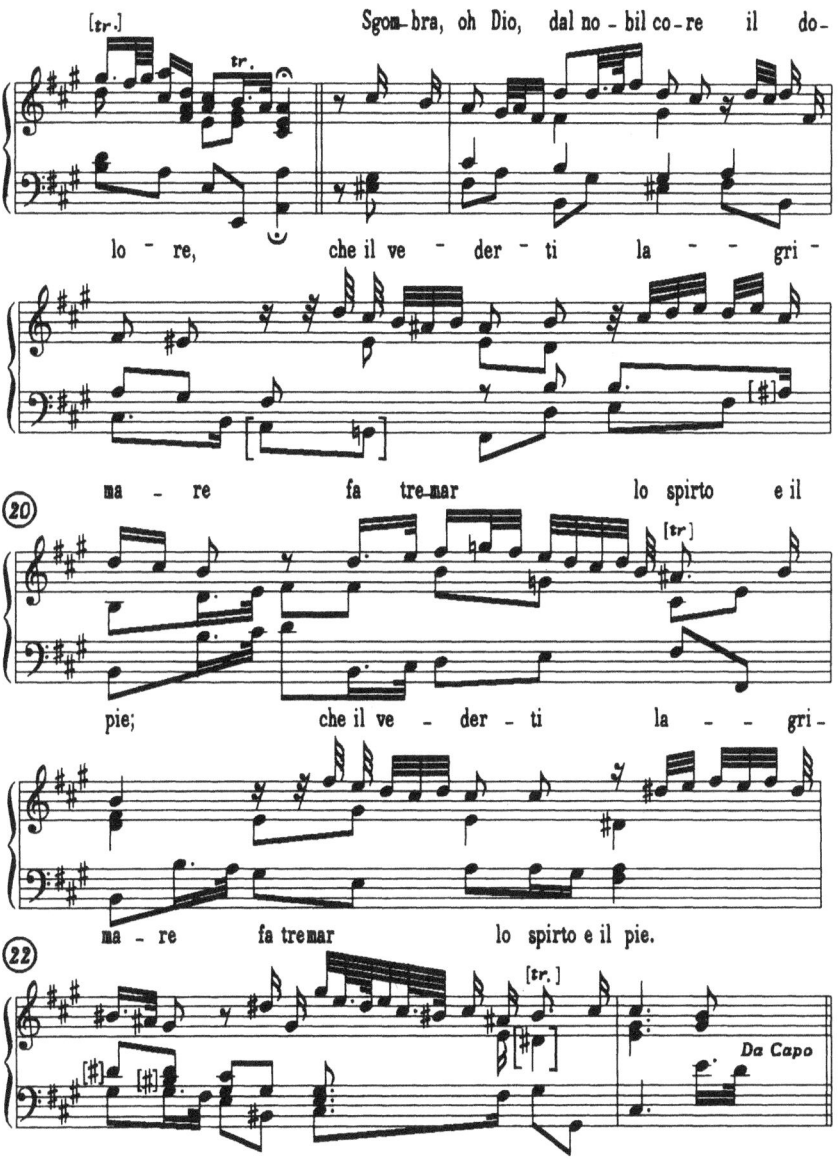

Reprinted by permission of the British Library

[Amen, alleluja], HWV 275
RM 20. f. 12., fol. 4

[Amen, alleluja], Continued

Figuring from this manuscript reproduced by permission of the British Library

Notes

Introduction

1. H-G 70: Vorwort; 84: i.
2. H-G 12: iv.
3. HHA, I/1.
4. HHA, II/8.
5. HHA, III/5: 58-64.
6. HHA, IV/2, 12, 14, 15, 18.
7. HHA, IV/18: 56.
8. These mostly anonymous scribes were first described and delineated by Jens Peter Larsen in *Handel's "Messiah": Origins, Composition, Sources*, 2d ed. (New York: W. W. Norton, 1972); see especially pp. 261-74. Larsen identified the hands of Smith Sr., Smith Jr., thirteen other scribes of the Smith circle (which he designated S1-13), a Royal Music Collection series (RM), a BL Department of MSS series (BM), a Hamburg series (Hb), and others.
9. Winton Dean, "Handel's Early London Copyists," in *Bach, Handel, Scarlatti: Tercentenary Essays*, ed. Peter Williams (Cambridge: Cambridge University Press, 1985), p. 97. In this aricle Dean also identified other important pre-1725 scribes.
10. These include S1-5, Hb1 and 2, H1-12. See Hans Dieter Clausen, *Händels Direktionspartituren* (Hamburg: Karl Dieter Wagner, 1972), p. 269 f. The H series of copyists was discovered by Clausen in the Hamburg conducting scores.
11. E.g., *St. John Passion, St. Matthew Passion*.
12. E.g., the four cantatas listed on p. 120.
13. For a remarkable instance of this, see J. S. Bach's *St. John Passion*, NBA, II/4: 33, m. 64.
14. This type was described and illustrated by C. P. E. Bach in the *Versuch über das wahre Art das Clavier zu spielen* (Berlin, 1753/1762; reprint, Wiesbaden: Breitkopf und Härtel, 1981), part 2, chap. 32, paragraph 12.
15. F. T. Arnold, *The Art of Accompaniment from a Thorough-Bass* (London: Oxford University Press, 1931), p. 66. The italics are mine, for emphasis. Original:

Auch geben diejenigen/ welche sagen: die *Signaturen* wären im *General-Basse* über den Noten gar nicht nütze und nöthig/ keine kleine *Ignoranz* und Thorheit an den Tag; denn es ist ja unmüglich [sic]/dass ein wohl = geübter/ so den natürlichen Lauff der *harmonie* und *Composition* verstehet/ alles nach eines andern Meynung solte treffen/ denn die *Progressiones* und *Resolutiones* können auff viererley Arth geschehen. (Frankfurt and Leipzig, 1702, p. 65)

16. (London: Oxford University Press, 1931; reprint, New York: Dover Publications, 1965).

17. Rev. ed. (Ann Arbor: UMI Research Press, 1986).

18. 2 vols. (Edinburgh: Edinburgh University Press, 1970).

19. New Version (London: Faber and Faber, 1975).

20. (London: Novello, 1965), pp. 150-52.

21. (New York: St. Martin's Press, 1969), pp. 128-34, 171-84. See also the critical report for Tobin's edition of *Messiah*, HHA I/17: Kritischer Bericht, pp. 104-8.

22. (University of Toronto, 1977).

23. Mayo, "Handel's Italian Cantatas," pp. 146-50.

24. "The Organ Parts to Handel's *Alexander's Feast*," *Music and Letters* 59 (April 1978): 159-79.

25. See chap. 1, note 10.

26. Donald Burrows, "Sources, Resources and Handel Studies," in *Handel: Tercentenary Collection*, ed. Stanley Sadie and Anthony Hicks (Ann Arbor: UMI Research Press, 1987), p. 23.

Chapter 1

1. Martha Ronish, "Continuo Groupings in the Handel Autographs," a paper delivered at the Maryland Handel Festival, College Park, Maryland, 9 November 1984.

2. A. Hyatt King, *Handel and his Autographs* (London: British Museum, 1967), pp. 17, 19.

3. See chap. 5.

4. See chap. 2.

5. HHA Supplement/I: 13. Terence Best, "Further Studies on Handel's Solo Sonatas," *Händel-Jahrbuch* (1984): 76-77. Best's dating of the Fitzwilliam thoroughbass exercises has been confirmed by the recent research of Donald Burrows into watermarks and rastra. (Letter to this writer, 1 July 1988.)

6. The relationship between Handel's figuring of *Rodelinda* and the Cluer printed edition will be discussed in the following chapter.

7. The so-called "pedagogical" cantatas; discussed later in this chapter.

8. Winton Dean, *Handel's Dramatic Oratorios and Masques* (London: Oxford University Press, 1959), p. 89.

9. Francesco Gasparini, *L'Armonico pratico al cimbalo* (Venice, 1708; reprint, New York: Broude Brothers, 1967), pp. 89-90; Johann David Heinichen, *Der General-Bass in der*

Composition (Dresden, 1728; reprint, Hildesheim: Georg Olms Verlag, 1969), pp. 540, 770, 774-78.

10. "Eine Kompositionslehre von Händel," *Händel-Jahrbuch* (1964/65): 35-57; HHA Supplement/1; "Bach and Handel as Teachers of Thorough-Bass," in *Bach, Handel, Scarlatti: Tercentenary Essays*, ed. Peter Williams (Cambridge: Cambridge University Press, 1985), pp. 245-57.

11. University of Toronto, 1977, pp. 146-50. Mayo seems unable to decide if the pedagogical cantatas were intended for a "none too experienced continuo player" (p. 148) or a more capable one. On p. 149 he writes: "There would be no better test of a continuo player than the accompaniment of one of these works."

12. An example is discussed on p. 144.

13. HHA Supplement/1: 11-12.

14. In the prefaces to the H-G editions of *Joseph*, p. iv, and *Jephtha*, p. v.

15. These are catalogued and described in J. A. Fuller Maitland and A. H. Mann, *Catalogue of the Music in the Fitzwilliam Musuem, Cambridge*.

16. Examples will be quoted later in the chapter. Cf. Dean, *Handel's Dramatic Oratorios*, p. 531.

17. A. Hyatt King, *Handel and his Autographs*, p. 25. See also pp. 26-27 for a useful chart on the composer's dating of the autographs.

18. Donald Burrows, "Paper Studies and Handel's Autographs: a Preliminary Report," *Göttinger Händel-Beiträge*, 1 (1984): 109.

19. Dean, *Handel's Dramatic Oratorios*, pp. 88-89.

20. H-G 42: iv. Dean, *Handel's Dramatic Oratorios*, p. 89.

21. See document 5.

22. See chap. 3.

23. For example, the cantatas *La Lucrezia* and *O lucenti o sereni occhi* in the British Library manuscript RM. 19. e. 7., fols. 85-88, fol. 93v. See also the second volume of solo cantatas in H-G, pp. i-ii.

24. HHA I/13: Kritischer Bericht, pp. 154-56.

25. RM. 20. c. 11., fol. 49. H-G facsimile edition of *Jephtha*, p. 199. The *Jephtha* example is from the aria "Waft her, angels, through the skies," which is four pages long in the facsimile edition and contains several rejected passages.

26. H-G 44: v.

27. H-G 70: 58, 59.

28. See chap. 10.

29. John Tobin, *Handel at Work* (London, 1964), p. 79. See also notes 14 and 20.

30. Arnold, *The Art of Accompaniment*, pp. 258-59, 274-75, and 810-13. The F Major Sonata for recorder (HHA Supplement/1, p. 81) does contain the figuring $\begin{smallmatrix}6\\4\\3\end{smallmatrix}$ on the

246   Notes for Chapter 3

supertonic in a similar passage; but in contrast to the example quoted above, the bass ascends in simple quarter notes, without the repeated off-beat on the dominant.

31. This occurs several times in *Rodelinda*; see p. 48.
32. This useful term was coined by Arnold, *The Art of Accompaniment*, p. 880.
33. See chap. 9 and "Remarks on Specific Groups of Formulas," Group VIII in chap. 10.

Chapter 2

1. Clausen, *Händels Direktionspartituren*, pp. 6-9.
2. H-G 12: iv; 66: i.
3. H-G 70: Vorwort; 44: v.
4. Fitzwilliam Museum MS 30 H 7, pp. 1-54.
5. Clausen, *Direktionspartituren*, pp. 51, 230. Original: "[D]ie Bezifferung des Basses hat er bisweilen berichtigt oder ergänzt."
6. H-G 44: 170-73.
7. This recitative does contain one interesting example of an obsolete figure. On p. 173, m. 2 of the H-G edition, the first eighth note was originally (i.e., in the autograph) figured 4^+, implying $\genfrac{}{}{0pt}{}{6}{\genfrac{}{}{0pt}{}{4^+}{2}}$, rather than $\genfrac{}{}{0pt}{}{4^+}{3}$, implying $\genfrac{}{}{0pt}{}{6}{\genfrac{}{}{0pt}{}{4^+}{3}}$, as given in the string parts, H-G, and presumably the conducting score.
8. The dating is based on Winton Dean's dating of the revisions to "Dove sei?" in "Handels Kompositorische Entwicklung in den Opern in der Jahre 1724/1725," *Händel-Jahrbuch* (1982): 30-33. Handel figured the first version (fol. 26v), with the long opening ritornello, and Dean dates the first revision before December 1725.
9. Clausen, *Händels Direktionspartituren*, p. 210.
10. H-G 70: Vorwort. Original: "Die auffallend reiche Bezifferung findet sich nur in dem Handexemplare als ein späterer Zusatz, von Händel selbst geschrieben und offenbar bestimmt, einem unkundigen Begleiter, den er bei der Aufführung dieser Oper benutzen musste, als Wegweiser zu dienen."
11. H-G 12: iv; 84: 1.
12. I am indebted to Anthony Hicks for discussions that helped to generate this hypothesis.
13. Otto Erich Deutsch, *Handel: a Documentary Biography* (London: A. and C. Black, 1955), p. 179.
14. Bernd Baselt, *Händel-Handbuch* (Kassel: Bärenreiter, 1978-), 4: 132. See also chap. 5.

Chapter 3

1. Several other miscellaneous sets of Handel parts have survived in public and private collections, e.g., oratorio parts in the Library of Congress, Chandos Anthems, and arias from *Radamisto* in the Coke Collection.

Notes for Chapter 3   247

2. Information on the dating of the *Cembalopartituren* has been gleaned from Clausen, *Händels Direktionspartituren*.

3. Clausen, *Händels Direktionspartituren*, p. 64. The copyists are (in approximate order of frequency in the *Cembalopartituren*): Smith Sr., S1, Hb1, H9, S2, H8, Hb2, S3, S4, and Smith Jr.

4. Winton Dean and J. Merrill Knapp, *Handel's Operas 1704-1726* (London, New York: Oxford University Press, 1987), pp. 198-200.

5. Donald Burrows, "The Composition and First Performance of Handel's *Alexander's Feast*," *Music and Letters* 64 (July-October 1983): 209.

6. Arnold, *The Art of Accompaniment*, p. 67.

7. At this point the organ part is marked *tasto solo*, which indicates that only the bass line should be played.

8. G. F. Handel, *Alexander's Feast*, ed. Donald Burrows (Sevenoaks, Kent: Novello, 1982), p. vi.

9. Cooper, "Organ Parts," p. 170.

10. Winton Dean, quoted in Cooper, "Organ Parts," p. 159.

11. In the "Musical Dictionary" of *The Modern Musick Master* (London, 1731), Peter Prelleur defined organo as follows: "[It] signifies properly an Organ, but when it is written over any Piece of Musick, then it signifies the Thorough Bass."

12. However Donald Burrows has published information on the dating and derivation of the Flower vocal parts for *Messiah*. See "The Autographs and Early Copies of *Messiah*," *Music and Letters* 66 (July 1985): 205-6. Regarding the *Saul* parts, see Anthony Hicks, "Handel, Jennens and *Saul*: Aspects of a Collaboration," in *Music and Theatre: Essays in Honor of Winton Dean*, ed. Nigel Fortune (Cambridge: Cambridge University Press, 1987). Also, the recently published study, *Handel's Operas 1704-1726* by Winton Dean and Merrill Knapp, contains information on the actual or probable derivation of several sets of Aylesford opera parts.

13. Winton Dean, "Handel's *Sosarme*, a Puzzle Opera," *Essays on Opera and English Music in Honour of Sir JackWestrup* (Oxford: B. Blackwell, 1975), pp. 130-31.

14. Arthur D. Walker, *George Frideric Handel: the Newman Flower Collection*, foreword by Winton Dean (The Manchester Public Libraries, 1972), p. ix.

15. Dean, "Handel's *Sosarme*," p. 129.

16. Winton Dean, "A French Traveller's View of Handel's Operas," *Music and Letters* 55 (April 1974): 175. Robert Donington, *The Interpretation of Early Music*, New Version (London: Faber and Faber, 1975), p. 663-64.

17. I am extremely indebted to Graydon Beeks for providing detailed information on the four Library of Congress items. My thanks also to Winton Dean who graciously shared information on copyists in the two Manchester cembalo parts which are not by S2, i.e., *Alcina* and *Ariodante*.

Chapter 4

1. I have not been able to examine all the manuscripts listed. *Handel's Operas 1704-1726*, by Winton Dean and John Merrill Knapp, brought to light several figured sources which were not known to me; the book also provided many valuable details concerning the figuring in MSS which were originally on the list. William Gudger generously shared his notes on the Lennard Collection. The following have also been very helpful: Watkins Shaw, "Handel's *Messiah*"; J. Merrill Knapp, "The Hall Handel Collection," *Princeton University Library Chronicle*, 36 (1974): 3ff; David Ray Stutzenberger, "*Belshazzar*, an Oratorio by George Frideric Handel," 2 vols. (Ph.D. diss., University of Maryland, 1980); the critical reports of the HHA editions of *Messiah*, the *Brockes Passion*, and *Amadigi*. Also, the large collection of Handel sources on microfilm at the University of California, Berkeley Music Library has been of considerable assistance.

2. Letter to this writer, 11 February 1984.

3. Clausen, *Händels Direktionspartituren*, pp. 91, 99, 109, and 196. Donald Burrows, "Sources for Oxford Handel Performances," *Music and Letters* 61 (April 1980): 181.

4. E.g., Cooper, "Organ Parts," p. 164. Cooper states that the Flower full score of *Alexander's Feast* in Manchester "was mostly copied from the [Walsh 1737] printed edition: the extent to which the bass is figured is sufficient evidence to show this." But only a portion of the Flower score is figured like the print; the remainder is only sparsely figured (see the appended list of MS scores).

5. For an explanation of this term, see p. 38.

Chapter 5

1. In this chapter, I will not be considering the various collections of "favourite songs" which were issued with great frequency and often pirated.

2. Donald Burrows, "Walsh's editions of Handel's Opera 1-5: the texts and their sources," in *Music in Eighteenth-Century England*, ed. Christopher Hogwood and Richard Luckett (Cambridge: Cambridge University Press, 1982), p.79.

3. Burrows, "Walsh's editions," p. 95. However, Barry Cooper believes that the conducting score for *Alexander's Feast* was copy for the 1737 Walsh edition. (Cooper, "Organ Parts," p. 165.)

4. This manuscript contains crosses and Xs in pencil, some of which seem to relate to the formatting of the Cluer edition, e.g., cuts of abbreviated ritornelli, division of arias into pages and systems. In the Fitzwilliam Museum Lennard Collection there are four items which William Gudger has identified as engraver's copy for the Wright oratorio editions of the 1780s: *Deborah, Solomon, Susanna,* and *Theodora.*

5. Charles Humphries and William C. Smith, *Music Publishing in the British Isles* (New York: Barnes and Noble, 1970), pp. 23-24.

6. Humphries and Smith: *Music Publishing*, pp. 16, 295.

7. Burrows: "*Walsh's editions*," p. 79.

8. See chap. 2.

9. Deutsch, *Handel*, pp. 438, 451f.

10. Ibid., p. 179 ff.

11. Baselt, *Handbuch*, 4: 134.

12. The table is intended to give only a representative sample of the Royal Academy printed editions.

13. Baselt, *Handbuch*, 4: 143.

14. H-G 66: Preface.

15. William C. Smith, *Handel: a Descriptive Catalogue of the Early Editions* (London: Cassell, 1960), p. 31.

16. Dean and Knapp, *Handel's Operas*, p. 517. I am grateful to Anthony Hicks for bringing this to my attention.

17. Ibid., p. 517.

18. Ibid., p. 561f.

Chapter 6

1. Arnold, *The Art of Accompaniment*, pp. 414-17; Donington, *Interpretation*, pp. 323-24.

2. Manfred Bukofzer, *Music in the Baroque Era* (New York: W.W. Norton, 1947), p. 323.

3. Handel, *Messiah*, H-G: 62-65. John Tobin, *Handel's "Messiah,"* p. 133.

4. NMA, X/2: 64-69. Mozart's orchestration of *Messiah* is not cited as evidence regarding Baroque performance practice.

5. Handel, *Alexander's Feast*, ed. Burrows, p. viii. Handel, *Athalia*, H-G: 142, 195, and 199.

6. Frederick Neumann, *Essays in Performance Practice* (Ann Arbor: UMI Research Press, 1982), p. 6.

7. C. P. E. Bach, *Essay on the True Art of Playing Keyboard Instruments*, trans. William J. Mitchell (New York: W.W. Norton, 1949), p. 313. Unless otherwise noted, the Mitchell translation of Bach's *Versuch* is quoted. Original: "Nichts destoweniger hat man mit Verwunderung angemerkt, dass einige Componisten, bey der Bezeichnung ihrer Grundstimmen, diese Progressionen im Einklange nicht allzeit andeuten. Man findet zuweilen Ziffern über den Bass gesesset, wo keine gegriffen werden sollen" (*Versuch*, Part Two, p. 172).

8. Bach, *Essay*, p. 314. Original: "Wenn also alle Stimmen eines Stückes im Einklange fortgehen: so ist nichts natürlicher, als dass auch der Accompanist diesem Einklange folget, und die Harmonie weglässet" (*Versuch*, Part Two, p. 174).

9. Arnold, *The Art of Accompaniment*, p. 416.

10. Bach, *Essay*, p. 314. I have found it necessary to revise the Mitchell translation in several places. He translates "sondern dadurch wohl gar einen besondern Glanz erhält" as "but attains its affect through the use of it." This is certainly an interpretation, rather than a translation; the use of "affect"—a specialized term in Baroque theory—is clearly not justified by Bach's text. Also, Mitchell uses the phrase "broken chords" in the first sentence; this can be confusing at first reading. Original:

[S]o giebet man auf die Melodie der Ripienstimmen genau Acht, ob sie so beschaffen ist, dass die nöthigsten Intervallen der Grundharmonie, besonders die Dissonanzen mit ihrer Auflösung, in der gebrochenen Harmonie darinnen berühret werden; ist dieses leztere, so bleibet man auch bey der Begleitung im Einklange. Wenn aber der die Hauptstimme begleitende Gedanke simpel ist, und nicht allein Harmonie verträget, sondern dadurch wohl gar einen besondern Glanz erhält: so wählt man die mehrstimmige Begleitung. (*Versuch*, Part Two, p. 174).

11. Bach, *Versuch*, Part Two, p. 323. Here again I have found it necessary to alter Mitchell's translation, p. 427, by substituting a more literal translation of the first clause. Original: "[M]üssen die Grundnoten eine Harmonie mit vielen und guten Bindungen bey sich haben, damit darüber eine sangbare Hauptstimme gebauet werden könne. Die Gänge, wobey viele Septimen- Quintquarten- Sextquinten- und Nonenaccorde vorkommen, sind besonders vorzüglich."

12. Bach, *Essay*, p. 428. Original:

    Die Bassthemata werden entweder von den übrigen Instrumenten im Einklange begleitet, oder blos von den Bässen allein ausgeführet. In jenem Falle lässet der Accompanist die Harmonie weg, und spielet seine vorgeschriebenen Noten ebenfalls in Octaven mit beyden Händen: wenn aber der Componist *aus guten Ursachen* Ziffern über den Bass gesetzt hat, weil die Bindungen, welche dabey angebracht werden können, gerne gehöret seyn wollen, und das Thema nicht allein nicht verdunkeln, sondern vielmehr erklären, so muss man sie mitspielen. Gewisse Themata sind so beschaffen, dass ein verständiger Zuhörer nur ein halbes Vergnügen spüret, wenn die Harmonie dazu fehlt, weil dieseletztere in der Vorstellung seiner Seele von den Tönen, die er höret, untrennbar ist. Die Orgel ist alsdenn, sowohl wegen der Bindungen, als auch wegen der durchdringenden Stärke zur Begleitung das vorzüglichste Instrument. Im zweyten Falle, welcher bey zweystimmigen Sing= und Spielsachen vorkommt, ist eine harmonische Begleitung nöthig. (*Versuch*, Part Two, p. 324)

13. The *Rodelinda* conducting score is discussed extensively in chap. 2.

14. Harvey P. Reddick, "Johann Mattheson's Forty-eight Thorough-bass Test-pieces: Translation and Commentary" (Ph.D. diss., The University of Michigan, 1956), 2: 26-27, 119-20. A modern facsimile edition of Mattheson's original treatise has been published by Georg Olms Verlag, Hildesheim, 1968.

15. NBA, I/1: 55f.

16. G. P. Telemann, *Musikalische Werke*, Vol. 18, Zwölf Pariser Quartette Nr. 1-6, ed. Walter Bergmann, pp. 49, 56.

17. However, in the Gerald Coke Collection there is a manuscript keyboard arrangement of this aria, probably contemporary with the composer, which contains some chordal filling-in of *unisono* passages.

Chapter 7

1. The term "secco" when applied to recitative has incorrect and slightly pejorative connotations; it is also unhistorical. The expression "secco recitative" was not used until the nineteenth century. See Edward Downes, "Secco Recitative in Early Classical Opera Seria," *Journal of the American Musicological Society* 14 (1961): 50f. In the present chapter, "plain recitative" and "simple recitative"—the usual eighteenth-century translations of *recitativo semplice*—will be used instead.

Notes for Chapter 7 251

2. C. P. E. Bach (*Versuch*, vol. 2, chap. 38, paragraph 6) allows the keyboardist to ignore incidental harmonic alterations, such as 8 7♭, in *recitativo accompagnato*. Arthur Mendel, in the preface to his vocal score of J. S. Bach's *St. John Passion* (New York: Schirmer, 1951), p. xxxii incorrectly applied this license to theatrical recitative as a whole.

3. Winton Dean, "A French Traveller's View," 172-78.

4. Ibid., pp. 174-75.

5. I am very grateful to Prof. J. Merrill Knapp for this information.

6. Some of these markings are contained in the H-G edition, pp. 118 and 119. Those not given by Chrysander are: 1) a staccato directive which should appear in H-G p. 120, m. 3, and 2) a sostenuto marking which should appear on p. 120, m. 10.

7. Fitzwilliam Museum, Handel Autograph Sketches and Fragments, 6 I 15, p. 61. The cantata was evidently part of a pasticcio titled "Oratorio," presented by Handel on 28 March 1738. For further particulars, see Dean, *Handel's Oratorios*, pp. 212, 224, 238-39, 261, and 269-70.

8. Francesco Gasparini, *The Practical Harmonist at the Harpsichord*, trans. Frank S. Stillings (New Haven: Yale School of Music, 1963), p. 78. The italics are my own, for emphasis. Original:

   Nei Recitativi si deve avere una particolare attenzione alla parte Composta, cioè alla parte, che canta. Si troverà spesse volte, che in una nota ferma del fondamento la parte farà una dissonanza, e movendosi per più, e diverse false tornerà in Consonanza, senza che il Basso mai si mova. Quando dunque la parte cominciando in Consonanza anderà a portarsi in una Seconda, si darà alla nota tutto in un tempo Seconda, Quarta, e Settima maggiore, e similmente se la parte anderà in una di queste false, cioè in Quarta, o Settima maggiore, non si darà una senza l'altra, sostenendo poi queste false fin che la parte risolvendosi vada in Consonanza, cioè in Terza, o in Quinta, o in Ottava. Se con queste false si unirà appresso la Quarta anche la Quinta, farà buon' effetto. (*L'Armonico pratico*, pp. 88-90)

9. In the illustrative musical example which follows the quotation, Gasparini uses the figuring $\begin{smallmatrix}7\\5\\4\\2\end{smallmatrix}$ $\begin{smallmatrix}8\\5\\3\end{smallmatrix}$ for this progression. This is an unusually complete figuring, probably used for pedagogical purposes. Heinichen (*Der General-Bass*, p. 256 f.) also allows the fifth to be added to the $\begin{smallmatrix}7\\4\\2\end{smallmatrix}$ chord, while the Johann Peter Kellner MS, "Rules . . . for Playing Thorough-Bass . . . by Herr Johann Sebastian Bach," clearly states: "With $\begin{smallmatrix}7\\2\end{smallmatrix}$ nothing else is played." See Philipp Spitta, *Johann Sebastian Bach* (London: Novello and Co., 1899), 3: 316).

10. Gasparini, *L'Armonico pratico*, p. 90. The original actually reads: ". . . queste Cantilene di Recicativi [*sic*]. . . ."

11. Gasparini, *The Practical Harmonist*, pp. 83-84. Compare Gasparini's accompaniment with Telemann's treatment of the same progression (ex. 7.6). Gasparini's original:

   [C]ome appunto io studiando ritrovai potersi fare in una falla un' acciaccatura raddoppiata con toccar quattordici tasti in un colpo; e sarà Ver. Gr. quando nel Recitativo si trova il passo di Settima maggiore. . . . Questo però serva più di bizzaria, che di esempio, o regola generale, potendosi qualche volta usare, ma distinguer tempo, luogo, e persone. Queste, e simili false, o durezze pare, che diano campo al buon Cantore di meglio esprimere gli affetti, e il buon gusto delle Composizioni. (*L'Armonico pratico*, pp. 96-97)

12. Gasparini, *The Practical Harmonist*, p. 80. Original: "[T]utte le note poste tra due linee, servono per un sol colpo, e si fanno tutte insieme" (*L'Armonico pratico*, p. 92).

13. Gasparini, *The Practical Harmonist*, p. 79. Original: "Per introdur gli accompagnamenti ne' Recitativi con qualche sorte di buon gusto si deve distender le Consonanze quasi arpeggiando, ma non di continuo; perche quando si è fatta sentire l' Armonia della nota, si deve tener fermi i tasti, e lasciar, che il Cantore si sodissi, e canti col suo comodo, e secondo, che porta l' espressiva delle parole." (*L'Armonico pratico*, p. 91).

14. Peter Williams, "Continuo," in *New Grove Dictionary of Music and Musicians*, 4: 694.

15. Reinhard Strom, *Essays on Handel and Italian Opera* (Cambridge: Cambridge University Press, 1985), pp. 84-85, 115.

16. Mendel, preface to *St. John Passion*, p. xvii.

17. Buelow, *Thorough-Bass Accompaniment*, pp. 22, 182-83, and 186.

18. Ibid., pp. 182-83, 186-87.

19. Ibid., pp. 182, 187.

20. Ibid., pp. 248-74.

21. George J. Buelow, "*Johann David Heinichen's Der General-Bass in der Composition*" (Ph.D. diss., New York University, 1961), p. 427. Original:
    "Wird der Sass des andern Tactes zwar im Recitativ auch von grossen Meistern vielfältig gebrauchet, jedoch will man ihn eben nicht vor allzu legal ausgeben, weil die über der ersten Bass-Note befindliche 5ta min. nothwendig über der folgenden resolviren muss, und also 2. verbothene 5ten machet. Zur Entschuldigung aber kan dienen, dass dieser 5ten-Fehler, 1) nicht in denen 2. componirten Stimmen erscheinet, 2) im Recitativ bey einem stillstehenden Basse und verschwindenden Clavicimbal-Tonenicht hervor ragend ist, und 3) durch einen vollstimmigen Griff, im Accompagnement leicht kan verdecket werden. (*Der General-Bass*, p. 953)

22. Nicolo Pasquali, *Thorough-Bass Made Easy* (Edinburgh, 1757; facs. ed., London: Oxford University Press, 1974), plate XXIV.

23. Ibid., pp. 47-48.

24. Williams, "Continuo," *New Grove*, 4: 697.

25. Unfortunately, the standard Mitchell translation of the *Versuch* has clouded the issue by an incorrect reading of the conclusion of paragraph three. (The mistranslated portion was not quoted here because it is irrelevant to the present discussion.) Mitchell's mistranslation gives the impression that the topic is *recitativo accompagnato*. The "new version" of Robert Donington's *Interpretation*, pp. 663-64, contains a correct interpretation of the passage.

26. Bach, *Essay*, pp. 421-22. I have altered one phrase of the Mitchell translation; "lange daurender Harmonie" has been changed from "sustained chords" to "long lasting harmonies." Original:
    3. Declamirt der letztere hurtig, so muss die Harmonie auf das bereiteste da seyn, besonders alsdenn, wenn sie bey den Absätzen der Hauptstimme vorgeschlagen werden muss. Der Anschlag einer neuen Harmonie muss auf das geschwindeste geschehen, so

bald die vorige Harmonie zu Ende ist. Hierdurch wird der Sänger in seinem Affecte, und in dem daher nöthigen geschwinden Vortrage niemals gestöhret, weil er bey Zeiten die Modulation und Beschaffenheit der Harmonie beständig voraus weiss. Wenn man unter zweyen Uebeln wählen müste, so würde hier das Eilen dem Schleppen vorzuziehen seyn. Doch besser ist allezeit besser. Bey der geschwimden Declamation muss sich der Accompagnist des Harpeggierens enthalten, zumal wenn sich die Harmonie oft ändert. Man hat hierzu keine Zeit, und wenn man sie auch hätte, so würde der Clavierist selbst, der Sänger und Zuhörer leicht dadurch in eine Verwirrung gerathen. Dieses Harpeggiren ist auch alsdenn unnöthig, weil es blos ausser diesem Falle, und bey langsamen Recitativen und lange daurender Harmonie gebrauchet wird, um den Sänger zu erinnern, dass er in derselben Harmonie bleiben soll, anstatt dass er widrigenfalls durch die Länge der Dauer gar leicht aus dem Tone kommen, oder in eine Veränderung der Harmonie gerathen könnte. . . .
4. Die Geschwindigkeit und Langsamkeit des Harpeggio bey der Begleitung hänget von der Zietmaasse und dem Inhalte des Recitatives ab. Je langsamer und affectuöser das letztere ist, desto langsamer harpeggirt man. Die Recitative mit aushaltenden begleitenden Instrumenten vertragen das Harpeggio besonders wohl. So bald aber die Begleitung, statt der Aushaltungen, kurze und abgestossene Noten krieget, sogleich schlägt auch der Clavierist die Harmonien, ohne Harpeggio, kurz und trotzig mit vollen Händen an. Wenn auch schon in diesem Falle weisse gebundene Noten da stehen solten, so bleibet man dennoch bey dem kurz abgestossenen Vortrag. (*Versuch*, Part Two, pp. 314-15).

27. Mendel, ed., *St. John Passion*, p. xviii; "On the Keyboard Accompaniments to Bach's Leipzig Church Music," *Musical Quarterly* 36: 339-62. See also NBA I/23: 84, 87, and 102-3.

28. *Bach's Continuo Group: Players and Practices in His Vocal Works* (Cambridge, Massachusetts: Harvard University Press, 1987), pp. 76-89.

29. "The Length of Bass Notes in J.S. Bach's Secco Recitatives," abstract of a paper delivered at the national meeting of the American Musicological Society, Denver, November 1980.

30. Georg Philipp Telemann, *Singe- Spiel- und Generalbass Übungen* (Hamburg, 1733-34; facs. ed., Kassel: Barenreiter Verlag, 1983), nos. 39-40.

31. E. g., Peter Williams, "Continuo," *The New Grove Dictionary of Musical Instruments* (Publishers Limited, 1984) 1: 489. Dreyfus, "The Length of Bass Notes," Table.

32. Telemann, *Generalbass-Übungen*, no. 41.

33. Frankfurt-am-Main, Staats und Universitäts Bibliothek, Ms ff Mus 807, 953, 1187, and 1474. All four cantatas have one or more scores and three continuo parts: cello, transposed organ, and untransposed organ. In all of these scores and parts the notation of the bass as simple recitative is consistent: quarter notes and rests.

34. Telemann, *Musikalische Werke*, vol. 20, ed. Bernd Baselt (Kassel: Barenreiter Verlag, 1967), p. xiv.

35. Mendel, ed., *St. John Passion*, p. xix.

36. Richard Petzoldt, *G. P. Telemann*, trans. Horace Fitzpatrick (New York: Oxford University Press, 1974), p. 174.

37. Williams, "Continuo," in *New Grove*, 4: 697. Williams does not give examples of works in which the recitative is varied in this way. For a fuller discussion, see Williams, "Basso Continuo on the Organ," Part II, *Music and Letters* 50 (1969), 239-40. Examples include:

BWV 30, "Freue dich, erlöste Schar," and BWV 30a, "Angenehmes Wiederau." In both cases one recitative is written with quarter notes and rests in the continuo, while the others have the conventional notation.

38. Gasparini, *The Practical Harmonist*, p. 79. Original: "[E] non infastidirlo, o disturbarlo con un continuo arpeggio, o tirate di passaggi in sù, e in giù, come fanno alcuni" (*L'Armonico pratico*, p. 91).

39. Telemann, *Generalbass-Übungen*, no. 41. Original: "Alles lauf-werk u. alle manierchens müssen beÿm recitatif-spielen nachbleiben."

40. Bach, *Essay*, p. 422. Original: "Ausser der gebrochnen Harmonie brauchet man auch auf den übrigen Clavierinstrumenten zu der Begleitung der Recitative keine andere Manier und Zierlichkeit" (*Versuch*, Part 2, p. 316).

41. Bach, *Essay*, pp. 421, 423.

42. Ibid., pp. 422-24.

43. J. J. Quantz, *Versuch einer Anweisung die Flöte traversiere zu spielen* (Berlin, 1752; reprint, Kassell: Bärenreiter, 1953), tab. 23, fig. 5.

44. J. J. Quantz, *On Playing the Flute*, trans. Edward Reilly (New York: Free Press, 1966), p. 265. Original:
Bey einem Recitativ so auswendig gesungen wird, geschieht dem Sänger eine grose Erleichterung, wenn der Accompanist die ersten Töne desselben bey einem jeden Einschnitte voraus nimmt, und ihm, so zu sagen, in den Mund leget; indem er nämlich erstlich den Accord durch eine geschwinde Brechung anschlägt, doch so, dass des Sängers erste Note, wo möglich, in der obersten Stimme liege; und gleich darauf ein Paar der nächsten Intervalle, die in der Singstimme vorkommen, einzeln nachschlägt; s. Tab XXIII. Fig. 5. Dieses kömmt dem Sänger, so wohl wegen des Gedächtnisses, als auch wegen der Intonation, sehr zu statten. (*Versuch*, p. 238)

45. *Proceedings of the Royal Musical Association*, Twelfth Session (1885-86): 40.

46. Pasquali, *Thorough-Bass*, plates 27 and 28.

47. Ibid., p. iv.

48. Heinichen, *Der General-Bass*, pp. 776, 772, 778, and 656.

49. John Mayo, "Einige Kantatenrevisionen Händels," *Händel-Jahrbuch*, 1981, pp. 63-75.

50. Bach, *Essay*, p. 422.

51. Jack Allan Westrup, "The Cadence in Baroque Recitative," *Natalicia Musicologica Knud Jeppesen*, ed. Bjørn Hjelmborg and Søren Sørensen (Copenhagen: Wilhelm Hansen, 1962), pp. 243-52.

52. Sven Hostrup Hansell, "The Cadence in 18th-Century Recitative," *Musical Quarterly* 54 (April 1968): 246-47.

53. Heinichen, *Der General-Bass*, p. 674.

54. E. g., Winton Dean, "The Performance of Recitative in Late Baroque Opera," *Music and Letters* 58 (October 1977): 396.

55. Quantz, *Playing the Flute*, p. 292. Original: "Dieser muss überhaupt bey allen Cadenzen des theatralischen Recitativs, es mag ein mit Violinen begleites, oder nur ein gemeines seyn, seine zwo Noten, welche mehrenteils aus einem fallenden Quintensprunge bestehen,

unter der letzten Sylbe anfangen, und nicht zu langsam, sondern mit Lebhaftigkeit anschlagen" (*Versuch*, p. 272).

56. This is demonstrably true in the second case and highly likely in the first. The second reference is illustrated with a musical example which is obviously accompanied recitative (Quantz, *Playing the Flute*, p. 293). The first reference includes a description of a type of passage which is more characteristic of accompanied than plain recitative: "[T]he accompanying parts enter only at the caesuras, when the singer has completed a phrase." (Original: "[D]ie begleitenden Stimmen fallen . . . bey den Einschnitten, wenn der Sänger eine Periode geendiget hat.") Also, immediately following the first reference there is a qualification drawn from accompanied recitative: "If, however, the violins have a short rest instead of a note on the downbeat. . . ." ("Sofern aber die Violinen anstatt der Note im Niederschlage eine kurze Pause haben. . . .")

57. Dean, "Performance of Recitative," p. 398.

58. Heinichen, *Der General-Bass*, p. 824; Telemann, *Generalbass-Übungen*, no. 40; Pasquali, *Thorough-Bass*, plates 24, 27, and 28. Pasquali's *realizations* of recitative cadences in his book are consistently delayed.

59. E. g., H-G 51: 69, 143. The former is an unusually lyrical cadence; perhaps the appoggiatura was not intended. Several examples can be found in the Flower cembalo part of *Samson* (Manchester Public Library, Newman Flower Collection, MS. 130 Hd4 v. 275). Examples abound in the works of Alessandro Scarlatti; see Edward Dent, *Alessandro Scarlatti* (London: E. Arnold, New Impression, 1960), pp. 78, 100, and 140.

60. Arnold, *The Art of Accompaniment*, p. 421f.; Donington, *Interpretation*, pp. 315-19.

61. Heinichen, *Der General-Bass*, pp. 672-74. References to "die bekante Cadenz": pp. 730, 826, and 832; to "die gewöhnliche Cadenz:" pp. 808, 821, 825, 827, and 828.

62. Ibid., p. 716.

63. Ibid., p. 824. Cf. the recitative cadence on p. 699.

64. Hansell, "18th-Century Recitative," p. 229.

65. Gasparini, *The Practical Harmonist*, p. 82.

66. Hansell, "18th-Century Recitative," p. 230.

67. Buelow, *Thorough-Bass Accompaniment*, pp. 182, 186-87. Peter Williams, "The Harpsichord Acciaccatura," *Musical Quarterly* 54 (October 1968): 503f.

68. Hansell, "18th-Century Recitative," p. 246.

Chapter 8

1. Donington, *Interpretation*, p. 323.

2. Williams, *Figured Bass Accompaniment*, 2: 85.

3. Williams, "Basso Continuo on the Organ," part 2, *Music and Letters* 50 (1969): 238.

4. Bach, *Essay*, p. 188.

5. An example from *E partirai, mia vita?* is given below.

6. John Mayo, "Einige Kantatenrevisionen Händels," *Händel-Jahrbuch* 27: 63–77. See above, pp. 7f and 22.

7. Bach, *Essay*, p. 188.

8. H-G 50: 85.

9. HHA Supplement/1: 25, 30, 34, and 35.

10. See C. P. E. Bach, *Essay*, p. 418. Original: "Das Vorschlagen mit der Harmonie in der rechten Hand zu kurzen Pausen in der Grundstimme ist oft notwendig, die Ordnung zu erhalten und eine gute Ausnahme zu befördern" (*Versuch*, Part Two, p. 309).

11. Gasparini, *The Practical Harmonist*, p. 31. Original: "Quando vi è la pausa di un sexdecimo [*sic*], o sedicesimo, o quarto di sospiro, in quel tempo si battono le Consonanze della prima nota con la mano destra, e con la sinistra si passano, e fa buon effetto" (*L'Armonico pratico*, pp. 36–37).

12. Heinichen, *Der General-Bass*, pp. 383, 384, 388, 390, 391, 394, 395, 399, 401, 406, 407, 411, 413, 414, etc.

13. Reddick, "Mattheson's Test-Pieces," 2: 40–41. Original:
    Hernach ist auch zu erinnern/ dass die rechte Hand nothwendig vorshlagen muss/ wenn in der fünfften Zeile zu Anfang der Mensur/ eine Sechzehn = Theil = Pause steht: weil sonst der leere Raum dem Gehör zuwider/ als welches vornehmlich wünschet/ das alles fein ordentlich aneinanderhange/ erfüllet/ und nicht zerrissen werde. Durchgehends kann im accompagniren/ ausser wenigen Vorfällen/ wo man des Verfassers Meynung ansehen muss/ dieser*) Vorschlag bey dergleichen kurzen Pausen gebraucht werden.
    *) Allhier, und in der Harmonie, bedeutet das Wort *Vorschlag*, musicalisch genommen, ganz was anders, als in der Melodie, wie ein jeder aus der obigen Beschreibung abnehmen kann. (*Grosse General-Bass-Schule*, pp. 236–37)

14. Reddick, "Mattheson's Test-Pieces," 2: 68–69. Original:
    [I]st nothwendig zu erinnern/ dass/ da dieser Styl allezeit Bindungen und Rückungen erfordert/ auch darauf mit der rechten Hand müsse gesehen/ und Z. E. die über der ersten Note stehende 5/ oder der Accord/ nicht zu derselben sondern zur Pause vorher/ geschlagen werden/ die darauf folgende Bass-Note/ b/ schlägt sodann allein/ und die Beziefferung der 6. und 4. hernach; kurz/ die Hände schlagen eine um die andere an allen Orten/ wo die Zieffern nicht gerade über den Noten stehen. (*Grosse General-Bass-Schule*, pp. 260–61)

15. Reddick, "Mattheson's Test-Pieces," 2: 125. Original: "Im zehnten und folgenden Tact schlägt die rechte Hand allemahl vor/ wo die Pause stehet/ solches giebt eine gar angenehme Brechung" (*Grosse General-Bass-Schule*, p. 319).

16. Arnold, *The Art of Accompaniment*, p. 444.

17. Reddick, "Mattheson's Test-Pieces," 2: 209. Original:
    Die ersten zween Täcte nun sähe man gerne ganz schlecht gespielet/ so/ dass der Haupt-Sass vernehmlich heraus käme/ zu Folge dem in der Natur und Vernunfft gegründeten Ausspruch: *Dass aller Anfang einfach/ schlecht und deutlich seyn muss*. Durch das schlechte Spielen wird hauptsächlich verlanget/ dass zu jeden sechs Noten in besagten Täcten nur einmahl mit der rechten Hand vor-und zugeschlagen werde/ wobey erinnerlich seyn mag/ dass der Vorschlag die Pause angehet. (*Grosse General-Bass-Schule*, p. 403)

18. Reddick, "Mattheson's Test-Pieces," 2: 61. Original: "Wenn aber in den letzten Zeilen dieses Exempels/ oder sonstwo/ das Achtel zum Pausen häuffig vorkommt/ so muss derjenige Accord/ oder diejenige Signatur/ welche zur nächsten Note gehöret/ zum Voraus/ bey währender Pause/ mit der rechten Hand angeschlagen werden" (*Grosse General-Bass-Schule*, p. 253).

19. Reddick, "Mattheson's Test-Pieces," 1: 9, 24–28, and 2: 124.

20. Mattheson, *Grosse General-Bass-Schule*, pp. 308, 316.

21. Telemann, *General-Bass Übungen*, no. 12. The translations from the Telemann treatise are mine. Original: "Dergleichen anschlagen über pausen ist alsdann sehr gut, wan es, wie hier, das gewicht des tactes zu unterhalten abzielet."

22. Ibid., no. 21. Original: "Durch den ersten theil dieser aria findet man oben beÿ den pausen eine gleiche bewegung mit dem basse, beÿ (a), hingegen eine andere; die letztere ist beÿ zärtlichen ausdrückungen u. zu unterhaltung des tactes die beste."

23. Ibid., no. 47. Original: "Dass auch beÿ pausen angeschlagen werde, zeigen (d) (e) (f); es ist aber behutsam am dabeÿ zu verfahren, wann sie nicht beziefert sind: denn bisweilen wird die pause mit der vorhergehenden note gebunden (d); oft aber gehöret sie zur harmonie der folgenden (e) (f)."

24. Ibid., nos. 45 and 46.

25. Arnold, *The Art of Accompaniment*, pp. 417–21.

26. Bach, *Essay*, pp. 418–20.

Chapter 9

1. Donington, *Interpretation*, p. 324. The last set of italics is my own, for emphasis.

2. Williams, *Figured Bass Accompaniment*, 1: 52.

3. Ibid., Original: "Man beziffert die Orgelpunkte nicht leicht, sondern fertige sie mit dem *tasto solo* ab. Wer sie beziffert, muss sich gefallen lassen, dass man sie dem ohngeacht *tasto solo* spielet" (*Versuch*, Zweiter Teil, p. 20).

4. Williams, "Basso Continuo," p. 240.

5. Arnold, *The Art of Accompaniment*, pp. 798–801.

6. H-G: 92f.

7. H-G: 60f.

8. G. P. Telemann, *Singe-, Spiel- und Generalbase Übungen*, no. 14. Original:
   Die liegenden bässe, da inzwischen die obere stimme moduliret, welche bisweilen die creuz u. die quere durch die harmonischen creÿse gehet, werden selten beziefert; u. da thut man am besten, wenn man die rechte hand gar ruhen lässt, u. mit der linken nur dann u. wann den untern ton angiebt, mithin das völlige aushalten etwa dem Violoncell überlässt. Hier aber, beÿ einer partitur, haben wir zuvörderst getrachtet, das gewicht zu unterhalten; also schlagen wir oben immer im auf= u. nieder= tacte an, welches auch im basse geschehen mag, wan er nicht auf pfeif=werken gespielet wird, da er aushält. Im solcher obigen absicht lassen wir etliche neben= figuren unberüret, als beÿ (a) (b) (c) (d).

Notes for Chapter 9

9. Heinichen, *Der General-Bass*, pp. 392, 403, 414, 425, 436-37, 447-48, 459, 470-71, 482-83, and 506-7.

10. Heinichen, *Der General-Bass*, p. 948. Original:
    Unter dergleichen beständig liegende *Bass-Claves*, worüber die obern Stimmen so mancherley *Syncopationes* machen, wie wir hier zum nüsslichen *Exercitio* mit lauter gebräuchlichen Sässen gethan, schreibet man sonst gern ein: *Tasto solo*, und lässet alle Ziffern weg, zum Zeichen, dass der *Accompagnist* nur den *Bass-Clavem* alleine solle halten, ohne einziges *Accompagnement*, bis die *Harmonie* weiter gehet.

11. Bach, *Essay*, p. 286. First set of italics mine. Original:
    Wir werden weiter unten davon besonders handeln, und melden hier nur zum Voraus denen zum Trost, welchen die Bezifferung davon zu fürchterlich vorkommt, dass die rechte Hand bey diesen Orgelpuncten zu ruhen pflegt, und dass man sie daher nicht beziffert, sondern bloss *tasto solo* darüber setzet. Hier ist die Vorbildung der Ziffern nöthig, um die Fortschreitungen der Stimmen, und die Veränderungen der Harmonie anzuzeigen. (*Versuch*, Part Two, p. 138)

12. Bach, *Essay*, pp. 319-20. Original:
    4. Man beziffert die Orgelpunkte nicht leicht, sondern fertige sie mit dem *tasto solo* ab. Wer sie beziffert, muss sich gefallen lassen, das man sie dem ohngeacht *tasto solo* spielet. Es ist hieran nicht allein eine **sehr nöthige** Bequemlichkeit, sondern oft die **Unmöglichkeit** Schuld: und gesesset, man könnte alle Orgelpunkte mit der rechten hand begleiten: so würde doch der Dank dafür lange noch nicht so gross seyn, wie die Angst und Mühe, die es manchem dabey kostet.
    5. Bey dem t. s. in den Orgelpunkten hat das Auge nicht nöthig, so viele übereinander gethürmte Ziffern und ungewöhnliche Aufgaben zu übersehen. Oft ist die Einrichtung der Harmonie so beschaffen, dass eine Stimme die andere übersteigt, welches eine Verwechslung der Stimmen im Generalbasse veranlassen kann, die deswegen nicht erlaubt ist, weil man sonst dadurch viele Fehler vertheidigen könnte, ohne dass dem ohngeacht das Ohr zufrieden wäre; man müste also bey diesem Falle, wenn die rechte Hand nicht zu tief herunter kommen sollte, den ganzen Orgelpunkt wegen der richtigen Vorbereitung und Auflösung im getheilten Accompagnement der Harmonie so geschwinde hintereinander, dass sie beynahe nicht heraus zu bringen sind, wenn man sie auch mitspielen wollte. (*Versuch*, Part Two, p. 182-83)

13. Bach, *Essay*, p. 320. Original: "Folgende Exempel, wobey die Ziffern gesetzet sind, um von der Einrichtung der Harmonie einen deutlichen Begriff zu geben" (*Versuch*, Part Two, p. 183).

Bibliography

Collected Editions

G. F. Händel's Werke. Leipzig, 1858–94. Reprint. Ridgewood, N. J.: Gregg Press, 1965.
Hallische Händel-Ausgabe. Kassell: Bärenreiter, 1955–.
Neue Bach-Ausgabe. Kassell: Bärenreiter, 1954–.
W. A. Mozart: Neue Ausgabe Sämtlicher Werke. Kassell:Bärenreiter, 1955–.
Telemann, Georg Philipp. *Musikalische Werke.* Kassell: Bärenreiter, 1950–.

Eighteenth-Century Sources

Handel Autographs and Scribal Copies:

Royal Music Library Collection and Department of Manuscripts, British Library, London.
Royal College of Music, London.
Autograph Sketches and Fragments, Fitzwilliam Museum, Cambridge.
Newman Flower Collection, Manchester Public Library.
Conducting Scores, Carl von Ossietzky Staats- und Universitäts-Bibliothek, Hamburg.

First Editions of Handel Operas

Radamisto. London: Meares, 1720.
Floridante. London: Walsh, 1722.
Ottone. London: Walsh, 1723.
Flavio. London: Walsh, 1723.
Giulio Cesare. London: Cluer, 1724.
Tamerlano. London: Cluer, 1724.
Rodelinda. London: Cluer, 1725.
Scipione. London: Cluer, 1726.
Alessandro. London: Cluer, 1726.
Admeto. London: Cluer, 1727.
Riccardo Primo. London: Cluer, 1728.

Thoroughbass Treatises

Bach, Carl Philipp Emanuel. *Versuch über das wahre Art das Clavier zu spielen.* Berlin, 1753/ 1762; reprint, Wiesbaden: Breitkopf und Härtel, 1981. Trans. William J. Mitchell as *Essay on the True Art of Playing Keyboard Instruments.* New York: W. W. Norton, 1949.

Gasparini, Francesco. *L'Armonico pratico al cimbalo*. Venice, 1708. Reprint. New York: Broude Brothers, 1967. Trans. Frank S. Stillings as *The Practical Harmonist at the Keyboard*. New Haven: Yale School of Music, 1963.

Heinichen, Johann David. *Der General-Bass in der Composition*. Dresden, 1728. Reprint. Hildesheim: Georg Olms Verlag, 1969.

Mattheson, Johann. *Grosse General-Bass Schule*. Hamburg, 1731. Reprint. Hildesheim: Georg Olms Verlag, 1968.

Pasquali, Nicolo. *Thorough-Bass Made Easy*. Edinburgh, 1757. Reprint. Oxford: Oxford University Press, 1974.

Quantz, Johann Joachim. *Versuch einer Anweisung die Flöte traversiere zu spielen*. Berlin, 1752. Reprint. Kassell: Bärenreiter, 1953. Trans. Edward Reilly as *On Playing the Flute*. New York: Free Press, 1966.

Telemann, Georg Philipp. *Singe-Spiel und Generalbass Übungen*. Hamburg, 1733-34. Reprint. Kassell: Bärenreiter, 1983.

Twentieth-Century Sources

Arnold, Frank Thomas. *The Art of Accompaniment from a Thorough-Bass*. London: Oxford University Press, 1931.

Baselt, Bernd. *Händel-Handbuch*. 4 vols. to date. Kassel: Barenreiter, 1978-86.

Best, Terence. "Further Studies on Handel's Solo Sonatas." *Händel-Jahrbuch* (1984): 75.

Buelow, George. *Thorough-Bass Accompaniment according to Johann David Heinichen*. Rev. ed. Ann Arbor: UMI Research Press, 1986.

───. "Johann David Heinichen's *Der General-Bass in der Komposition*." Ph.D. diss., New York University, 1961.

Bukofzer, Manfred. *Music in the Baroque Era*. New York: W. W. Norton, 1947.

Burrows, Donald. "Sources, Resources and Handel Studies." In *Handel: Tercentenary Collection*, ed. Stanley Sadie and Anthony Hicks. Ann Arbor: UMI Research Press, 1987.

───. "The Autographs and Early Copies of *Messiah*." *Music and Letters* 66 (July 1985): 201.

───. "Paper Studies and Handel's Autographs." *Göttinger Händel Beiträge* 1 (1984): 103.

───. "The Composition and First Performance of Handel's *Alexander's Feast*." *Music and Letters* 64 (July-October 1983): 206.

───. "Walsh's editions of Handel's Opera 1-5: the texts and their sources." In *Music in Eighteenth-Century England*, ed. Christopher Hogwood and Richard Luckett. Cambridge: Cambridge University Press, 1982.

───, ed. *Alexander's Feast*, by G. F. Handel. Sevenoaks, Kent: Novello, 1982.

───. "Sources for Oxford Handel Performances." *Music and Letters* 61 (April 1980): 177.

Clausen, Hans Dieter. *Händels Direktionspartituren*. Hamburg: Karl Dieter Wagner, 1972.

Collins, Michael. "Cadential Structures and Accompanimental Practices in 18th-Century Italian Recitative." In *Opera & Vivaldi*, ed. Michael Collins and Elise K. Kirk. Austin: University of Texas Press, 1984.

Cooper, Barry. "The Organ Parts to Handel's *Alexander's Feast*." *Music and Letters* 59 (April 1978): 159.

Dean, Winton. "Handel's Early London Copyists." In *Bach, Handel, Scarlatti: Tercentenary Essays*, ed. Peter Williams. Cambridge University Press, 1985.

───. "Händels kompositorische Entwicklung in den Opern in der Jahre 1724/1725." *Händel-Jahrbuch* (1982): 23.

───. "The Performance of Recitative in Late Baroque Opera." *Music and Letters* 58 (October 1977): 389.

───. "Handel's *Sosarme*, a Puzzle Opera." In *Essays on Opera and English Music in Honour of Sir Jack Westrup*. Oxford: B. Blackwell, 1975; pp. 115-47.

———. "A French Traveller's View of Handel's Operas." *Music and Letters* 55 (April 1974): 172.
———. *Handel's Dramatic Oratorios and Masques*. London: Oxford University Press, 1959.
Dean, Winton, and J. Merrill Knapp. *Handel's Operas 1704-1726*. Oxford: Clarendon Press, 1987.
Dent, Edward J. *Alessandro Scarlatti*. London: E. Arnold, New Impression, 1960.
Deutsch, Otto Erich. *Handel: a Documentary Biography*. London: A. & C. Black, 1955.
Donington, Robert. *The Interpretation of Early Music*. New Version. London: Faber and Faber, 1975.
Downes, Edward. "Secco Recitative in Early Classical Opera Seria," *Journal of the American Musicological Society*, 14 (1961): 50.
Dreyfus, Laurence. "The Length of Bass Notes in J. S. Bach's Secco Recitatives." Paper delivered at the national meeting of the American Musicological Society. Denver, November 1980.
———. *Bach's Continuo Group: Players and Practices in His Vocal Works*. Cambridge, Massachusetts: Harvard University Press, 1987.
Fuller-Maitland, J. A., and A. H. Mann. *Catalogue of the Music in the Fitzwilliam Museum, Cambridge*. London, 1893.
Hansell, Sven Hostrup. "The Cadence in 18th-Century Recitative." *Musical Quarterly* 54 (April 1968): 228.
Hicks, Anthony. "Handel, Jennens and *Saul*: Aspects of a Collaboration." In *Music and Theatre: Essays in Honour of Winton Dean*, ed. Nigel Fortune. Cambridge University Press, 1987.
Humphries, Charles and William C. Smith. *Music Publishing in the British Isles*. New York: Barnes and Noble, 1970.
King, A. Hyatt. *Handel and his Autographs*. London: British Museum, 1967.
Knapp. J. Merrill. "The Hall Handel Collection." *Princeton University Library Chronicle* 36 (1974): 3.
Larsen, Jens Peter. *Handel's "Messiah": Origins, Composition, Sources*. 2d ed. New York: W. W. Norton, 1972.
Lenneberg, H., and L. Libin. "Unknown Handel Sources in Chicago." *Journal of the American Musicological Society* 22 (1969): 85.
Macfarren, Sir George. [Description of Handel's Recitative Accompaniment.] *Proceedings of the Royal Musical Association*, Twelfth Session (1885-86): 40.
Mann, Alfred. *Theory and Practice: The Great Composer as Student and Teacher*. New York: W.W. Norton & Co., 1987.
———. "Bach and Handel as Teachers of Thorough-Bass." In *Bach, Handel, Scarlatti: Tercentenary Essays*, ed. Peter Williams. Cambridge: Cambridge University Press, 1985.
———. *Aufzeichnungen zur Kompositionslehre*, HHA Supplement/1.
———. "Eine Kompositionslehre von Händel." *Händel-Jahrbuch* (1964/65): 35.
Mayo, John. "Handel's Italian Cantatas." Ph.D. diss., University of Toronto, 1977.
Mendel, Arthur, ed. *St. John Passion*, by J. S. Bach. New York: Schirmer, 1951.
Neumann, Frederick. *Essays in Performance Practice*. Ann Arbor: UMI Research Press, 1982.
Petzoldt, Richard. *G. P. Telemann*. New York: Oxford University Press, 1974.
Reddick, Harvey. "Johann Mattheson's 48 Thorough-Bass Test-Pieces: Translation and Commentary." Ph.D. diss., The University of Michigan, 1956.
Roberts, John H. "Handel and Charles Jennens's Italian Opera Manuscripts." In *Music and Theatre: Essays in Honour of Winton Dean*, ed. Nigel Fortune. Cambridge: Cambridge University Press, 1987.
Ronish, Martha. "Continuo Groupings in the Handel Autographs." Paper delivered at the Maryland Handel Festival. College Park, Maryland, 9 November 1984.

Shaw, Watkins. *A Textual and Historical Companion to Handel's "Messiah."* London: Novello, 1965.
Smith, William C. *Handel: a Descriptive Catalogue of the Early Editions.* London: Cassell, 1960.
Spitta, Philipp. *Johann Sebastian Bach.* London: Novello, 1899.
Squire, W. Barclay. *Catalogue of the King's Music Library.* Vol. 1, *Handel Manuscripts.* London: British Museum, 1927.
Strom, Reinhard. *Essays on Handel and Italian Opera.* Cambridge: Cambridge University Press, 1985.
Stutzenberger, David Ray. "*Belshazzar*, an Oratorio by G. F. Handel." 2 vols. Ph.D. diss., University of Maryland, 1980.
Tobin, John. *Handel's "Messiah."* New York: St. Martin's Press, 1969.
_____ . *Handel at Work.* London, 1964.
Walker, Arthur D. *George Frideric Handel: the Newman Flower Collection.* The Manchester Public Libraries, 1972. Foreword by Winton Dean.
Westrup, Jack Allan. "Recitative." In *The New Grove Dictionary of Music and Musicians*, vol. 4, 1980.
_____ . "The Cadence in Baroque Recitative." In *Natalicia Musicologica Knud Jeppesen.* Ed. Bjørn Hjelmborg and Søren Sørensen. Copenhagen: Wilhelm Hansen, 1962, p. 243.
Williams, Peter. "Continuo." In *The New Grove Dictionary of Musical Instruments*, and in *The New Grove Dictionary of Music and Musicians*, vol. 4, 1980.
_____ . *Figured Bass Accompaniment.* 2 vols. Edinburgh: Edinburgh University Press, 1970.
_____ . "Basso Continuo on the Organ." *Music and Letters* 50 (1969): 136, 230.
_____ . "The Harpsichord Acciaccatura." *Musical Quarterly* 54 (October 1968): 503.

Index

Acis and Galatea: complete printed edition of, 85; figuring in the autograph of, 14, 21; foreshortened cadences not required for, 135; unfigured aria in the autograph of, 21; *unisono* texture for dramatic effect in, 108

Admeto: Chrysander's treatment of figuring in, 43; figuring in the Newman Flower keyboard part for, 61; figuring in manuscript copies of, 16; performance of, as described by Fougeroux, 110–11; Royal Academy print of, 88; supplementary figuring in various sources for, 66–67, 69, 70–76, 105

Agrippina: figuring in the autograph of, 14; figuring in the Newman Flower keyboard part for, 61; sparse figuring for *unisono* passages in, 105; suggested harmonization of an excerpt from, 184; supplementary figuring in the Aylesford full score of, 66; unfigured continuo arias in the autograph of, 20

Ah, crudel nel pianto mio: sparse figuring for *unisono* passages in, 105

Alcestis: figuring in the autograph of, 15

Alcina: two cembalo parts for, in the Newman Flower Collection, 61; discarded figurings in, 35; figuring in the autograph of, 17

Alessandro Severo: Cembalopartitur for, 54; Cluer print of, 47; Royal Academy print of, 88

Alexander's Feast: Chrysander's treatment of figuring in, 43; complete printed edition of, 85; continuo parts for, used under the composer's direction, 53; figuring from the Walsh edition of, 2; figuring in the harpsichord part for, 55–56, 57–58, 61; figuring in the Newman Flower keyboard continuo part for, 63; figuring in the organ continuo part for, 56, 58–59, foreshortened cadences not required for, 135; *organo tasto solo* markings in, 96–97; problems in the figuring of, 8

L'Allegro: cembalo tasto solo marking in, 97; delayed or semidelayed cadence in, 136; discarded figurings in, 35; figuring in the autograph of, 14, 16; sparse figuring for *unisono* passage in, 105; *tasto solo* in, 97

Amadigi: incomplete figuring in the autograph of, 38; Knapp's edition of, 2

Ameln, Konrad: and the figuring in *Alexander's Feast,* 2

Anne, Princess (of England): and Handel's pedagogical cantatas, 22, 23

Arianna: Hamburg *Cembalopartitur* for, 54

Ariodante: two cembalo parts for, in the Newman Flower Collection, 61; Hamburg *Cembalopartitur* for, 54

Arminio: discarded figurings in, 35; Handel's repeated figurings for recitatives in, 134

Arnold, Frank Thomas: on accompaniment over a pedal point, 155–56; *The Art of Accompaniment from a Thorough-Bass,* 5–6

"As Pants the Hart": discarded figurings in, 35; figuring in the autograph of, 15

Atalanta: figuring in the autograph of, 15; Handel's repeated figures for recitative in, 134

Athalia: discarded figurings in, 35; figuring in the autograph of, 14, 15, 16, 17; *organo tasto solo* markings in, 96–97, 156; pedal points in, 156, 160; sparse figuring for *unisono* passages in, 105

Autograph Sketches and Fragments, Fitzwilliam Museum, Cambridge: discarded figurings in, 35; Handel's thoroughbass exercises in, 4, 15, 16, 21, 144; Handel's works in, 14, 24, 112; Hendrie's use of, 2

Autographs, Handel's (composition scores): bass figuring in, 14–41; discarded figurings in, 34–38; frequently-used figurings in, 14; inconsistency of figuring in, 14; Jennens and, 78–81; obsolete figures in, 25, 29–34; signifi-

cant amounts of figuring in, 14–15; small amounts of figuring in, 2, 3, 14; and sustained chords for recitatives, 111–12
Aylesford Collection
—Jennens and, 3, 78–81
—keyboard parts in, 61–64, 197–210; Dean on, 62; differences from full scores, 62; format of, 61; location of, 61
—as sources containing supplementary figures, 81
—vocal and instrumental parts in, 3

Bach, Carl Philipp Emanuel, *Versuch über das wahre Art das Clavier zu spielen:* on accompaniment for recitatives, 117, 119, 123, 134; on accompaniment over pedal points, 155–56, 157–59; on figures that may be ignored, 251n.2; on rests in the continuo line, 141, 147, 148, 152–53; on *unisono* passages, 97–100
Bach, Johann Sebastian: and the accompaniment of recitative, 110, 119, 120; and bass themes, 100; figuring in works by, 3; *Nun komm, der Heiden Heiland,* 105–6; *St. John Passion,* 119, 156; *St. Matthew Passion,* 119; *Schwingt freudig euch empor,* 41
Bass line, realization of figures over rests in, 141–53; C. P. E. Bach on, 141, 147, 148, 152–53; Donington on, 141; Gasparini on, 147–48; Handel's practice in, 142–47; Heinichen on, 147; Mattheson on, 147, 148–51; Telemann on, 151–52; Williams on, 141–42. *See also Unisono* textures: bass themes and
Bates, Joah: recollections of, 126
Belshazzar: discarded figurings in, 29; Handel's revisions in the autograph of, 27; obsolete figurings in, 35; retrospective figuring in the autograph of, 38, 41; *unisono* theme in, 107
Berenice: Handel's repeated figures for recitatives in, 134
Best, Terence: editorial practice of, 2–3; on the work of scribes, 65
La bianca rosa: delayed or semidelayed cadences in, 136
British Library Add. 38002: source for *Admeto,* 69
British Library, London. *See* Royal Music Library Collection
Buelow, George: *Thorough-Bass Accompaniment according to Johann David Heinichen,* 6
Bukofzer, Manfred: on accompaniment for *unisono* passages, 96
Burrows, Donald: on Handel's relationship to Walsh, 83; on the Newman Flower vocal parts for *Messiah,* 247n.12; on R. M. 19. a. 10., 56

Cadences
—delayed: vs. foreshortened, 134–37; in some operatic recitatives, 136; Pasquali on, 255n.58
—foreshortened: vs. delayed, 134–37; harmonization of, 137–40, 255n.59; in opera, 135–37; in oratorios, 135. *See also* Recitative, thoroughbass realization for: foreshortened cadences
—semidelayed, 135–36
Caporale, Andrea (cellist), 56
Cecilia, "Volgi un sguardo": proper treatment of rests in the bass line of, 146
Cembalopartituren (harpsichord scores): collection of, in Hamburg, 53–55
Chandos Anthems: Hendrie's edition of, 2; figuring in the autograph of, 14
Chrysander, Friedrich: and editorial procedures concerning figures, 2, 43–45; on figures in *Jephtha,* 25, 29; on figuring in the conducting score of *Rodelinda,* 44–45; and problems of Handel's figuring, 23–25; on Handel's *Cembalopartituren,* 53–55; and treatment of rests in the continuo line, 142, 143; on *unisono* passages, 96
Churchill, John: on the reliability of Pasquali's directives, 126
Clausen, Hans Dieter: on Handel's *Cembalopartituren,* 54–55, 247n.3; on Handel's conducting scores, 43
Cluer: instrumental movements in editions of operas by, 47; orchestral accompaniments in editions by, 88; becomes the regular publisher for Handel, 90
Cluer and Creake: printed edition of *Rodelinda* by, 47–51
Composition, Handel's method of, 23–29; and figuring in autographs, 4, 16–20. *See also* Autographs, Handel's
Concerti, Op. 4: Walsh edition of, 84
Concerti Grossi, Op. 6: discarded figurings in, 15; figuring in the autograph of, 14, 15, 29, 41; obsolete figures in, 30
Concerto, Op. 4, No. 6: continuo part for, 56
Concerto Grosso, Op. 6. No. 3: incompatible figures in the autograph of, 41; *unisono* passages in, 105
Concerto Grosso, Op. 6, No. 6: obsolete figures in, 29
Concerto Grosso, Op. 6, No. 7: figuring over pedal points in, 161
"Concerto in *Alexander's Feast*": continuo part for, 56, 58
Conducting scores *(Handexemplare):* bass figuring in, 3, 43–51; location of, 43
Continuo parts, bass figuring in, 3–4, 53–64; in

Index   265

the Aylesford keyboard parts, 61–64; in the late Baroque period, 3–4; in the Hamburg *Cembalopartituren,* 53–55; in the Royal College of Music Collection (MS. 900), 55–56; in the Royal Music Library Collection (British Library), 56, 58
Cooper, Barry: on the organ part for *Alexander's Feast,* 56, 58; on problems of Handel's figuring, 8
Coronation Anthems: figuring over bass line rests in (Anthem II), 144, 146; discarded figurings in, 35; figuring in the autograph of, 14, 15, 16; figuring over pedal points in (Anthem IV), 160

Dean, Winton: on the accompaniment of Handel's recitative, 110; on foreshortened cadences, 135–36; on Handel's copyists, 3; on Handel's figuring, 7, 20; on the Newman Flower keyboard parts, 62; on stages of composition, 24
Deborah: figuring in the autograph of, 16; Handel's repeated figures for recitative in, 134; the horizontal line in Wright's edition of, 178; pedal points in, 156, 160
Deidamia: bass-line rests in plain recitatives of, 112; discarded figurings in, 35; Handel's revisions in the autograph of, 25–27; obsolete figures in, 30
De Marzis, Pasqualino: possible mention of, in RCM 900, 56
Dolce pur d'amor: possible pedagogical purpose in figuring for, 22
Donington, Robert, *The Interpretation of Early Music,* 6–7; on accompaniment over pedal points, 155; on foreshortened cadences, 137; on rests in the continuo line, 141
Dreyfus, Laurence: on shortened accompaniment in the music of Bach, 119

E partirai, mia vita?: delayed or semidelayed cadences in, 136; figuring over bass line rests in, 144; Handel's repeated figures for recitatives in, 134; pedagogical cantata, 22
Esther: figuring in the autograph of, 14
Ezio: Hamburg *Cembalopartitur* for, 54; Handel's repeated figures for recitatives in, 134

Faramondo: Hamburg *Cembalopartitur* for, 54
Figuring, Handel's: in the autographs, 3; customary editorial practices concerning, 1–3; in keyboard continuo parts, 3–4; purposes for, 1, 4–5. *See also* Autographs, Handel's; Conducting scores; Continuo parts; Printed editions; Scribal copies

Fitzwilliam Museum. *See* Autograph Sketches and Fragments, Fitzwillian Museum, Cambridge
Flavio: Handel's repeated figures for recitatives in, 134; Royal Academy print of, 86
Floridante: figuring in different copies of, 69
Flower Collection. *See* Newman Flower Collection
Formulas: in Handel's bass figuring, 165–77
Fougeroux, Pierre Jacques: on Handel's accompaniments for recitative
Funeral Anthem: discarded figurings in, 35

Gardiner, John Eliot: and foreshortened cadences in *Acis and Galatea,* 110
Gasparini, Francesco, *L'Armonico pratico al cimbalo:* on cadences for recitatives, 140; influence of operas by, on Handel, 115; against ornamentation in the accompaniment of recitative, 123; on realization of bass lines having short rests, 147–48; standard progression in, 165, 175; on sustained chords in recitatives, 110, 114–15, 265n.9
Giulio Cesare: Cluer print of, 47, 84–85; figuring in the autograph of, 15; figuring in the Royal Academy print of, 90; Royal Academy print of, 86; supplemental figuring in various sources for, 68–69; suggested harmonization of an excerpt from, 178–83
Giustino: bass theme in, 99; detached and sustained chords for recitative in, 111; discarded figurings in, 35
Granville collection, Eg. 2924: source for *Admeto,* 69
Graun, Carl Heinrich: and bass themes, 100

Hallische Händel-Ausgabe (HHA): policy on bass figuring in, 2
Hamburg *Cembalopartituren:* Handel's works in, 53–55
Händel-Gesellschaft (H-G): continuo figuring in, 1–2
Handexemplare. See Conducting scores
Hansell, Sven: on foreshortened cadences, 134, 139–40
Harpsichord scores. *See Cembalopartituren*
Harpsichord Suites: Cluer edition of, 84
Hasse, Johann Adolf, *Artaserse:* foreshortened and delayed cadences in, 134
Heinichen, Johann David: on accompaniment over a pedal point, 156–57; Buelow's study of, 6; on deceptive cadences, 169; on foreshortened cadences, 137–39; on harmonic support in recitative, 126–28; on realization of figures over bass line rests, 148; on

sparsely figured parts, 56; on sustained vs. detached accompaniments for recitatives, 116, 251n.9
Hendrie, Gerald: supplementary figuring used by, 2
Hercules: delayed or semidelayed cadence in, 136; *unisono* theme in, 107
Hogwood, Christopher: and foreshortened cadences in *Messiah,* 110
Hudson, Frederick: editorial practices of, 2–3

Imeneo: discarded figurings in, 35; figuring in the autograph of, 15; obsolete figures in, 29, 30, 33; *unisono* passage in, 96
Israel in Egypt: bass-line rests in plain recitative of, 112; figuring in the autograph of, 15, 16; foreshortened cadences not required for, 135

Jennens, Charles: original owner of the Aylesford Collection, 53, 61; supplemental bass figuring by, 79–82
Jephtha: autograph figuring in the conducting score of, 43, 44; deleted passage in, 28
Joseph: delayed or semidelayed cadence in recitative from, 136; figuring in the autograph of, 16, 41; figuring in the Newman Flower keyboard part for, 61, 63; Handel's repeated figures for recitatives in, 134; Hamburg Manuscript for, 55; obsolete figures in, 25, 30; supplemental figuring in, 69; *unisono* theme in, 107
Judas Maccabeus: figuring in the Newman Flower keyboard continuo part for, 63; Hamburg Manuscript for, 55; sparse figuring for *unisono* passages in, 105

Kellner, Johann Peter: "Rules . . . for Playing Thorough-Bass . . . by Herr Johann Sebastian Bach," 251n.9; shortened accompaniment preferred by, 119; standard bass pattern used by, 173
King, Alexander Hyatt: on the British Library collection of Handel's autographs, 14
Knapp, J. Merrill: editorial amplifications of figuring by, 2
Koopman, Ton: and thoroughbass realization for plain recitative, 109
Krause (eighteenth-century theorist): shortened accompaniment preferred by, 119

Leonhardt, Gustav: and thoroughbass realization for plain recitative, 109
Linike (copyist for Handel's works), 3
London, British Library, Royal Music Collection. *See* Royal Music Library Collection
London, Royal College of Music MS. 900. *See* Royal College of Music, London
Lucio Papiro: Hamburg *Cembalopartitur* for, 54
La Lucrezia: bass-line rest in plain recitatives of, 112; Handel's figured recitative from, 131; sustained chords called for, in recitative from, 111
Lungi dal mio bel Nume: discarded figurings in, 35; figuring over bass-line rests in, 143–44; pedagogical cantata, 22
Lustig (eighteenth-century theorist): and preference for shortened accompaniment, 119

Macfarren, Sir George: on Handel's practice in accompanying recitative, 126
Manchester collection. *See* Newman Flower Collection
Mann, Alfred: and Handel's figured bass exercises, 21
Mattheson, Johann, *Grosse General-Bass Schule:* on realization of bass lines having short rests, 147, 148–51; *unisono* passage in, 105
Mayo, John: on Handel's pedagogical cantatas, 7–8, 22, 131, 245n.11
Mendel, Arthur: on detached chords for recitatives, 119; on disregarding figures in the thoroughbass for recitatives, 251n.2
Messiah: delayed or semidelayed cadences in recitative from, 136; discarded figurings for, 35; figuring in the autograph of, 14, 17, 38; foreshortened cadences not required for, 135; Handel's figuring for recitatives in, 129, 131, 134; Jennens's supplementary figuring for, 80–81; obsolete figures in, 30; parts for, bequeathed to the Foundling Hospital, 53; suggested harmonization of an excerpt from, 186–87
Mi palpita il cor: detached and sustained chords for recitatives in, 112; possible pedagogical purpose in the figuring for, 22; Smith Sr.'s cello continuo part for, 112, 113
Mozart, Wolfgang Amadeus: orchestration of *unisono* passages in *Messiah* by, 96
Muzio Scevola: figuring in the autograph of, 15

Neidt (eighteenth-century theorist): detached chords in recitative recommended by, 120
Neumann, Frederick: on the proper use of treatises, 97
Newman Flower Collection, Manchester Public Library: score for *Admeto* in, 69, 71–75; keyboard parts in, 61–64; cembalo part for *Scipione* in, 91; supplementary figures in, 68–69

Ninfe e pastori: figuring over bass-line rests in, 143; pedagogical cantata, 22; Handel's figured recitatives from, 131, 134
"No di voi non vuo' fidarmi": figuring in the autograph of, 15

Occasional Oratorio: Hamburg manuscript for, 55
Ode for St. Cecilia's Day: figuring in the autograph of, 15, 24; figuring over a pedal point in, 160; sustained chords for recitative in, 111
O numi eterni: Handel's repeated figures for recitatives in, 134
Opus 5, No. 5; sparse figuring for *unisono* passages in, 105
Oreste: Hamburg *Cembalopartitur* for, 54
Organ Concerto, Op. 4, No. 3: obsolete figures in, 30
Organ continuo: Handel's treatment of, 58
Organo: as the continuo part, 61
Orlando: unfigured continuo solo in the autograph of, 20
Ormisda: Hamburg *Cembalopartitur* for, 54
Ottone: Chrysander's treatment of figuring in, 43; figuring in the autograph of, 15; Royal Academy print of, 86, 89; figuring for *unisono* passages in, 102; short rests in the bass line of, 146; *unisono* theme in, 107, 250n.17

Il Parnasso in Festa: Hamburg *Cembalopartitur* in continuo format for, 54, 55
Parti, l'idolo mio: delayed or semidelayed cadence in, 136
Parts, vocal and instrumental: location of, 53, 246n.1
Pasquali, Nicolo, *Thorough-Bass Made Easy,* 56; and delayed cadences, 255n.58; on Handel's practice in accompanying recitative, 126; and length of chords for recitative, 117
Pasqualini. *See* De Marzis, Pasqualino; Pasquali, Nicolo
Il Pastor Fido: Cembalopartitur for, 54, 55; lack of accompaniment in, 63; unfigured continuo arias in the autograph of, 20; *unisono* passage in, 102
Pedagogical cantatas: Handel's figuring for, 15, 21, 22–23. *See also E partirai, mia vita?; Lungi dal mio bel Nume; Mi palpita il cor; Ninfe e pastori; Sento la che ristretto; Se pari è la tua fè*
Pedal points: the playing of chords over, 155–64; Arnold on, 155–57; C. P. E. Bach on, 155–56, 157–59; Donington on, 155; in Handel's music, 159–64; Heinichen on, 156–57; Telemann on, 156; Williams on, 155
Performing scores. *See* Conducting scores

Plain recitative: thoroughbass realization of, 109–40, 251n.1
—foreshortened cadences in, 110, 134–40
—detached or sustained chords for the accompaniment of, 109, 110–22; Handel and, 110–13; theorists on, 112–22
—melodic and harmonic support in, 109–10, 123–34; evidence for, in Handel's figuring, 128–31, 134; the role of the accompanist, 123–24, 131–32, 134; theorists' writings on, 123, 124–29
Poro: bass-line rests in plain recitative of, 112; discarded figurings in, 35; figuring in the autograph of, 14; Hamburg *Cembalopartitur* for, 54; Hamburg manuscript for, 55; Handel's repeated figures for recitative in, 134
Presentation copies: collections of Handel's works in, 3
Printed editions: additional figuring in, 83–92; Cluer and, 83, 84–85, 86–88, 89–90, 91, 92
—in Royal Academy editions, 85–92; Smith and, 84, 85; Walsh and, 83, 84, 85, 88, 89, 90

Quantz, Johann Joachim, *Versuch einer Anweisung die Flöte traversier zu spielen:* on cadences, 135, 255n.56; on length of chords for recitative, 117; on melodic support for the singer of recitative, 124
"Quel fior che all' alba ride": figuring in the autograph of, 15

RCM 900. *See* Royal College of Music, London
Radamisto: figuring of *unisono* passage in, 100–101; Royal Academy print of, 86, 88–89; short rests in the bass line of, 146–47
Recitative, plain. *See* Plain recitative
Recitative, secco. *See* Plain recitative
La Resurrezione: figuring in the Newman Flower keyboard continuo part for, 63; supplementary figuring for, 67, 68, 81
Riccardo Primo: Cluer print of, 92; discarded figurings in, 34, 35; figuring in the autograph of, 14, 15, 16; figuring for *unisono* passage in, 102; Jennens's supplementary figuring for, 81; obsolete figures in, 30; Royal Academy edition of, 92
Rinaldo: Cembalopartitur for, 54–55; figuring in the autograph of, 15; lack of accompaniment in, 63; obsolete figures in, 30
Rodelinda: Cluer print of, 47–51, 85; discarded figurings in the performing score of, 34; figuring in the autograph of, 15–16; figuring in the conducting score of, 40, 46–47, 50–51; figuring for *unisono* passages in, 100, 102, 103–4, 105, 107; obsolete figures in, 31; Royal Acad-

emy print of, 87, 91; sparse figuring for *unisono* passages in, 105
Rodrigo: Continuo arias in, 20
Royal Academy: printed editions of Handel's operas by, 85–92
Royal College of Music, London: harpsichord part for *Alexander's Feast* (in MS. RCM 900), 55–58, 247n.7
Royal Music Library Collection (British Library, London): collection of Handel's autographs in, 14; MS. RM 18. c. 1., 81; MS. RM 18. d. 9., 71–79; MS. RM 19. a. 1., 56, 59; MS. RM 19. a. 10., 56, 58–59; MS. RM 19. c. 2., 69; MS. RM 19. c. 7., 68–69; MS. RM 19. e. 2., 111; MS. RM 20. d. 12., 21; MS. RM 20. e. 5., 21

Samson: delayed or semidelayed cadences in, 136; discarded figurings in, 35; figuring in the autograph for, 15; figuring in the Newman Flower keyboard part for, 61, 63; figuring over pedal points in, 161; Handel's repeated figures for recitative in, 134; length of chords for recitative in, 112; sparse figuring for *unisono* passages in, 105
Saul: deleted passage in, 28; discarded figuring in, 35; figuring in the autograph of, 16, 17, 20; figuring in the Newman Flower keyboard part for, 63; Jennens's additions to the autograph of, 78; Smith Sr.'s copy of, 75–78; *unisono* passage in, 108
Scarlatti, Alessandro, *Lascia, deh lascia al fine:* realization of, 6, 116, 139
Scipione: autograph figuring in the conducting score of, 43–44; figuring in the Newman Flower keyboard part for, 61; Handel's repeated figures for recitative in, 134; Royal Academy print of, 87, 91–92
Scribal copies: Jennens and, 78–81; the Smith circle and, 65, 68, 69, 75–78, 80; supplementary figuring in, 65–80, 211–17
Se pari è la tua fè: figuring over bass-line rests in, 144; pedagogical cantata, 22
Se per fatal destino: delayed or semidelayed cadence in, 136; suggested harmonization of an excerpt from, 188–89
Sei pur bella: pedagogical cantata, 22
Semele: figuring in the autograph of, 15; figuring over pedal points in, 161
Sento la che ristretto: Handel's repeated figures for recitative in, 134; pedagogical cantata, 2
Serse: autograph figuring in the conducting score of, 43–44; Hamburg *Cembalopartitur* for, 54; obsolete figures in, 31

Shaw, Watkins, *A Textual and Historical Companion to Handel's "Messiah":* on problems of figuring in, 7
Siroe: accompaniment for *unisono* passages in, 105; delayed or semidelayed cadence in recitative from, 136; figuring in the autograph of, 14, 15; Fougeroux on a performance of, 110–11; Handel's figured recitative from, 131; obsolete figures in, 31
Smith circle: presentation copies by, 3; supplemental figuring used by, 65–68, 69, 75–78, 80. *See also* Smith, John Christopher, Sr.
Smith, John Christopher, Sr.: cello continuo part by, 112, 113; conducting score of *Rodelinda* copied by, 44, 100, 102; conducting score of *Samson* copied by, 112; copyist for Handel's works, 3, 84; harpsichord part for *Alexander's Feast* copied by, 55; performance scores copied by, 44, 65; copy of *Saul* by, 71–79. *See also* Smith circle
Solomon: obsolete figures in, 29
Son gelsomino (Il Gelsomino): pedagogical cantata, 22
Songs in "Messiah"; earliest printed edition of *Messiah* excerpts, 7
Sonata in B-flat (recorder): discarded figurings in, 37–38
Sonata in F Major (recorder): figuring in, 246n.30
Staats- und Universitäts-Bibliothek Carl von Ossietzky, Hamburg: *Cembalopartituren* in, 53; Handel's conducting scores in, 43
Standard progression: Handel's figuring of, 20–21
Stölzel (eighteenth-century theorist): detached chords in recitative recommended by, 120
Susanna: complementary figures in the autograph of, 41; delayed or semidelayed cadences in recitative from, 136; length of chords for recitative in, 111

"Tacete, ohimè, tacete": figuring in the autograph of, 15; obsolete figures in, 31
Tamerlano: Cluer edition of, 85; deleted passage in, 28; figuring in the autograph of, 15; Handel's repeated figures for recitative in, 134; obsolete figures in, 31; Royal Academy print of, 87, 91
Telemann, Georg Philipp: on accompaniment over a pedal point, 156; on the accompaniment of recitative, 110, 123; and bass themes, 100; and detached chords, 120, 253n.33; figuring for *unisono* passages by, 107; figuring in works by, 4; on realization of figures over

bass rests, 151–52; and sustained chords, 120, 122
Teseo: unfigured continuo arias in the autograph of, 20
Theodora: figuring in the autograph of, 20
Tobin, John: on the accompaniment of *unisono* passages, 96; on problems of figuring, 7
Tolomeo: discarded figurings in, 35, 36–37; Fougeroux on a performance of, 110–11; Jennens's supplementary figuring for, 80; obsolete figures in, 31
Il Trionfo: figuring in the autograph of, 15; Newman Flower keyboard part for, 63

Udite il mio consiglio: suggested harmonization of an excerpt from, 190–93
Unisono textures, 95–108; C. P. E. Bach on, 97–100; bass figuring and, 96–97, 100–108; bass themes and, 98–100; defined, 95; Handel and, 100–108; Mozart and, 96; options for the performer of, 96; realizations not always appropriate for, 107–8; various scholars on, 96

Vedendo amor: figuring in the autograph of, 16
Venceslao: Hamburg *Cembalopartituren* for, 54
Vivaldi, Antonio: figuring for *unisono* passages in concerti by, 107
Voigt (eighteenth-century theorist): on detached chords in recitative, 120

Walsh: figuring in printed editions by, 2; printer of Handel's works, 83, 84; replaced by Cluer, 90
Westrup, Jack: on foreshortened vs. delayed cadences, 134
Werckmeister, Andreas: *Harmonologia musica:* on the necessity for figuring, 5
Williams, Peter: on accompaniment over pedal points, 155; *Figured Bass Accompaniment,* 6; on Gasparini, regarding recitative, 115; on the length of chords for recitative, 117, 120, 254n.37; on rests in the bass line, 141–42

This pioneering study examines aspects of figured bass notation and continuo realization in the High Baroque, especially with respect to the operas and oratorios of G. F. Handel. Contemporary treatises, Handel's manuscripts, original performance material, and other early sources provide clarification and guidance for the modern performer.

Part one is an overview of figured bass in Handel source materials: autograph manuscripts, performing scores, original keyboard parts, 18th century scribal copies, and early editions. Part two treats in depth continuo realization problems that are often overlooked and can be troublesome in modern performances. The author defines the most common bass patterns, or formula-progressions, in Handel's music, together with the precise harmony the composer intended.

The author attempts to show that continuo figuring can serve different functions depending on context. Much of the figuring that comes down to us in secondary sources may derive from the composer, or it may reflect valid contemporary practice. Modern editions, in the main, are too selective in this regard: they only include bass figuring from primary sources, leaving the modern performer frequently without sufficient guidance in the continuo part to improvise a stylistic accompaniment.

Appendices include brief examples of continuo realization by Handel.

Patrick J. Rogers is an active keyboard player and former Fulbright Scholar who studied Handel under Theodor Göllner, Roland Jackson, Terence Best, and the late J. Merrill Knapp.

www.ingramcontent.com/pod-product-compliance
Lightning Source LLC
Chambersburg PA
CBHW071242230426
43668CB00011B/1556